W9-CCM-353

THE BEST AMERICAN RECIPES 2004–2005

The Year's Top Picks

from Books, Magazines,

Newspapers, and the Internet

THE BEST AMERICAN RECIPES 2004–2005

Fran McCullough

and

Molly Stevens

Series Editors

Foreword by

Bobby Flay

Houghton Mifflin Company
Boston New York
2004

Visit our Web site: www.houghtonmifflinbooks.com.

Library of Congress Cataloging-in-Publication Data is available.

ISSN: 1525-1101
ISBN: 0-618-45506-X

Designed by Anne Chalmers
Cover photograph by Jim Scherer
Tiger Cake (page 252)

Printed in the United States of America

VB 10 9 8 7 6 5 4 3 2 1

contents

foreword

WE'VE SEEN *IRON CHEF;* we've read the tell-all tales. The kitchen can be a battlefield. Fighting to feed the masses, the professional cook combats leaping flames and unbearably hot conditions. Soldiers of the kitchen hurl expletives across the room, all the while brandishing huge knives. Yet somehow, through it all, we manage to give our diners the impression of effortless culinary perfection—or at least that's the goal. I love the kitchen of a busy restaurant on a Friday night—the frenzied energy, the mounting pressure, the imperative teamwork. But it's not my favorite kind of cooking.

Yes, I'm a professional chef, but the thing I love best is creating a meal at home that I've planned especially for the people who will be eating it. A home-cooked meal carries much more weight than just the food on the plate. When you sit down with friends and family around the kitchen table and eat together, you're not just offering food; you're offering a part of yourself. Your time, care, thought, and energy all marry with the ingredients you've chosen to become something greater than the sum of its parts.

The editors of *The Best American Recipes 2004–2005* understand that. From the easy to the complex, from Indian curries to the sweetest desserts, it's all here. And it's all doable. The editors have selected recipes that truly represent the best of American food. Following a recipe from this book means that you can be sure you're bringing your best to the table.

Many of these dishes are classics turned on their heads. Take Caribbean-Style Shrimp Cocktail with Jalapeño-Lime Dipping Sauce, for example. Big flavors are used to kick-start this perennial favorite. With subtle heat from jalapeños, a jolt of ginger, and some brown-sugar sweetness, this is a version for the ages. And you know that the recipe will be perfect, because it's from the staff of *Cook's Illustrated.* They are the kings and queens of the test kitchen, offering precise, well-tested recipes every time.

Once the weather turns cool, I just can't get enough soup. I know my good friend Tom Valenti's Roasted Butternut Squash Soup will find its way onto my table as soon as the leaves start changing. Savory, smoky, and satisfying, this meal-within-a-soup is perfect for a crisp fall evening. And there's something else I can't get enough of: bourbon. (Well, maybe I'm exaggerating just a little!) Still, whether it's on the rocks or in the marinade for Drunken Steak, bourbon has a flavor I find hard to resist.

The Best American Recipes does a couple of things that I really admire—it highlights some of America's best chefs and some of America's emerging trends. Chef Debra Ponzek's Charred Pesto Shrimp is a perfectly simple example of gutsy, bright, fresh American food. I can't wait to get these shrimp hopping on my grill. I also applaud the inclusion of grits. Like polenta twenty years ago, grits are being noticed and given a prominent place in the kitchen, and it's about time they got the respect they deserve. If you haven't tried them yet, start cooking the Green Chile–Cheese Grits now. They're creamy, zesty, and just plain delicious. I promise that this recipe will be only a starting point for you.

Although I'm not a baker, that doesn't mean I don't have a shot at baking every now and then. I'm intrigued by the white pepper and olive oil (these are my kinds of ingredients) in the Tiger Cake. I may well have to give it a try.

You see? That's what this book does. It intrigues, and it encourages you to try new ideas, new techniques, and new ingredients. *The Best American Recipes* demystifies the complex and glorifies the simple. With this book, you don't need restaurant drama to create good food. You don't need a professional range or a top-of-the-line Hobart mixer. And you don't need a team of ten to produce a meal you won't forget. *The Best American Recipes* is the perfect book for anyone who loves to cook at home.

—BOBBY FLAY
New York City

introduction

WE NEVER QUITE KNOW what we're going to find when we begin combing through hundreds of cookbooks, magazines, and newspapers looking for the best recipes of the year — which is a good part of why this is such an exciting enterprise. It's not unlike a massive culinary treasure hunt. Sometimes the treasures are anything but obvious, such as the Manhattan chef Waldy Malouf's pasta with mushrooms and chives — a recipe that looks so plain-Jane on paper that we almost passed it by. Yet as soon as we tested this easy recipe, we immediately fell for its clean but complex flavors. It's one of those can't-stop-eating-it dishes that we make again and again — a definite "best."

One of the most intriguing aspects of our search is recognizing the *hot* dishes of the year that seem to pop up everywhere. Once we identify these, we take it upon ourselves to test our way through as many versions as it takes to find the very best one out there. For instance, we knew early on that good old-fashioned crispy fried chicken was a big passion this year, partly because the food writer Jeffrey Steingarten fried his way through some two hundred chickens and devoted an entire column in *Vogue* to his findings. After testing plenty of different recipes, the one that stole our hearts was Fried Chicken Littles — crunchy, tender morsels served with a zingy, eye-opening dipping sauce.

It also didn't take us long to notice that granita, the sparkling Italian ice that up until now seems to have been waiting in the wings, was suddenly everywhere and in every imaginable flavor. This super-simple frozen dessert easily displaced sorbet and even ice cream this year. Taste the grapefruit and star anise granita in the dessert chapter, and you'll know why.

These are, of course, very homey dishes. And without a doubt, "homey" is the watchword this year. But that doesn't mean plain, and it certainly doesn't mean boring. From shrimp cocktail and chicken noodle soup, to burgers and meatballs, to crisps and crumbles, the recipes that delight us may be familiar, but each has a sophisticated global twist. Shrimp cocktail comes glazed with a spicy-sweet jalapeño-lime sauce, green chiles show up in macaroni and cheese, burgers are made from fresh salmon and dolloped with a snappy aïoli, and old-fashioned chiffon layer cake is flavored with ginger and mango.

We also were struck by a corresponding

and equally unmistakable trend: the revival of old recipes that had been forgotten or had fallen out of favor. We freely admit to having a huge preservationist streak, and we were thrilled to find others sharing the same passion. Resurrecting old recipes is not just an exercise in historic preservation; some are just too good to do without, including the mild southern curry called Country Captain. We tested several and chose a particularly elegant version.

You probably won't find a trifle on your favorite restaurant menu, but this big holiday treat from England has been gathering a lot of interest on this side of the ocean. The one we love most is Nigella Lawson's summer blackberry trifle, which brilliantly simplifies this gorgeous, impressive dessert.

Not that every standout recipe of the year falls into the old-fashioned, homey category. There are plenty of thrilling new recipes as well, such as Paula Wolfert's ethereal asparagus, cooked slowly in its own delectable juices with a touch of fresh tarragon.

A quick scan through the recipes that made their way into this collection reveals an impressive facility with global flavors that is no longer limited to chefs or hard-core foodies. We were happily surprised to see how mainstream several cuisines have become: Spanish and Mexican, in particular, but also West Indian (one reason ginger beer is turning up everywhere). Possibly the most exotic cuisine we encountered is Scandinavian, which brings its own refined excitement to our tables. These influences are changing the contents of our pantries, where you're now likely to encounter pimentón (Spanish smoked paprika), chipotles (smoked jalapeños) in adobo sauce, chorizo, pancetta (the unsmoked bacon of Italy), and panko (wonderfully crisp Japanese bread crumbs). Tomatillos, exotic mushrooms, and an assortment of fresh and dried chiles have entered the everyday realm and are now available in supermarkets almost everywhere. Americans have been slow to recognize the charms of pecorino Romano, the earthier cousin of Parmigiano-Reggiano. But this year we're making up for lost time — pecorino turns up everywhere.

At the same time, once-unfamiliar techniques are becoming commonplace. For instance, five years ago only the most dedicated cooks would undertake grinding their own spices to season a dish. Today a mortar and pestle or a little electric spice grinder (or a coffee grinder) is standard equipment in any well-appointed kitchen. The flavor dividends for the moments it takes to grind your own are simply amazing.

Even after compiling this book for six years in a row, we are seduced (a lot more often than we should be) by recipes that look good on the page but simply don't deliver in the kitchen. The proof really is in the pudding. We can assure you that all of the recipes in this collection have not only been kitchen-tested but meet our standards for dishes we want to make again and again. For those recipes that made the cut, we've added our own notes from the testing, to give you an idea of what to expect and offer suggestions about how you can play with them. And once again we present our favorite ten recipes from the book, so you won't miss them.

—FRAN McCULLOUGH
and MOLLY STEVENS

the top ten recipes

SAVORY FIG TART—This gem turned up in a flyer at our local Whole Foods Market. It's a golden puff pastry tart with a thin layer of fig spread, ribbons of prosciutto, little bits of goat cheese, and fresh thyme. It's stunning to look at, can be made in just a few minutes, and is perfect for entertaining.

MINTED PEA SOUP WITH CRISPY PANCETTA, BREAD, AND SOUR CREAM—This addictive soup is the brainchild of Jamie Oliver, the hot young British chef who has leaped across the ocean with great success. Is it the fresh-tasting (actually, frozen) peas, the touch of mint, or the crunch of croutons strewn with roasted pancetta that makes it unforgettable? We're not sure, but you can make this divine soup in just a few minutes.

MAC AND CHEESE SALAD WITH BUTTERMILK DRESSING—The Seattle chef Tom Douglas dreamed up this wonderful pasta salad that's loaded with herbs and zesty greens. The "mac" is actually farfalle or fusilli, and the cheese is ricotta salata, a lightly salted Italian sheep's milk cheese that's good with pasta. A dressing made with buttermilk, sour cream, and fresh dill makes it all sing.

BRAISED BEEF SHORT RIBS CHINESE STYLE—Recipes for braised short ribs abounded this year, and we fell in love with this novel version from the cookbook author Leslie Revsin. The flavors of soy sauce, dry sherry, star anise, fresh ginger, and garlic penetrate the ribs as they slowly braise, leaving them irresistibly meaty, sweet-salty-spicy, and tender beyond belief. Best of all, the ribs are even better when made ahead.

BUTTERNUT SQUASH ROUNDS WITH SAGE—This sensationally simple recipe from Annie Somerville at Greens, the famous San Francisco vegetarian restaurant, is one of those can't-stop-making-it dishes. It's so pretty and so easy that it constantly suggests itself for dinner. It also works perfectly for Thanksgiving.

SPINACH AND ARTICHOKE CASSEROLE—If you're thinking, "Oh no, I hate to prep spinach and artichokes," think again. The *New York Times Magazine* columnist Julia Reed, who has New Orleans roots, has carefully preserved her mother's fifties vegetable casserole, which is made with embarrassing ingredients such as frozen spinach, canned artichokes, cream cheese, and (gasp!) Ritz crackers. We loved it, and so did our guests. Everyone who tastes it will ask for the recipe.

CINNA-MYRON CARAMEL SWEET ROLLS —These sensational sticky buns come from Iowa, where apparently they know a thing or two about what makes a good breakfast treat. They're gooey, yeasty, sticky, and studded with chopped pecans. We can't imagine a better start to the day.

POPCORN FOCACCIA—One of the tenderest, airiest focaccias we've ever tasted. Don't pass it by, thinking it sounds too gimmicky. This intriguing recipe, from a gifted young writer named Jeremy Jackson, is made with ground popcorn. No kidding!

FOOD DANCE CAFÉ'S DOUBLE-CHOCOLATE PUDDING—Ari Weinzweig, a co-founder of Zingerman's Deli in Ann Arbor, Michigan, spends a lot of time traipsing around the world seeking the very best ingredients to sell in his store. So when he points us to a certain recipe, we take notice. You should, too. This pudding is creamy, chocolaty nirvana.

CRANBERRY MARGARITA—Leave it to the TV superstar Bobby Flay to come up with a zingy margarita that works for the holidays once the limes have all gone south. This flashy drink should replace the cosmopolitan.

—FRAN McCULLOUGH
and MOLLY STEVENS

TOOL OF THE YEAR

Silicone seems to have abandoned the implant business and trotted right into the kitchen, which is a good thing. All of a sudden, our kitchens are full of brilliantly colored silicone tools: pot grabbers; giant mitts that let you dive right into a pot of boiling water to grab an ear of corn; lipstick-red nonstick muffin pans that bend and flex and don't get hot; spatulas with the same virtues; and, best of all, the French baking mats called Silpats.

If you don't have a Silpat, you can use parchment paper (which works because it's coated with silicone) to keep foods from sticking to the pan. But if you do much baking, you really should consider investing in one (or more) of these mats. Silpats have been used in professional kitchens, especially bakeries, for decades, but they've just recently appeared on the home market. Nothing sticks to a Silpat—not burned-on food, not even caramel. Whatever you've baked slides off the mat, and after baking, everything rinses right off. Dough doesn't stick either. You can roll out your pie dough on a baking mat without using any flour at all, then just flip it into the pie plate and peel off the Silpat. You can also freeze the dough right on the Silpat. Be sure to store your Silpat flat. Right inside the baking sheet is a good place.

starters

SOURCE: *New York Times*

COOK: Amanda Hesser

cheese ball with cumin, mint, and pistachios

AMANDA HESSER HAS TAKEN A SECOND LOOK at that stalwart of the fifties cocktail party and given it an eastern Mediterranean makeover, with excellent results. The cheeses here (cream cheese, goat cheese, and pecorino Romano) seem lighter than the standard old chewy cheddar, and the flavors—lemon, coriander and cumin seeds, and fresh mint—are much more intriguing. Hesser's cheese ball gets a final cloaking in coarsely ground pistachio nuts, a sure sign that this is not your mother's cheese ball.

serves 8

- 1 8-ounce package cream cheese, at room temperature
- 4 ounces fresh goat cheese, at room temperature
- Grated zest of 1 lemon
- 1 tablespoon fresh lemon juice
- 1/2 cup freshly grated pecorino Romano cheese, preferably Fulvi
- 1 teaspoon toasted and ground coriander seeds
- 1 teaspoon toasted and ground cumin seeds
- 1/2 cup thinly sliced celery hearts with leaves
- 1/3 cup chopped fresh mint
- 1/4 teaspoon freshly ground black pepper
- Sea salt
- 1/3 cup salted pistachio nuts, coarsely ground
- Thin plain crackers for serving

In a large bowl, beat the cream cheese and goat cheese with a wooden spoon until creamy and light. Beat in the lemon zest and lemon juice. Fold in the pecorino, coriander, cumin, celery, mint, and pepper. Season with salt to taste.

Lay a large piece of plastic wrap on the counter. Using a spatula, scrape the cheese mixture onto the center of the plastic wrap. Pull the sides up and form the cheese into a ball. Wrap tightly, place in a bowl, and refrigerate for at least 2 hours.

Pour the ground pistachios into a shallow bowl. Unwrap the cheese ball and roll it in the nuts until coated. Place the ball on a serving plate, cover with plastic wrap, and chill until ready to serve. About 30 minutes before serving, unwrap the cheese ball and let it come to room temperature. Serve with crackers.

notes from our test kitchen

- If you have trouble forming the cheese ball, it may be too warm. Let it sit in the refrigerator and try again. You can also form it into a perfect mound by placing it in a small bowl, such as a mortar.
- Guests are sometimes reluctant to plow into something so perfect-looking. You may need to take the first swipe at it yourself and spread a few crackers on the serving plate.
- Leftovers are delicious in scrambled eggs.

SOURCE: *Delights from the Garden of Eden* by Nawal Nasrallah

COOK: Nawal Nasrallah

spicy eggplant dip

THIS RECIPE FROM A COMPREHENSIVE BOOK on the history of Iraqi cuisine is a prime example of how something simple and good will never go out of style. According to Nawal Nasrallah, a native of Iraq and a literature professor, the dip dates back to the ninth or tenth century. She goes on to explain, however, that eggplant was not an immediate hit, as many cooks found it too bitter to be trusted. And if you've ever tasted undercooked eggplant, you can understand. Fortunately, cooks soon learned that thorough cooking renders it soft and delightfully sweet. One early writer likened its taste to that of a lover's kiss.

Perhaps our only complaint about this deliciously creamy, aromatically spiced dip is that the recipe doesn't make enough. Fortunately, it is easily doubled, or even tripled, for a larger, or hungrier, crowd.

serves 4

- 1 large eggplant (about 1½ pounds)
- 2 tablespoons olive oil
- ½ teaspoon salt
- ¼ teaspoon freshly ground black pepper
- 1 garlic clove, grated
- ½ teaspoon ground cumin (see notes)
- ½ teaspoon ground coriander (see notes)
- ½ teaspoon coarsely chopped crushed dried chile (see notes)
- Chopped fresh parsley, tomato slices, and/or pomegranate seeds for garnish (optional)
- Warm bread for serving

Preheat the oven to 450 degrees. Wash the eggplant and pierce the skin with a sharp knife in 2 or 3 places, so that it will not burst in the oven. Bake the eggplant directly on an oven rack, turning it once or twice, until soft, about 45 minutes. Set aside to cool.

Once the eggplant is cool, cut off the stem and remove the peel. Discard any juices and remove as many of the seeds as you can without losing any pulp. Place the remaining pulp in a medium bowl and mash with a fork.

Heat the olive oil in a small skillet or saucepan until it sizzles and pour it over the eggplant puree. Add the salt, pepper, garlic, cumin, coriander, and chile. Mix well. Spread the mixture on a plate in a layer about 1 inch thick. Garnish with parsley, tomato, and/or pomegranate seeds. Serve cool with warm bread.

VARIATION

spicy eggplant puree with onion: For a more complex version, coarsely chop 1 medium onion and sauté it in the olive oil. Add it to the eggplant with the oil.

notes from our test kitchen

- For maximum flavor, start with whole coriander and cumin seeds. Toast them briefly in a small skillet and then grind them before adding them to the dip. This small amount of effort will deliver a big flavor return.
- For the chile, we use crushed red pepper flakes.
- Left ungarnished, the dip is rather plain-looking, so we urge you to try at least one or two of the garnishes. Our favorite combination is pomegranate seeds and chopped parsley. Very festive.

tip

Eggplant normally needs 40 to 50 minutes of roasting before it can be turned into a dip. If you'd like to speed things up, here's a version of baba ghanoush from Tara Duggan of the *San Francisco Chronicle*. It won't have the same deep flavor as the traditional recipe, but it's fine in a pinch. Pierce a large eggplant (1½ pounds) in a few places and cover with plastic wrap. Microwave on high for 4 minutes. Turn over and microwave for 4 minutes longer. If the eggplant is still not very soft all over, microwave for 1 to 2 minutes more per side. Scrape out the softened eggplant flesh and place it in a food processor along with 1 minced garlic clove, ⅓ cup tahini, ¼ cup fresh lemon juice, and ¼ cup extra-virgin olive oil. Puree until completely combined. Season with salt to taste and pulse a few times. If the baba ghanoush has a bitter edge, add ¼ cup plain whole-milk yogurt. Transfer to a bowl and drizzle with more olive oil. Serves 6.

SOURCE: *Good Food No Fuss* by Anne Willan

COOK: Anne Willan

giant goat cheese gougère

GOUGÈRES ARE BEST DESCRIBED as savory cream puffs—traditionally made with bits of Gruyère cheese folded into the dough and piped out into little bite-size nibbles to serve with drinks. As much as we love these tender, airy puffs, we're not always up for taking the time to load up the pastry bag and pipe out individual pastries. So we were thrilled to discover that Anne Willan had solved our problem by baking the dough in one big round. The pastry won't puff up as much as an individual gougère. Think of it more as a flat, light pizza with a crisp, airy perimeter. The center remains somewhat denser, which makes a perfect foil for the goat cheese and herb topping.

We like to pass thin slivers with a round of drinks. You can also serve thicker wedges as a sit-down first course, perhaps accompanied by a simple tossed salad. Gougères also make a fine light meal with a hearty soup or vegetable salad.

makes one 10- to 11-inch gougère;
serves 8 to 10 as an hors d'oeuvre, 6 as a first course

- 1 tablespoon olive oil, plus more for the pan
- 4 1/2 ounces Gruyère cheese
- 1 cup all-purpose flour
- 3/4 cup milk
- 5 tablespoons unsalted butter, cut into pieces
- 1/2 teaspoon salt
- 4 large eggs
- 1 tablespoon chopped fresh thyme, rosemary, sage, or tarragon
- 1 garlic clove, crushed (optional)
- 4 1/2 ounces fresh goat cheese, cut into 6–8 slices (see notes)

Adjust the rack to the middle and preheat the oven to 375 degrees. Brush a 10- to 12-inch tart pan (preferably with a removable base) with some oil. (For a more rustic-looking gougère, oil a baking sheet.) Cut the Gruyère into small dice.

Sift the flour onto a sheet of wax or parchment paper. In a small saucepan, heat the milk, butter, and salt until the butter is melted. Bring to a boil, remove from the heat, and immediately add all the flour. Beat vigorously with a wooden spoon for a few moments until the mixture pulls away from the sides of the pan to form a ball. Beat for 30 seconds to 1 minute over low heat to dry the dough slightly, just until it starts to stick to the base of the pan. Remove from the heat and let cool for 2 to 3 minutes.

Using the wooden spoon or a hand-held electric mixer, beat 3 of the eggs, one by one, into the dough. Adding just the right amount of egg is key, so break the remaining egg into a small bowl, whisk it with a fork to mix, and add a little at a time to the dough—you may not need all of it. At the end, the dough will be shiny and should just fall from the spoon. Beat in the diced Gruyère.

Spread the dough evenly in the tart pan (or into a round shape on the baking sheet, if using), using the back of a spoon. Sprinkle with the herbs and garlic (if using), leaving a 3/4-inch border around the edges. Top the herbs with the goat cheese—the dough will show through the cheese. Brush the cheese with the tablespoon of olive oil.

Bake the gougère until the dough is crusty and browned and the cheese is toasted, 45 to 50 minutes. The gougère will puff, then deflate slightly as it cools. Serve warm, cut into wedges.

notes from our test kitchen

- Unflavored dental floss makes neat work of slicing fresh goat cheese. Slide a 6- to 8-inch piece of floss under the goat cheese log to where you want to slice off a disk. Then bring the 2 ends up, cross them, and pull in opposite directions.
- The gougère is best served immediately, but it can be baked 2 to 3 hours ahead and reheated in a moderate oven.
- For a dressier first course, scoop the dough out onto an oiled baking sheet in 6 individual portions. Flatten each into a rustic round shape, top as directed, and bake for 30 to 40 minutes.

SOURCE: *New York Times*
COOK: Melissa Clark after Marily Mustilli
STORY BY: Melissa Clark

parmesan crackers

WHAT TO SERVE WITH WINE BESIDES CRACKERS AND CHEESE? Melissa Clark found the perfect answer at the Mustilli winery in Sant'Agata de' Goti in the Italian region of Campania. At first she thought the Americans were being served cookies with their wine. They were, but these were Parmesan cookies—the crackers and cheese together. What makes these shortbread cookies so unusual is that they get a quick second browning at high heat, which caramelizes the cheese.

They are intense, rich, and perfect with a good red wine. Better yet, they're made in a food processor, and you don't roll them out. Just shape the dough into a log and chill until you're ready to slice and bake them.

makes 40 crackers

- 8 tablespoons (1 stick) unsalted butter, plus more for the pan
- 1 cup all-purpose flour
- 1 cup freshly grated Parmigiano-Reggiano cheese

Combine all the ingredients in a food processor and pulse until the dough comes together. Turn the dough out onto a piece of plastic wrap and form it into a log 1½ inches in diameter. Chill until firm, at least 2 hours.

Adjust the rack to the middle and preheat the oven to 325 degrees. Butter two baking sheets. Cut the log into ¼-inch-thick slices and place them 1 inch apart on the sheets. Bake until firm, 12 to 13 minutes. Remove the baking sheets from the oven and raise the temperature to 500 degrees. When the oven is ready, return the sheets to the oven and bake for about 3 minutes, until the crackers are deeply golden brown all over. Let cool on a wire rack.

SOURCE: *Gourmet*

COOK: Lori W. Powell

mustard-cheese crackers

THESE SNAPPY, CRISP, RICH CRACKERS have appealing flavors. Beyond one or two of them with drinks, you'll spoil your dinner. There are three kinds of mustard here punching things up: Dijon, mustard seeds, and dry mustard. Swiss cheese is the right foil for all the mustards as well as the rich dough.

Fortunately, you can make the dough in the food processor in minutes, then freeze the logs, slice, and bake. The crackers are especially good with beer.

makes about 60 crackers

- 8 tablespoons (1 stick) cold unsalted butter, cut into tablespoon-size pieces, plus more for the pan
- 8 ounces Swiss cheese, coarsely grated (2 1/4 cups)
- 1 cup all-purpose flour
- 3 tablespoons Dijon mustard
- 2 teaspoons dry mustard
- 1 1/2 teaspoons mustard seeds
- 1 teaspoon salt

Blend the butter and cheese in a food processor until almost smooth. Add the remaining ingredients and pulse until just combined. Divide the dough between two sheets of wax paper and roll each half into an 8-inch log. Wrap in wax paper and then foil, and freeze until firm, 1 1/2 to 2 hours.

Adjust the racks to the upper and lower thirds and preheat the oven to 350 degrees. Butter two large baking sheets. Cut 1 log crosswise into 1/4-inch-thick slices and arrange the slices 1 inch apart on the sheets. Bake, switching positions halfway through the baking, until the edges are golden brown, about 15 minutes. Transfer the crackers to a wire rack to cool. Repeat with the remaining log.

note from our test kitchen

The mustard seeds and flour tend to clump up at the bottom of the food processor, so be sure to stop it and scrape them back into the dough.

SOURCE: *Whole Foods Holiday Entertaining Guide*
COOK: Whole Foods Market

savory fig tart

IF YOU'D LIKE TO PRESENT YOUR GUESTS with a professional-looking savory tart warm from the oven with a minimum of fuss, this is your recipe. Puff pastry is the key ingredient here—golden brown and barely covered with a figgy spread. The top accents are crumbled goat cheese, ribbons of prosciutto, and fresh thyme.

The tart is perfect for entertaining, since you can do the initial baking early in the day and just finish it in a couple of minutes, slide it into the oven, and let it cool briefly before serving.

You can make a rustic-looking tart and let the top notes fall where they may, or a more formal one, with the ribbons of prosciutto forming an elegant pattern and the cheese scattered in between. Either way, the tart looks irresistible.

serves 8

All-purpose flour for dusting
7 ounces frozen puff pastry, thawed
1/2 cup fig spread (see notes)
4 ounces crumbly fresh goat cheese
4 slices prosciutto, cut into thin strips
Freshly ground black pepper
Fresh thyme leaves

Adjust the rack to the middle and preheat the oven to 375 degrees. Line a baking sheet with parchment paper. Lightly dust the work surface and the pastry with flour. Roll the pastry out to a 7-x-15-inch rectangle. Brush the perimeter with water.

Fold all four edges over, creating a 1/2-inch overlapping "frame" around the pastry. Transfer to the baking sheet.

Poke the pastry all over with a fork, then bake until firm and golden brown all over, 25 to 30 minutes. Remove from the oven and let cool for 5 minutes.

Preheat the broiler. Fill the pastry with the fig spread. Crumble the goat cheese over the top and drape strips of prosciutto on the cheese. Broil for about 4 minutes, until the prosciutto starts to brown and the cheese melts. Let cool for 15 minutes.

Cut into 8 bars, sprinkle with black pepper and thyme leaves, and serve warm.

notes from our test kitchen

- Fig spread isn't the same thing as fig jam; it's quite a bit less sweet. You'll find it in gourmet stores and cheese shops.
- What to do with your leftover puff pastry dough? Make Cinnamon Sacristains, the crunchy cinnamon-sugar cookies on page 262.

tip

We love the sweet, concentrated taste of figs in all sorts of savory dishes, so we were more than delighted to discover them in an incredibly simple and irresistible bruschetta topping, Anchoiade with Figs and Walnuts, in an article by the California cook Tasha Prysi in *Fine Cooking*. In a food processor, combine 3 ounces chopped dried figs (about 8 figs, stems removed), 1 ounce (1/4 cup) walnut halves, 8 to 10 oil-packed anchovy fillets, 3 garlic cloves, and 1/4 teaspoon kosher salt. Process until finely chopped. Add 1/4 cup extra-virgin olive oil, 2 teaspoons cognac, and a few grinds of black pepper. Process again to make a somewhat coarse paste. Taste and adjust the salt and pepper, if necessary. Brush 1/2-inch-thick slices of rustic country bread with extra-virgin olive oil and grill or toast until golden brown on both sides. Spread the *anchoiade* on the grilled bread, top with a few shavings of Parmigiano-Reggiano or Manchego cheese (made with a vegetable peeler), and serve. The *anchoiade* will keep for days in a tightly covered container in the refrigerator.

SOURCE: www.rusticocooking.com

COOK: Micol Negrin

roasted pepper boats with pancetta and pecorino

NOW THAT PANCETTA, THE UNSMOKED ITALIAN BACON, is available almost everywhere, it's easy to make this delicious, very rustic appetizer. The pepper boats make a fantastic presentation if you use red, yellow, and orange peppers, but they're also pretty using just one or two colors. Skip green peppers, which are a bit overwhelming in this dish.

The pepper boats look great on a platter. This is gather-round-the-table food, and light eaters will be happy to have it as a meal, with lots of bread to sop up the delicious juices. Just add a salad, wine, and a second platter of salami and cheese.

serves 4 to 6

- 3 tablespoons extra-virgin olive oil, plus more for the pan
- 1 red bell pepper, halved, seeded, and cut into 8 long strips
- 1 yellow bell pepper, halved, seeded, and cut into 8 long strips
- 1 orange bell pepper, halved, seeded, and cut into 8 long strips
- 3/4 cup freshly grated pecorino Romano cheese
- 12 thin slices pancetta, halved
- 1/2 teaspoon freshly ground black pepper

Preheat the oven to 450 degrees. Lightly oil an 11-x-17-inch baking sheet. Arrange the pepper strips flesh side down on the sheet. Drizzle with the olive oil, sprinkle with the pecorino, and top with the pancetta. Season with the pepper.

Roast for about 20 minutes, until the peppers soften and the pancetta is lightly browned. Don't let it burn, or the dish will taste acrid. Serve hot.

notes from our test kitchen

- We especially like the Fulvi brand of pecorino.
- If you can't find pancetta, you can use small pieces of bacon, but not a heavily smoked kind.

SOURCE: *Kitchen of Light* by Andreas Viestad
COOK: Andreas Viestad

cumin-baked parsnips with salmon roe

THE SCANDINAVIAN CHEF ANDREAS VIESTAD creates a miraculously complex-tasting dish with humble parsnips. The trick, he says, is to roast them covered with foil, which brings out their sweetness and delicacy. Adding cumin, lemon juice, and olive oil to the packet intensifies the flavors even more.

While the parsnips are cooling off a bit, you make a quick sauce of parsley, olive oil, and just a touch of garlic. The elegant garnish is a gorgeous spoonful of salmon roe—a salty counterpoint to the sweet parsnips.

This is a perfect starter for a fall or winter meal, but it's also—without the roe—a terrific side dish for meats and rich fish such as salmon. The recipe serves two as a side and is easily doubled; just make up a second packet.

serves 4

- 2 parsnips, peeled and halved lengthwise
- 2 teaspoons ground cumin
- 3 tablespoons fresh lemon juice
- 3 tablespoons olive oil
- 2 tablespoons finely chopped fresh parsley
- 1 small garlic clove
- 4–6 tablespoons salmon roe, to taste

Preheat the oven to 350 degrees. Place the parsnips in a small baking dish. Sprinkle with the cumin, lemon juice, and 2 tablespoons of the olive oil. Cover with foil and bake for about 40 minutes, until soft and sweet. Let the parsnips cool until nicely warm.

Meanwhile, with a mortar and pestle or a mini blender, crush or pulse the parsley, garlic, and remaining 1 tablespoon oil until you have a smooth sauce.

Place the parsnips cut side up on individual plates. Spoon the parsley sauce over the top, add the salmon roe, and serve.

note from our test kitchen

If you can't find salmon roe, bright orange capelin roe, widely available in jars at supermarkets and in bulk at fish stores, will work for this dish.

SOURCE: *The Way We Cook* by Sheryl Julian and Julie Riven

COOK: Arlene Jacobs

roasted asparagus with panko bread crumbs

IF YOU'RE LOOKING FOR A UNIQUE HORS D'OEUVRE that takes almost no time to put together and will be the hit of your party, here it is. Coat thick spears of fresh asparagus with a zingy mustard-mayonnaise mixture, then roll them in the super-crunchy Japanese bread crumbs known as panko and bake until tender and golden. Besides being a cinch to assemble, the asparagus can be made ahead and cooked once your guests arrive. Don't be surprised if these crunchy spears disappear in seconds flat.

We sometimes like to arrange a few spears on a plate and top them with a poached or fried egg and call it supper. In that case, the recipe will make only four servings.

serves 6

- 1/4 cup mayonnaise
- 2 tablespoons Dijon mustard
- 1 teaspoon fresh lemon juice
- 1/2 teaspoon coarse salt (kosher or sea salt), plus more to taste
- 1/4 teaspoon freshly ground black pepper, or to taste
- 1 cup Japanese panko bread crumbs (see notes)
- 2 tablespoons olive oil, plus more for the pan
- 1 pound thick asparagus spears, fibrous stems snapped off (see notes)

Preheat the oven to 450 degrees. In a large, shallow bowl wide enough to hold the asparagus, whisk together the mayonnaise, mustard, lemon juice, salt, and pepper. Put the bread crumbs in another shallow bowl.

Oil a large rimmed baking sheet. Roll the asparagus in the mayonnaise mixture to coat, then in the bread crumbs so the spears are well breaded. Transfer the asparagus to the prepared baking sheet and sprinkle with the oil. (The asparagus can be covered and refrigerated for several hours before roasting.)

Roast the asparagus, turning halfway through, for 12 to 18 minutes, until the crumbs are golden brown and the spears are tender but have some bite. Sprinkle with salt and serve at once.

notes from our test kitchen

- Japanese panko bread crumbs are lighter, flakier, and crisper than ordinary bread crumbs. Made through a unique process in which a slightly sweet bread dough is sprayed onto the surfaces of a hot oven, panko is becoming popular in the United States as a coating and breading. You can find panko bread crumbs in Asian markets and increasingly in the international section of many large supermarkets. Use leftover panko as a coating for fish or as a topping for gratins.
- If you can't find panko, substitute unseasoned dry bread crumbs.
- When shopping for fresh asparagus, don't be tempted by the skinny spears that are so often in the market. The coating won't stick to thin asparagus. Besides, the thicker spears are tender and sweet and give you more surface for the crunchy coating.
- To remove the fibrous ends from the asparagus, hold a spear with both hands and bend gently until the end snaps off. It will break naturally. Pare off any stringy ends with a small knife.

SOURCE: *The Quick Recipe*
COOK: *Cook's Illustrated* staff

caribbean-style shrimp cocktail with jalapeño-lime dipping sauce

SHRIMP COCKTAIL DOESN'T BEGIN TO DESCRIBE how unusual these shrimp are. They're not just nude shrimp with a sauce. They're sautéed, glazed with a sweet-hot ginger-jalapeño-lime sauce for a second round in the skillet, and then dipped in the sauce once they've cooled.

The shrimp are great with beer, rum, or tequila. Your guests dip the shrimp by their tails, which are a bit sticky, so be sure to provide plenty of cocktail napkins—and plenty of shrimp. As someone in the test kitchen noted when these shrimp were being developed, "People will still be talking about these the next day." We certainly were.

serves 6

DIPPING SAUCE

- 1 medium garlic clove
- 1/8 teaspoon salt
- 1 1/2-inch piece fresh ginger, minced (about 1 1/2 tablespoons)
- 2 medium scallions, white and green parts, minced
- 1 large jalapeño chile, stemmed, seeded, and minced
- 1/4 cup fresh lime juice (from about 2 limes)
- 1/4 cup packed dark brown sugar

SHRIMP

- 1 tablespoon vegetable oil
- 1 pound extra-large shrimp (21–25 count per pound), peeled and deveined, tails left on
- 1/4 teaspoon salt
- 1/4 teaspoon freshly ground black pepper

MAKE THE DIPPING SAUCE:

Mince the garlic with the 1/8 teaspoon salt to make a paste. Mix the garlic paste with the remaining ingredients in a small serving bowl and set aside.

MAKE THE SHRIMP:

Heat the oil in a large, heavy-bottomed skillet over high heat until it begins to smoke. Season the shrimp with the 1/4 teaspoon salt and pepper. Add the shrimp to the hot pan and sauté until they are pink and cooked through, about 2 minutes. Remove the pan from the heat, add 2 tablespoons of the jalapeño-lime sauce to the hot pan, and toss to coat the shrimp. Spread the shrimp on a rimmed baking sheet to cool, about 5 minutes.

Once the shrimp have cooled, arrange them on a platter around the bowl of sauce and serve immediately.

SOURCE: *The Summer House Cookbook* by Debra Ponzek and Geralyn Delaney Graham

COOKS: Debra Ponzek and Geralyn Delaney Graham

charred pesto shrimp

A GREAT ADDITION TO YOUR SUMMER REPERTOIRE of easy entertaining dishes, guaranteed to win high praise. The pesto here is wall-to-wall herbs—a loud mix of basil, tarragon, cilantro, chives, and parsley—accented with a bit of lemon zest and pulled together with extra-virgin olive oil. There's none of the grated cheese or pine nuts that enrich traditional pesto, because these would distract from the herbs and make a mess of the grill. As is, the pesto remains light and bright—a perfect way to dress fat, juicy shrimp.

If you're serving the shrimp as an hors d'oeuvre, spear each one with a toothpick before passing. They're equally tasty hot off the grill or at room temperature. We also love to turn this into a main course by tossing the shrimp with thin pasta, such as linguine or angel hair, or by serving them over mounds of steamed white rice.

serves 4 to 6

- 1 cup packed fresh basil leaves
- 1/4 cup fresh tarragon leaves
- 1/4 cup fresh cilantro leaves
- 1/4 cup chopped fennel fronds (optional; see notes)
- 1/4 cup chopped fresh chives
- 1/4 cup chopped fresh flat-leaf parsley
- 1 tablespoon grated lemon zest
- 3/4 cup extra-virgin olive oil
- 1/2 teaspoon salt, preferably sea salt
- Freshly ground black pepper
- 24 jumbo shrimp, peeled and deveined (see notes)

Coarsely chop the basil and place in a blender or food processor. Add the tarragon, cilantro, fennel fronds (if using), chives, parsley, lemon zest, oil, salt, and pepper to taste. Process until smooth. You should have about 1 cup pesto; it will have a somewhat loose, saucelike consistency.

Place half the pesto in a large bowl, add the shrimp, and toss to coat thoroughly.

Prepare a medium-hot grill. When the grill is heated, grill the shrimp, turning once with tongs, until cooked through, about 2 minutes per side. Transfer the cooked shrimp to a platter and drizzle with the remaining pesto. Spear each shrimp with a toothpick for easy handling, then serve warm or at room temperature.

notes from our test kitchen

- Fennel fronds are the feathery tops that come on bulbs of fennel. They should be bright green and fresh-smelling. If you prefer, substitute 2 tablespoons chopped fresh dill.
- If you buy smaller shrimp, the authors suggest that you thread them onto skewers before grilling so they're easier to turn and won't fall through the grate.

SOURCE: *Patricia Unterman's San Francisco Food Lover's Guide* by Patricia Unterman

COOK: Joyce Goldstein

pickled salmon

THERE'S SMOKED SALMON, there's gravlax, there's lox—and there's this very wonderful pickled salmon, the easiest to make and arguably the tastiest of all. All you need is 3 or 4 days for the pickle to cure and about 5 minutes of work. (Like ceviche, the fish is "cooked" by the acid it's bathed in.) This is a light, slightly sweet pickle with lots of onion and a few spices—perfect with matzoh crackers and butter. It's excellent for the Jewish holidays or any other kind of celebration, for that matter.

Patricia Unterman suggests serving it with a cucumber salad made with sour cream. It also fits with deviled eggs, caviar, and Scandinavian fare.

serves 12

- 2 cups white vinegar
- 1 1/2 cups water
- 6 tablespoons sugar
- 2 tablespoons kosher salt
- 2 pounds salmon fillets, skinned
- 2 white or yellow onions, cut into 1/4-inch-thick slices
- 2 tablespoons pickling spices
- Matzoh crackers and softened butter for serving

In a small saucepan, bring the vinegar, water, sugar, and salt to a boil. Take the pan off the heat and let cool completely.

Meanwhile, cut the salmon fillets into pieces measuring about 1 x 2 inches. In a glass, ceramic, or plastic container, layer the salmon pieces with the onions and spices, ending with the onions on top. Pour the pickling liquid over all, seal, and refrigerate for 3 to 4 days.

To serve, remove the salmon pieces and onions from the liquid and arrange on a platter. Serve with matzoh crackers and softened butter. Return any unused salmon pieces to the pickling liquid and refrigerate; the salmon will keep for another day or two.

notes from our test kitchen

- If you don't want to buy pickling spices, here's a typical mix: coriander seeds, mustard seeds, whole allspice, dill seeds, whole cloves, crumbled bay leaf, fenugreek seeds, and chile flakes.
- The salmon looks especially pretty in a glass jar with a wide mouth.

SOURCE: *In a Roman Kitchen* by Jo Bettoja

COOK: Jo Bettoja

roman meatballs in "fake" sauce

JO BETTOJA IS AN AMERICAN COOK from small-town Georgia who's lived in Rome for decades. She always manages to find the most distinctive, refined versions of what people there are eating, and this recipe is a sterling example. In Rome they eat meatballs the way we eat hamburgers, and this terrific version, though very simple, has some extraordinary elements that offer different flavors with every bite: raisins, pine nuts, Parmesan, and fresh herbs, as well as a little pancetta. The sauce is "fake" as far as the Romans are concerned because it has no meat, except for a little pancetta to get it going in the pot.

You could, of course, use a store-bought tomato sauce with the meatballs, but Bettoja's is so good and so easy to make that you'd be cheating yourself out of some of the joy of this recipe. To turn this into a meal, serve the meatballs with bread, over spaghetti, or even over polenta (see tip), although the Romans wouldn't.

serves 6 to 8

SAVORY TOMATO SAUCE

- 2 ounces pancetta
- Small handful fresh parsley
- 1 small celery rib, trimmed
- 1 small carrot, peeled
- 1 small garlic clove
- 1/4 cup extra-virgin olive oil
- 1 small onion, finely chopped
- 3 pounds ripe tomatoes, peeled, seeded, and chopped, or two 28-ounce cans Italian plum tomatoes with juice
- Salt and freshly ground black pepper

MEATBALLS

- 1 1/2 pounds ground beef, ground twice (see notes)
- 2 large slices Italian bread
- 1 teaspoon salt
- 1/2 teaspoon freshly ground black pepper
- 1/4 teaspoon freshly grated nutmeg
- 1 ounce pancetta
- 1/2 small garlic clove
- Small handful fresh parsley
- 1 large sprig fresh marjoram, leaves stripped, or 1 teaspoon dried
- 2 large eggs
- 1/4 cup freshly grated Parmesan cheese
- 1/4 cup raisins, plumped in warm water and drained
- 1/3 cup pine nuts
- 1 cup fine dry bread crumbs, or more as needed
- 1/2 cup olive oil

MAKE THE SAUCE:

Chop together the pancetta, parsley, celery, carrot, and garlic, turning the ingredients with your knife and mixing as you chop.

Heat the olive oil in a large pot. Add the onion and cook over medium heat, stirring often, until it is softened and golden, about 5 minutes. Add the pancetta mixture and continue cooking over moderately low heat until the vegetables are very soft and the onion is golden, 7 to 10 minutes, adding 1 or 2 tablespoons of water every now and then to allow the seasonings to cook without burning.

Add the fresh tomatoes or the canned tomatoes with about three quarters of their juice. Season with salt and pepper to taste and finish cooking the sauce for 15 minutes over moderate heat, mashing the tomatoes with the back of a wooden spoon and stirring often.

MAKE THE MEATBALLS:

Put the ground beef in a large bowl. Trim the crusts from the bread and tear the bread into pieces. Soak the bread in cold water. Drain and squeeze out the water. Using your hands, mix the softened bread into the beef. Season with the salt, pepper, and nutmeg.

Chop together the pancetta, garlic, parsley, and marjoram and add to the meat. Beat the eggs and stir them into the meat along with the Parmesan, raisins, and pine nuts. Mix all the ingredients together thoroughly with your hands. Form 10 large meatballs about 3 inches in diameter, slightly flattened on top. Roll them in the dry bread crumbs until they are well coated.

Heat the olive oil to simmering in a large skillet and fit the meatballs into the pan. Sauté over medium-high heat, turning, until browned outside and cooked through, about 15 minutes. Drain on paper towels. Gently lower the meatballs into the tomato sauce and simmer for 5 to 8 minutes. Serve hot.

notes from our test kitchen

- If you don't have a butcher to grind the meat twice, give it a spin in the food processor.
- You can add some pork to the meatballs if you like. Use 1 or 2 sausages, removing the casings and crumbling the meat into the beef.

tip

Jo Bettoja passes along a foolproof way of making perfect polenta without all the stirring. The polenta will be a little loose, and you'll need to stir it again before serving.

Heat 5½ cups water with 1½ teaspoons salt until barely simmering. Remove the pan from the heat and gradually whisk in 1 pound polenta or finely ground cornmeal—a little at first, then the rest in 3 or 4 additions, stirring all the time to prevent lumps from forming. Return the pan to the heat and cook for a few minutes, stirring, until the polenta has thickened.

With a wooden spoon or spatula, make a hole in the center of the polenta all the way down to the bottom of the pan. Pour in 1 cup cold water, cover the pan tightly, and turn the heat down as low as possible. The polenta must go *plop-plop*. It will be ready in 45 minutes. Serves 6.

SOURCE: *César* by Olivier Said and James Mellgren with Maggie Pond

COOK: Maggie Pond

chorizo and apples in hard cider

RIGHT NEXT DOOR TO THE WORLD-FAMOUS CHEZ PANISSE in Berkeley is a fine tapas place called César, where this superb dish is served in the fall and winter. A tapa can be a little something to have with drinks or a lot of little somethings to make a meal on the fly. This one comes from the Spanish region of Asturias, where hard cider (*sidra*) is the famous local product. It's a whole new way of looking at apples and pork, those boon companions. Here the pork is spicy chorizo, and the apples are both in the cider, the cooking medium, and in little cubes that absorb all the delectable flavors. It's a hearty enough dish to make a small meal on its own.

serves 8

- 16 small (1-inch) links Spanish chorizo (see notes)
- 2 Gala apples, cored and each cut into about 16 cubes
- 2 cups hard cider

In a large Dutch oven or traditional *cazuela* (a flameproof terra-cotta casserole), combine all the ingredients. Bring to a boil, then reduce the heat and simmer until the apples are tender and the chorizo are cooked through, about 30 minutes.

Remove the apples and chorizo from the pan. Continue to cook the cider down to a thick syrup, reducing it to 1/2 cup, about 5 minutes. Return the chorizo and apples to the pan, reheating and glazing them with the syrup. Serve immediately on small plates.

notes from our test kitchen

- Be sure to get Spanish chorizo, not Mexican, which is an entirely different product. Spanish chorizo is smoked and firm. Mexican chorizo is looser and made with fresh pork, and it must be cooked. If you can find only larger chorizo, cut the sausage into 1-inch lengths.
- If you're not serving individual plates, the most appealing way to present the sausage is in a smallish shallow dish, such as a pasta plate.

SOURCE: *From Curries to Kebabs* by Madhur Jaffrey

COOK: Madhur Jaffrey

melt-in-the-mouth lamb kebabs

THESE SUCCULENT KEBABS are really little pan-fried meatballs, and they're a revelation. They truly do melt in the mouth, at which point they release their marvelous flavors. These particular kebabs originated in the Muslim courts of Awadh, now Uttar Pradesh, and were originally made with crushed green papaya to tenderize the meat—not a problem with American lamb.

Why are they so very good? The seasonings are delicious, but what takes them over the top is the onion. It's fried in peanut oil until crisp, drained thoroughly, and then ground in a spice mill and mixed with the meat. For extra flavor, the kebabs are cooked in the oniony oil.

In India kebabs would be served with bread, raw onion rings (see notes), and fresh mint chutney. You may want to offer these as a main course. In that case, serve them over rice and add a raita (a yogurt-cucumber salad). This amount will serve four.

serves 8

- 1 pound ground fatty lamb
- 1 1/2 tablespoons finely grated fresh ginger
- 1 tablespoon finely chopped fresh mint
- 3 garlic cloves, crushed to a pulp
- 1 1/2 teaspoons garam masala (see notes)
- 1 teaspoon cayenne pepper
- 1 teaspoon salt
- 1/2 teaspoon finely chopped fresh rosemary (optional)
- Peanut or corn oil for shallow frying
- 1 medium onion, halved and thinly sliced
- 4 teaspoons chickpea flour (see notes)
- 4 teaspoons plain yogurt
- About 2 tablespoons *kewra* (screw pine) water (optional; see notes)
- Raw onion rings for serving (see notes)
- Fresh Cilantro Chutney (recipe follows) for serving

Put the lamb in a medium bowl. Add the ginger, mint, garlic, garam masala, cayenne, salt, and rosemary (if using), and mix well. Cover and refrigerate for at least 3 hours or up to 1 day.

Pour enough oil into a medium pan to come to a depth of 1/8 inch and set over medium-high heat. When the oil is hot, add the sliced onion and fry, stirring and turning the heat down as needed, until the slices are reddish brown and crisp, 10 to 12 minutes. Remove the slices with a slotted spoon, saving all the oil left in the pan, and spread out on a double layer of paper towels. They will crisp further as they cool. Change the paper towels and spread out the onion slices again to get rid of most of the oil. Once the onions look dry, put them in a clean coffee or spice grinder and grind coarsely.

Put the chickpea flour in a small cast-iron pan and set over medium-high heat. Stir the flour around until it turns a very light golden brown and emits a faintly roasted smell. Remove the flour from the hot pan.

Take the meat out of the refrigerator and add the ground onions, roasted chickpea flour, and yogurt. Mix well. Wet your hands with *kewra* water, if using, and form about 20 meatballs that are about 1 1/4 inches in diameter. Flatten the balls to make patties that are about 1 3/4 inches in diameter and 2/3 inch thick. If not serving immediately, place the patties in a single layer on two plates, cover with plastic wrap, and refrigerate.

Meanwhile, strain the oil left over from frying the onion and reserve.

Just before serving, pour the reserved oil into a nonstick pan—it needs to come to a depth of 1/4 inch, so add more, if necessary. Set the pan over medium-low heat. When the oil is hot, slide in as many kebabs as the pan will hold easily and fry for 2 to 3 minutes on each side, until reddish brown. Fry all the kebabs this way. Drain on paper towels and serve hot with raw onion rings and chutney.

fresh cilantro chutney

serves 6 to 8

- 1 cup tightly packed fresh cilantro leaves
- 2–3 hot green chiles, chopped
- 1 large or 2 medium garlic cloves, chopped
- 1/2 teaspoon salt, or to taste
- 3 tablespoons water
- 1 tablespoon fresh lemon juice
- 1 cup plain yogurt

Combine the cilantro, chiles, garlic, salt, water, and lemon juice in a blender. Blend, pushing down with a rubber spatula as needed, until smooth.

Put the yogurt in a medium bowl. Beat lightly with a fork until smooth. Add the contents of the blender and mix well. Taste for seasoning and serve.

notes from our test kitchen

- To make your own garam masala, grind the following in a spice grinder or coffee grinder: 1 tablespoon cardamom seeds, 1 teaspoon black peppercorns, 1 teaspoon black cumin seeds, 1/3 whole nutmeg, and a 2- to 3-inch cinnamon stick (broken into pieces). Store in a tightly covered container away from heat and light. Note that black cumin seeds taste very different from regular cumin seeds; they have a subtle musty, smoky flavor.
- If you don't want to make your own garam masala, try a good-quality store-bought brand. It won't be quite as flavorful, but it will still be really good.
- You can find chickpea flour (*besan*) at Indian groceries, many natural food stores, and some supermarkets. Store it, tightly sealed, in the freezer; it's relatively fragile. Screw pine is available at any Indian market. Just use regular water if you can't find it. But it's worth seeking out some screw pine essence, which Jaffrey describes as having "an almost overpoweringly sensual, flowery aroma."
- Delicious as the kebabs are on their own, they are even better with accompaniments. To make raw onion rings, halve a small onion (less than 5 ounces) and finely slice into half rings. Put them in a bowl of cold water, cover, and refrigerate for 2 to 3 hours. Drain and pat dry.

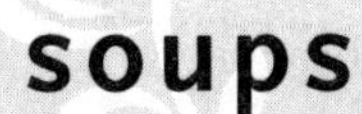

soups

chilled potato-chive soup

ONE OF THE BIGGEST (figuratively and literally) cookbooks to hit the shelves this year was Marcus Samuelsson's long-awaited *Aquavit*. It's a dramatic volume filled with lavish photographs and complex signature dishes, but the recipes that won our hearts were the simpler, homey creations like this cold soup, a version of vichyssoise, which Samuelsson adapted from a recipe of his Swedish grandmother's.

Chives grew wild on the coast of Sweden where he grew up, and so he learned to make the most of them. Not only do they add a bright oniony flavor to the soup, but they turn it a very pretty, pale, springtime green. The addition of fresh lime juice may seem unusual, but it gives the soup a welcome note of vibrancy and just the right lift.

serves 4

- 4 medium Yukon Gold potatoes, peeled and quartered (see note)
- 4 cups chicken stock
- 3 garlic cloves, peeled
- 1 cup finely chopped fresh chives
- 1 tablespoon finely chopped fresh tarragon
- 3 tablespoons fresh lime juice
- 1/2 cup sour cream
- Kosher salt and freshly ground white pepper

Put the potatoes in a medium pot, add the stock and garlic, and bring just to a boil. Reduce the heat slightly and simmer for 25 to 30 minutes until the potatoes are very soft.

Puree the soup with an immersion blender, or transfer to a regular blender, in batches, and puree. Add the chives, tarragon, and lime juice and blend well. Add the sour cream and puree. Season with salt and pepper to taste.

Transfer the soup to a bowl, cover, and refrigerate for 3 to 4 hours, or until thoroughly chilled, before serving.

notes from our test kitchen

- You'll want about 1¼ pound of potatoes; more, and the soup may turn out too thick.
- After chilling, the soup will thicken some. If it is too thick for your tastes, thin it with a bit of stock, water, or light cream.

SOURCE: *Jamie's Kitchen* by Jamie Oliver

COOK: Jamie Oliver

minted pea soup with crispy pancetta, bread, and sour cream

THIS IS A SOUP YOU'LL COME TO CRAVE. It's not the sludgy kind made from dried peas but a fresh-tasting baby pea soup with the zing of mint and a crunchy croutons-and-bacon topping. It's both subtle and hearty, and although it's not heavy, it can easily be a meal in itself.

Although Oliver used to make it with fresh spring peas, he quickly realized that frozen peas (he likes BirdsEye) work perfectly and make it possible to have the soup on the table speedily. Using frozen peas also means this can be served year-round, not just in the spring.

The rustic croutons and pancetta (the unsmoked Italian bacon, usually available at the deli counter) are a good trick to remember; they'd be great on other soups—such as lentil or potato soups—as well. Other herbs, such as basil and oregano, can be used.

serves 4 to 6

- 1/2 loaf stale white bread
- Extra-virgin olive oil
- 1 large handful of fresh mint, leaves stripped
- Sea salt and freshly ground black pepper
- 12 thin slices pancetta or bacon
- 1 bunch scallions, ends trimmed and roughly chopped
- 2 pats butter
- 1 pound 2 ounces frozen peas
- 1 quart chicken stock
- 7 tablespoons heavy cream
- 4 teaspoons sour cream

Preheat the oven to 350 degrees.

Take the crusts off the bread and pinch off irregular dice-size pieces. Put these into a roasting pan and drizzle with a little olive oil, scatter over some of the mint leaves, and season with salt and pepper. Chop the pancetta, add it to the roasting pan, and bake until the bread and pancetta are crunchy and golden—15 to 20 minutes.

Meanwhile, in a medium to large saucepan, slowly fry the scallions and remaining mint in the butter for about 3 minutes, or until soft. Turn the heat up, add the frozen peas and the chicken stock, and bring to a boil. Lower the heat, add the heavy cream, and simmer gently for 15 minutes.

Puree the soup until it's very smooth (you may want to do this in batches). Correct the seasoning very carefully to taste—really think about this a bit and get it just right. Remember: add, taste, add, taste. By this time the bread and pancetta should be nice and crisp, so ladle the soup into the bowls and sprinkle over the bread, mint leaves, and pancetta. Add a little sour cream and drizzle with some peppery extra-virgin olive oil.

notes from our test kitchen

- The size of pea packages varies: just come as close as you can to the amount specified here. Petite peas are the best-tasting.
- To make everything ready at the same time, put on the bread when the scallions begin to fry.
- Chopping the pancetta makes it a bit easier to work with.
- Oliver likes to use spinach and asparagus in the soup too.

tomato soup with spanish smoked paprika

THE "CREAM" in this quick soup is coconut milk, which gives it a light, complex quality. The subtle spice is the wonderful Spanish smoked paprika Pimentón de la Vera, but you can also use Hungarian sweet paprika. Top the soup with a little fresh goat cheese that melts in as you stir, and you have a deeply satisfying soup made from cans on your shelf.

Smoked Spanish paprika comes in sweet and hot versions; if you like things spicy, you can use all hot or half sweet and half hot smoked paprika.

serves 4

- 1 tablespoon olive oil
- 1/2 large onion, chopped
- 1 garlic clove, chopped
- Salt
- 1/2 teaspoon Spanish smoked sweet paprika, or Hungarian paprika
- 1/2 teaspoon dried oregano, crumbled, plus extra for garnish
- 1 pint cherry tomatoes, quartered, or one 14.5-ounce can diced organic tomatoes, including their juice
- 3 cups chicken stock
- 1 cup unsweetened coconut milk, well stirred
- Freshly ground black pepper
- 1/4 cup crumbled fresh goat cheese, such as Montrachet

Heat the olive oil in a soup pot. Add the onion and stir it well over medium heat until wilted, about 5 minutes. Add the garlic and 1/2 teaspoon salt and cook over medium-low heat for another few minutes, until the garlic is soft. Add the paprika and oregano and stir well, and cook for a few minutes more. Add the tomatoes and cook for a few minutes.

Add the stock and bring to a simmer. Let simmer, uncovered, for 15 minutes.

Pour the soup into a blender and puree it in batches (or puree it right in the soup pot using an immersion blender), leaving a few bits of tomato. Add the coconut milk and blend well. Return the soup to the pot (if necessary) and bring to a simmer. Check the seasoning, adding pepper to taste. Serve the soup in shallow plates, each garnished with a tablespoon of goat cheese and a pinch of oregano.

SOURCE: *Tom Valenti's Soups, Stews, and One-Pot Meals* by Tom Valenti and Andrew Friedman

COOK: Tom Valenti

roasted butternut squash soup with bacon

ROASTING WINTER SQUASH before pureeing it—as opposed to simmering it—concentrates its flavor and sweetness. And roasting it under a blanket of sliced bacon infuses this voluptuously smooth sweet autumn soup with an appealing smoky, savory dimension. The crispy bacon is crumbled and scattered on top. (Happily, there's more than you need as a garnish, and it makes a great little kitchen snack.)

This gem of a recipe comes from Tom Valenti, the New York City chef considered by many to be the grandmaster of comfort food. He points out that it's equally good with other winter squashes, such as acorn and Hubbard. The soup can be held for a few days in the refrigerator or frozen for up to 1 month.

serves 8

- 6 pounds butternut squash
- 6 tablespoons unsalted butter (see notes)
- Coarse salt and freshly ground black pepper
- 8 slices smoked bacon (see notes)
- 2 tablespoons olive oil
- 1 large Spanish onion, cut into small dice
- 3 thyme sprigs, plus extra for garnish
- 1 bay leaf
- 1 1/2 quarts chicken stock or broth
- 2 tablespoons heavy cream (optional; see notes)
- Sugar, if needed
- Extra-virgin olive oil, to drizzle

Preheat the oven to 400 degrees. Cut the butternut squashes in half lengthwise. Scoop out and discard the seeds. Place the squash halves cut side up on a rimmed baking sheet. Divide the butter among the hollowed-out seed cavities and generously season the squash with salt and pepper. Lay 1 to 2 strips of bacon lengthwise along the surface of each half. Roast, basting a few times by scooping the butter out of the cavity and spooning it over the bacon and squash, until the squash is tender and easily pierced by a sharp knife, 35 to 40 minutes (see notes).

Remove the baking sheet from the oven. Transfer the bacon to a paper-towel-lined plate to drain. Once cool, mince or crumble into small bits and set aside.

Once the squash have cooled slightly, scoop out the flesh with a tablespoon. Discard the skins.

Heat the olive oil in a large, heavy-bottomed pot over medium-high heat until hot but not smoking. Add the onion, season with salt and pepper, and cook, stirring, until softened but not browned, about 5 minutes. Stir in the thyme sprigs and bay leaf and then add the squash. Cook, stirring to integrate the flavors and keep the squash from scorching, for 1 to 2 minutes.

Add the stock to the pot, stirring to incorporate, and bring to a boil over high heat. Lower the heat and simmer for 15 minutes.

Using tongs or a slotted spoon, fish out and discard the thyme sprigs and bay leaf. Transfer the soup to a food processor. (You can also use a regular blender, working in batches.) Add the cream, if using, and process for several minutes until uniformly thick and creamy. Be careful not to overblend, which would turn the soup thin. If not serving immediately, let cool, cover, and refrigerate for a few days or freeze for up to 1 month.

Return the soup to the pot and gently reheat it. Taste and adjust the seasonings with salt, pepper, and sugar if necessary.

To serve, ladle the soup into bowls, and scatter some of the minced bacon over the surface. Top with fresh thyme leaves and a drizzle of extra-virgin olive oil. Serve at once.

notes from our test kitchen

- Tom Valenti uses double-smoked slab bacon and slices it himself. You can also use good-quality medium- to thick-sliced bacon here.
- Depending on the season, the squash may take as much as an hour to cook to tenderness. The longer the squash has been in storage, the more time it will take to cook.
- If the bacon gets crispy before the squash is tender, remove the strips and set them aside on paper towels to drain.

- There may be a fair amount of fat drippings on the baking sheet after roasting the squash. Discard or save for another use.
- This is one instance where an immersion blender is not recommended. Stick with the food processor or blender.
- Even though the heavy cream is listed as optional in the recipe, it goes a long way in pulling together the various flavors of the soup. We wouldn't dream of leaving it out.

tip

Tom Valenti suggests using this same technique to make a richly flavored butternut squash puree. Follow the recipe for the soup, omitting the stock and adding 2 tablespoons cold unsalted butter to the puree as it's blended in the food processor (the blender won't work for the puree). Season with a few pinches of light brown sugar, a dash of maple syrup, and ground cinnamon, allspice, or nutmeg, according to your taste. Serves 8 as a side dish.

french country cabbage soup

CABBAGE SOUP IS AN OLD FRENCH FARMHOUSE FAVORITE, but here's a version that will please the most urbane palate. Simmering thinly sliced green cabbage together with onions, carrots, celery, and potatoes in a light broth creates a soup that's as lovely in the bowl as it is comforting to eat. The bit of white wine added to the pot lends a light, tangy note.

In southwestern France, cooks might crumble bits of Roquefort or other blue cheese into each bowl. Marlena Spieler prefers the taste of grated pecorino or locatelli Romano. We sometimes stir in a few bits of fresh goat cheese instead. In truth, this soup is good without any cheese at all. Whatever you do, serve it with slices of rustic bread—toasted or not.

serves 6 to 8

- 2 tablespoons butter, or vegetable oil, or fatty prosciutto bits
- 2 celery stalks with leaves, coarsely chopped
- 1 onion, coarsely chopped
- 1 medium carrot, thinly sliced
- 4 garlic cloves, coarsely chopped
- 1/2 small green cabbage, cored and thinly sliced
- 2 bay leaves
- About 1 tablespoon fresh thyme leaves
- 1 cup dry white wine
- 5 cups vegetable or chicken stock
- 2–3 medium red potatoes, cut into bite-size pieces
- 2 ounces prosciutto (about 4 thin slices), diced
- Salt and freshly ground pepper, to taste
- Freshly grated pecorino or locatelli Romano cheese for garnish

Heat the fat over medium heat in a soup pot. Add the celery, onion, carrot, and garlic and cook, stirring occasionally, until softened but not at all browned. Add the cabbage, bay leaves, and thyme and cook, stirring every so often, over medium heat until the cabbage is softened.

Pour in the wine and increase the heat to high. Simmer rapidly until the liquid almost completely evaporates, about 10 minutes. When the wine has evaporated, add the stock and lower the heat to medium-high. Simmer until the cabbage is tender. Add the potatoes and diced prosciutto and simmer until the potatoes are tender, another 10 minutes or so.

Discard the bay leaves, taste for salt and pepper, and serve in big shallow bowls, sprinkled with cheese.

note from our test kitchen

- The soup will have a deeper flavor if you add a pinch of salt and pepper to the onion-celery-carrot mix as it cooks, and again when you add the cabbage. This way, the soup probably won't need much seasoning before serving, other than a good shot of black pepper.

SOURCE: *Gulf Coast Kitchens* by Constance Snow
COOK: Constance Snow after Debra Hanus

creamy roasted poblano soup

THIS RECIPE COMES FROM DEBRA HANUS, a potter and yoga instructor who lives near Beeville, Texas. She declares it "a never-fail party starter," and we won't argue. Probably the only challenge to making this soup is deciding how many chiles to use. The book's author, Constance Snow, tells us to use one for a "slight kick," three for a "rowdy taste."

Besides being simple to throw together, this creamy pale green soup is equally delicious served hot or chilled. If you'd like to turn it into a more substantial dish, add roasted corn kernels or chunks of leftover chicken. We like a sprinkle of toasted pepitas (hulled pumpkin seeds) for a little textural contrast.

serves 4 to 6

- 1 large onion, chopped
- 2 tablespoons unsalted butter
- 3 cups chicken stock
- 1 8-ounce package cream cheese, chunked
- 1–3 poblano peppers, roasted, peeled, seeded, and chopped (see notes)
- 1 cup sour cream or plain yogurt
- Crumbled queso blanco, for garnish (see notes)
- Lime wedges for garnish

Cook the onion in the butter in a medium saucepan over medium heat until soft and golden but not browned. Add the chicken stock and cream cheese. Stir until the stock is hot and the cheese is melted; do not let the soup boil. Cool slightly, then puree with the roasted poblanos in a food processor or blender. (Do this in batches if necessary.) Return the soup to the pot; add the sour cream or yogurt and heat through, but do not boil. Serve hot or chilled, each bowl garnished with the crumbled cheese and a lime wedge.

notes from our test kitchen

- To roast and seed the poblano chiles, set them over a gas burner or under a broiler. Roast, turning with tongs, until the skin is blistering and charred all over. Transfer the roasted chiles to a bowl, cover tightly with plastic, and set aside to cool. Once cool, the skins will slide right off. Remove the stems and seeds and coarsely chop the chiles.
- *Queso blanco* is a simple, fresh white cheese with an pleasantly rubbery texture. Crumbled onto soups and other hot foods, it holds its shape and doesn't melt. If you can't find *queso blanco*, substitute *queso fresco,* or you can make your own or serve the soup without cheese. We have on many occasions and love it just as much—especially with few roasted pepitas on top.

tip

Constance Snow explains how to make your own cheese for the topping: Warm 1 gallon whole milk (preferably raw) in a stainless-steel pot until it reaches 175 degrees. Remove from the heat and slowly add 1/4 cup distilled white vinegar, stirring gently. A curd with a greenish yellow whey should quickly form. Drain the curd into a cheesecloth-lined colander. Tie the four corners of the cheesecloth together and hang the curd from the handle of a wooden spoon placed across a bowl. Set aside to drain for 1 hour. Refrigerate for up to 1 week. Makes 1 1/2 pounds.

SOURCE: *Gourmet*

COOK: **Shelley Wiseman**

spanish almond soup

WE LOVE TO START A MEAL WITH SOUP, but are often thwarted by the long simmering time required by many recipes. Here's a fabulously easy solution that comes together in a blender and simmers for no more than 5 minutes. One friend we served it to described this earthy soup as "Spain in a bowl," referring to the appealing combination of garlic, parsley, saffron, sherry vinegar, and roasted almonds. The almonds, along with seasoned croutons, thicken the soup, so there's no flour or cream to mask the purity of the ingredients. And because it simmers for only a short time, the flavors remain vibrant.

serves 4

- 3 tablespoons extra-virgin olive oil
- 1/2 cup (3 ounces) blanched almonds
- 2 cups 1/2-inch bread cubes (from a baguette; see notes)
- 2 tablespoons chopped fresh flat-leaf parsley
- 1 large garlic clove, finely chopped
- 1/4 teaspoon coarsely crumbled saffron threads (0.3 g)
- 2 cups chicken stock
- 2 cups water
- Salt, or to taste
- 1 teaspoon sherry vinegar, or to taste (see notes)

Heat the oil in a large heavy skillet over medium-high heat until hot but not smoking, then sauté the almonds, stirring constantly, until golden, 2 to 4 minutes. Transfer the almonds with a slotted spoon to a blender. Add the bread cubes, parsley, garlic, and saffron to the oil in the skillet and cook over medium heat, stirring constantly, until golden, about 2 minutes. Transfer about one fourth of crouton mixture to a small bowl for garnish, then transfer the remainder to the blender. Add the stock to the blender and puree until smooth.

Transfer the puree to a 2- to 3-quart heavy saucepan and stir in the water. Simmer, uncovered, stirring occasionally until slightly thickened, about 5 minutes. Stir in the salt and vinegar (start with 1/2 teaspoon and add more to taste). Serve the soup topped with remaining croutons.

notes from our test kitchen

- Shop for a high-quality artisan baguette for this soup. The squishy supermarket kind won't do as good a job of thickening and flavoring the soup.
- In the original recipe, the sherry vinegar is listed as optional. This is unthinkable to us, as it adds a much-needed flavor dimension to the soup.

SOURCE: *Family Circle*

COOK: **Donna Meadow**

roasted cauliflower soup

CAULIFLOWER SOUPS seemed to abound this year. They ranged from creamy and rich to rustic and brothy. In the end, this one stole our hearts for several reasons: it's incredibly simple to make, it's creamy without being excessively rich, and it's got a flavor we can't resist. Tossing the cauliflower with olive oil and then roasting it before transforming it into soup gives the whole thing a wonderfully sweet, caramelized flavor. Once the cauliflower is roasted, it's simply a matter of a brief simmer and a whir in the blender.

serves 6 to 8

- 1 large head cauliflower (about 3 pounds), cut into florets (about 10 cups)
- 1 large onion, sliced
- 2 garlic cloves, each halved
- 2 tablespoons olive oil
- 2 14½-ounce cans (3⅔ cups) chicken broth or homemade stock
- 1 cup water
- 1 bay leaf
- 1 teaspoon chopped fresh thyme
- 1 cup half-and-half
- 1 teaspoon salt, or to taste
- ⅛ teaspoon freshly ground black pepper or more to taste

Preheat the oven to 400 degrees. In a large roasting pan (or on a rimmed baking sheet), combine the cauliflower, onion, and garlic. Drizzle over the olive oil and toss to coat.

Roast, stirring after 15 minutes, until the vegetables begin to brown and soften, for 30 minutes.

In a large saucepan, combine the roasted cauliflower mixture with the chicken broth, water, bay leaf, and thyme. Cover and bring to a boil. Reduce the heat to a simmer and simmer, still covered, until the cauliflower is tender, 20 minutes.

Discard the bay leaf. Transfer the soup to a blender or food processor, in batches, and puree until smooth. Return the soup to the saucepan. Stir in the half-and-half. Season with salt and pepper, heat gently, and serve.

notes from our test kitchen

- Don't be shy when seasoning this soup. We find that it tastes best with a bracing shot of freshly ground black pepper just before serving.
- If you can't resist adding garnishes to a bowl of creamy soup, try a drizzle of heavy cream or extra-virgin olive oil and a sprinkling of fresh thyme leaves. Little croutons are good, too.

SOURCE: *Moosewood Restaurant Celebrates*
COOKS: The Moosewood Collective

north african tomato bulgur soup (shorba)

THE INSPIRATION FOR THIS SIMPLE, nourishing meal comes from the North African and Middle Eastern soups served to break the fast during Ramadan. The aromas that build as you prepare the soup are the perfect way to soothe any hunger pangs. The combination of spices—coriander, cardamom, and cinnamon—lends an exotic note and transforms an otherwise simple dish into something uniquely wonderful.

Although the feta and parsley are listed as optional garnishes, we encourage you to include them. The simple soup benefits greatly from their salty and sharp edge.

serves 4

- 2 tablespoons olive oil
- 1½ cups finely chopped onions
- 1 large garlic clove, minced or pressed
- 1 teaspoon salt, or more to taste
- ½ teaspoon freshly ground black pepper, or more to taste
- 1 teaspoon ground coriander
- ¼ teaspoon ground cardamom
- ½ teaspoon ground cinnamon
- ⅔ cup medium-grain raw bulgur
- 2 cups finely chopped fresh tomatoes (see notes)
- 3½ cups stock or broth (see notes)
- 1–2 tablespoons fresh lemon juice
- Grated feta cheese (optional)
- Chopped fresh parsley (optional)

Warm the oil in a 2-quart pot over medium heat. Add the onions and garlic, sprinkle with the salt, and sauté until the onions are soft and translucent, about 10 minutes. Add the pepper, coriander, cardamom, and cinnamon and cook, stirring constantly, for about 1 minute.

Add the bulgur and continue to cook, stirring, for another 1 to 2 minutes. Add the tomatoes and the stock, cover, and bring to a boil. Reduce the heat and simmer for about 10 minutes, covered, until the bulgur is tender. Remove from the heat and stir in the lemon juice. Taste for salt and pepper.

Serve immediately topped with feta cheese and fresh parsley, if desired.

notes from our test kitchen

- To boost the flavor of the soup, start with whole coriander seeds and cardamom pods. Lightly toast coriander seeds in a dry skillet until fragrant and then grind to a fine powder in a spice grinder or coffee grinder. Crack open the cardamom pods and grind the little black seeds to a powder as well.
- Since we often crave this soup in the winter, we make it with canned tomatoes in place of fresh. Use one 28-ounce can of whole, peeled tomatoes, drained and chopped.
- At the famed vegetarian Moosewood Restaurant in Ithaca, New York, this soup would always be made with vegetable broth or stock. We confess that we like it with chicken broth, but the decision is up to you.
- The bulgur will continue to absorb liquid as it sits, so if you make the soup ahead, you will want to add a little more stock or water when reheating it.

SOURCE: *Cooking from the Heart* by Michael J. Rosen

COOK: Jerry Traunfeld

oyster stew with ginger and leeks

WE'VE LONG CONSIDERED OYSTER STEW a special holiday luxury—or something we order once or twice a year at an oyster bar. Never would we have thought of it as a dish to make on a camping trip. But leave it to Jerry Traunfeld, the wonderfully talented and innovative chef at the Herbfarm in Woodinville, Washington, to do just that. Traunfeld does admit that it was car camping, but we're still impressed. Although we wouldn't discourage you from taking the fixings for oyster stew on your next camping trip, we're content making it at home in the shelter of our kitchens.

We love the way the fresh ginger and chopped tarragon play off the briny, sweet taste of the oysters and the rich, buttery flavor of the cream. Don't let the notion of pairing ginger and tarragon scare you. Just as star anise and ginger make a happy marriage in many Chinese dishes, the anise accent of the tarragon is a perfect mate for the ginger. This is a perfect example of how a single, unexpected twist on a classic recipe can lead to pure delight.

serves 2

- 2 tablespoons unsalted butter
- 1/2 leek, white part only, washed and thinly sliced (1 cup)
- 1 tablespoon finely chopped fresh ginger
- 1/4 cup dry white wine
- 1/2 cup heavy cream
- 10 ounces freshly shucked extra-small oysters
- 1/2 teaspoon sea salt
- 1 tablespoon coarsely chopped fresh tarragon
- 1 tablespoon fresh lemon juice
- Crusty French bread, for serving

Melt the butter in a medium nonreactive saucepan over medium heat. Add the leek and cook until translucent, about 3 minutes. Add the ginger and cook for 1 minute. Pour in the wine and simmer for 30 seconds. Add the cream and bring to a simmer. Add the oysters and heat gently until they are firm and heated through, about 3 minutes. Add the salt, tarragon, and lemon juice. Taste and adjust the seasonings if necessary.

To serve, spoon the oysters and sauce into two warmed bowls. Serve the bread on the side.

notes from our test kitchen

- Don't be tempted to grate the fresh ginger for this recipe. It won't have nearly the pleasing effect of the finely minced bits floating in the stew.
- Set a teakettle on to boil as you start the soup. When it boils, fill the soup bowls with water to warm them.

SOURCE: *A Taste of the Tropics* by Jay Solomon

COOK: Jay Solomon

pacific rim chicken noodle soup

WE EXPECT THAT EVEN A WHIFF of this enticing version of chicken noodle soup would cure just about any doldrums or nasty cold. But don't wait until you're under the weather to try it. It's seasoned with lemongrass, ginger, garlic, fish sauce, chiles, and lime juice. In place of the soft, thick noodles in traditional chicken noodle soup, this one includes delicately thin cellophane or rice noodles and shredded leafy greens for a perfect textural contrast to the fragrant broth.

serves 6 to 8

- 4 ounces cellophane or thin rice noodles
- 8 cups water (see notes)
- 1 chicken (about 3 pounds), cut into 6–8 pieces
- 2 cups chopped celery
- 1 large onion, diced
- 2 tablespoons vegetable oil
- 1 tablespoon minced fresh lemongrass (see notes)
- 2 garlic cloves, minced
- 2 teaspoons minced fresh ginger
- 1 chile pepper, seeded and minced (see notes)
- 4 scallions, chopped
- 1 cup shredded bok choy, kale leaves, or Chinese cabbage
- 1/4 cup Asian fish sauce
- 2 tablespoons fresh lime juice
- 1 tablespoon minced fresh cilantro

Put the noodles in hot water to soften, about 3 minutes, then drain. Cut the noodles into 2-inch sections. Set aside.

Combine the water, chicken pieces, celery, and onion in a large stockpot. Bring to a boil and simmer for 30 to 35 minutes over medium-high heat. Transfer the chicken to a plate and strain the stock through a sieve into a large bowl. Discard the vegetables.

After the chicken cools, remove the meat from the bones. Discard the skin and bones and add the meat to the bowl of stock. Clean the stockpot. Return the pot to the stove and add the oil, lemongrass, garlic, ginger, and chile pepper. Sauté over medium heat for 2 to 3 minutes, stirring frequently, until the seasonings are soft. Return the chicken and stock to the pot. Add the bok choy (or kale or cabbage), scallions, fish sauce, and lime juice. Bring the soup to a simmer and simmer until the greens are tender. Add the softened noodles and cilantro and simmer, stirring occasionally, for another 4 to 5 minutes over medium heat.

To serve, transfer the noodles (with tongs or a large slotted spoon) to soup bowls and ladle the soup over the noodles.

notes from our test kitchen

- To boost the flavor of this soup, we like to use half chicken stock and half water to simmer the chicken.
- When using fresh lemongrass, peel away the tough or dried outermost leaves to reveal the tender "heart." This is the part you want to mince and use in your cooking. Avoid the fibrous green top and tough root parts.
- The size and type of fresh chile is really a matter of taste, but we've had best results using a jalapeño or serrano.

salads

SOURCE: *Flavor* by Rocco DiSpirito
COOK: Rocco DiSpirito

heirloom tomatoes with orange zest

WE LOVE IT WHEN MASTER CHEFS overcome their urge to complicate. When the chips are down, the brilliant cooks make simple food that's simply dazzling — and that's the case here. Rocco DiSpirito, the star of the marathon restaurant-opening TV reality show *The Restaurant,* offers nature's best tomatoes, harvest heirlooms, with sherry vinegar and a perfect tomato partner, orange zest. No oil — just salt and pepper, and you're done.

Of course, it's hard to improve on a great heirloom tomato at its peak of flavor, but the Spanish accents of orange and sherry do make the tomatoes taste even more delicious. As DiSpirito says, anything more would be an insult to the tomatoes.

serves 6

4 large heirloom tomatoes, thinly sliced
Finely grated zest of 1 large or 3 small oranges
1 1/2 tablespoons sherry vinegar
Coarse sea salt and freshly ground black pepper

Arrange the tomatoes shingle style on individual plates or on a single platter. Scatter the orange zest over the tomatoes and dress them with the vinegar and salt and pepper to taste. Serve immediately.

tip

Unlikely as it sounds, another dynamite idea for peak-of-the-season sliced tomatoes is to serve them dressed in melted butter. Gabrielle Hamilton, the chef at Prune in Manhattan, came up with this one.

SOURCE: *New York Times*
COOK: Lori Longbotham
STORY BY: Melissa Clark

baby greens with broiled lemons

THIS SALAD IS FOR LEMON LOVERS, and it goes with virtually everything that's delicious with lemons—a broad category that ranges from fish to lamb.

To smooth out the pucker factor, the lemon slices mellow a little in salt and sugar for an hour before getting caramelized under the broiler, which both tames them and brings out more dimensions of their flavor. Their roasty edges from the broiling look especially appealing on the greens.

There's only one caveat here: the lemon slices really do need to be paper-thin. If they're not, you'll get too much chewiness and bitterness in every bite.

serves 6

- 2 lemons, cut into paper-thin slices and seeded (see note)
- 2 tablespoons sugar
- 1 teaspoon salt, or more to taste
- 8 cups baby greens such as arugula or mesclun, washed and thoroughly dried
- 2 tablespoons olive oil
- 1/4 teaspoon freshly ground black pepper
- Fresh lemon juice (optional)

Combine the lemons, sugar, and salt in a medium bowl and let stand for 1 hour, stirring occasionally.

Preheat the broiler. Place the lemons on a rimmed baking sheet in a single layer and spoon any liquid left in the bowl over them. Broil about 5 inches from the heat until lightly browned, 3 to 4 minutes, turning the pan, if necessary, so that the lemons brown evenly.

Meanwhile, place the greens in a serving bowl. Add the hot lemons and their liquid, along with the olive oil and pepper; toss well. Season with salt and lemon juice, if desired. Serve immediately.

note from our test kitchen

If you have trouble slicing the lemons paper-thin, it's easier to cut them in half lengthwise, place the cut side down on the cutting board, and slice paper-thin half-moons. Smaller lemons will be better than gigantic ones, which may have too much bitter white pith.

SOURCE: *Food & Wine*
COOK: **Fanny Singer after Alice Waters**
STORY BY: **Peggy Knickerbocker**

baby romaine with green goddess dressing

WHEN ALICE WATERS'S DAUGHTER, FANNY, went off to college at Yale, anyone familiar with the food culture in Berkeley, her hometown, might have predicted dining hall shock. Fanny literally cut her teeth at Chez Panisse, her mother's world-famous restaurant, and even her babysitters cooked with her. Shocked she was, but her reaction was highly positive. Fanny set about trying to improve the dining hall fare for everyone by working with a group of students who had already started lobbying for locally raised food. She also discovered her own inner cook, and that included some dishes her mother wouldn't dream of making, such as bacon-filled waffles.

This salad reflects her Berkeley upbringing, and Fanny says she could eat it every day. The dressing is an update on the classic green goddess, which everyone seemed to rediscover this year. In Fanny's version, there are five herbs and both lemon and lime juice. You'll have too much dressing; you can eat it the next day, too, as Fanny does. Serve it over cold poached fish, or dress lobster salad with it to make lobster rolls, Fanny's choice for her birthday dinner.

serves 6

- 1 small shallot, minced
- 1 garlic clove, minced
- 1 tablespoon white wine vinegar
- 1 tablespoon fresh lemon juice
- 2 teaspoons fresh lime juice
- 1 large egg yolk, at room temperature (optional)
- 1/2 cup extra-virgin olive oil
- 1/2 ripe avocado, mashed
- 3 tablespoons chopped fresh parsley
- 1 tablespoon chopped fresh tarragon
- 1 tablespoon chopped fresh basil
- 1 tablespoon chopped fresh cilantro
- 1 tablespoon chopped fresh chives
- Salt and freshly ground black pepper
- 1 1/2 pounds baby romaine lettuce heads, halved or quartered

In a small bowl, combine the shallot, garlic, vinegar, lemon juice, and lime juice. Let stand for 5 minutes.

In a medium bowl, beat the egg yolk, if using, with a whisk. Gradually add half the olive oil in a thin drizzle, whisking constantly. Add 1 tablespoon liquid from the shallot mixture, then whisk in the remaining olive oil. Add the avocado and mash it in with a fork. Whisk in the shallot mixture and herbs, then season with salt and pepper to taste.

Divide the lettuce among individual salad bowls, top with some of the dressing, and serve.

SOURCE: *Fine Cooking*

COOK: Joanne Weir

tomato and fresh green bean salad with crisp prosciutto

YOU MIGHT SAY THAT the San Francisco–based cooking teacher Joanne Weir wrote the book on tomatoes—or at least she wrote *a* book on them. And her passion for tomatoes is obvious in this brilliant little summer salad. There's only one word of caution: it may not thrill you if you make it with ordinary supermarket tomatoes. But in the summer, when markets are brimming with vine-ripened tomatoes, there's nothing better.

The idea behind this salad is to showcase a few varieties of fresh tomatoes—both for visual contrast and for taste—and to pair them with crunchy green beans and a bit of crisp prosciutto. Ideally, you want juicy slicing tomatoes cut into fat wedges and tossed with a mix of red and yellow cherry or other bite-size tomatoes. The crispy prosciutto topping is quickly made by baking the ham in a hot oven—we love it so much that we sprinkle it on all sorts of other salads and soups to provide a savory crunch. It's similar to crumbled bacon but more delicate.

serves 6 to 8

- 6 medium-size ripe tomatoes, each cut into 6 wedges
- 1 tablespoon kosher salt (see notes)
- 4 thin slices prosciutto (about 2 ounces)
- 12 ounces fresh green beans, trimmed and cut into 2-inch pieces
- 3 tablespoons chopped fresh summer savory (see notes)
- 2 garlic cloves, minced
- 2 tablespoons sherry vinegar
- 1/4 cup extra-virgin olive oil
- Freshly ground black pepper
- 1 1/2 cups yellow and orange cherry tomatoes (or other bite-size tomatoes), halved
- Fresh summery savory sprigs for garnish

Preheat the oven to 400 degrees. Put a large pot of salted water on to boil. Put the tomato wedges in a colander set over a bowl. Sprinkle with the salt, toss, and let stand for 30 minutes.

Slice the prosciutto crosswise into 1/2-inch strips. Arrange on a baking sheet in a single layer and bake until crisp and light golden, 8 to 10 minutes. Set aside.

Meanwhile, when the water comes to a boil, add the beans and cook until tender, 4 to 6 minutes. Drain and let cool.

In a small bowl, whisk together the chopped savory, garlic, and vinegar. Whisk in the olive oil to blend. Season with salt and pepper to taste.

Combine the tomato wedges, cherry tomatoes, and green beans in a bowl. Add the vinaigrette, toss, and season with salt and pepper to taste. Transfer to a shallow serving bowl or platter, sprinkle with the prosciutto, and garnish with the summer savory sprigs. Serve immediately.

notes from our test kitchen

- If you stock *fleur de sel,* the delicately flaky French sea salt, this would be a good place to use it. Its light crunch is perfect on juicy tomatoes.
- If you can't find fresh summer savory, use thyme or marjoram, or a mixture of both.
- Watch the prosciutto carefully as it cooks. It can become overdone and tough, instead of crisp, in a matter of minutes. The timing will depend some on just how thinly it was sliced.

tip

Joanne Weir reminds us *never* to refrigerate tomatoes. Whether they're cherry tomatoes from the supermarket or heirloom varieties from the farmers' market, keep them away from the cold. Chilling destroys their flavor and turns the texture mealy. The ideal way to store fresh tomatoes is out of any direct light and at around 50 degrees.

SOURCE: *Once Upon a Tart* by Frank Mentesana and Jerome Audureau with Carolynn Carreño

COOKS: Frank Mentesana and Jerome Audureau

crunchy cucumber, celery, and red bell pepper salad with cumin and fresh mint

THIS COLORFUL AND REFRESHING SALAD from Once Upon a Tart . . . , a popular café and bakeshop in New York City, is something we make year-round. It's best, of course, in the summer, with fresh local peppers and cucumbers, but we also rely on it in the winter when we're craving something crunchy and bright. The dash of cumin and mint in the dressing provides just the right note to make this salad something quite special.

Feel free to exercise your creativity with the elements here. For instance, thinly sliced mushrooms, shaved radishes, or even julienned sticks of jicama are good additions.

serves 6

SALAD

- 6 celery ribs, cut into 1/4-inch-thick slices
- 3 cucumbers, peeled, halved, seeded, and cut on the diagonal into 1/4-inch-thick slices
- 3 scallions, white and green parts, cut into 1/4-inch-thick slices
- 1 red bell pepper, halved, seeded, and julienned
- 1/2 red onion, halved again and thinly sliced

VINAIGRETTE

- 1 tablespoon Dijon mustard
- 1 garlic clove, minced
- 1/4 cup white wine vinegar
- 1 teaspoon ground cumin
- 1 teaspoon salt
- Freshly ground black pepper
- 1/4 cup olive oil
- 2 tablespoons finely chopped fresh flat-leaf parsley
- 2 tablespoons finely chopped fresh mint

MAKE THE SALAD:

Toss the vegetables into a big bowl as you cut them.

MAKE THE VINAIGRETTE:

In a small bowl, whisk together the mustard, garlic, vinegar, cumin, salt, and a few grinds of pepper. Add the olive oil in a slow, steady, thin stream, whisking as you go. This will form an emulsion and thicken the dressing. Stir in the parsley and mint.

ASSEMBLE THE SALAD:

Just before you're ready to serve the salad, pour the vinaigrette over the vegetables. Using a large metal spoon or your hands, toss until everything is evenly coated. Taste to see if the salad needs more of anything, particularly salt, and serve.

notes from our test kitchen

- Kirby cucumbers, the smaller pickling type, tend to have more crunch and fewer seeds than the larger standard varieties. They also are not waxed, so you don't have to deal with that unpleasantly slick peel. English cucumbers, the seedless variety sold wrapped in plastic in supermarkets, work well here, too.
- Starting with whole cumin seeds will greatly improve the taste of the dressing. Toast them briefly in a dry skillet over medium-high heat until fragrant. Then grind to a fine powder in a spice or coffee grinder (or using a mortar and pestle) and add to the dressing.

SOURCE: *Food & Wine*

COOK: Laura Chenel

sweet pepper salad with manchego and almonds

IF YOU LIKE GOAT CHEESE, CHANCES ARE YOU'VE BOUGHT some of Laura Chenel's award-winning fresh California goat cheese. Chenel loves all kinds of cheese, however, and here her recipe features Manchego, the sheep's milk cheese from Spain that seems to have taken America by storm. This is basically a Spanish salad, using typical ingredients such as almonds, roasted red peppers, capers, and sherry vinegar.

To say what's in it, however, doesn't really convey the appeal of this salad, which is stunning to look at and wonderful to eat. It demands some good bread to sop up all the delectable juices. Indeed, this could be lunch all by itself, leaving some room for dessert. Best of all, it goes together in much less than half an hour—even less if you cheat a bit as we did (see notes).

serves 4

- 2 teaspoons vegetable oil
- 1/2 cup whole blanched almonds
- 2 cups roasted red peppers cut into 1/2- x 2-inch strips (see notes)
- 1/4 cup extra-virgin olive oil
- 2 tablespoons sherry vinegar
- 1 large garlic clove, minced
- 1 1/2 teaspoons chopped drained capers
- 1/2 teaspoon finely chopped fresh thyme
- 1/2 teaspoon minced fresh marjoram
- Salt and freshly ground black pepper
- 20 small pitted green olives
- 4 ounces Manchego cheese, cut into 1/4-inch-thick slices
- 1 tablespoon minced fresh flat-leaf parsley
- Crusty bread for serving

Heat the vegetable oil in a medium skillet over medium heat. Add the almonds and cook, stirring, until golden, about 5 minutes. Transfer to paper towels and let cool, then coarsely chop.

Arrange the peppers on plates. In a small bowl, combine the olive oil, vinegar, garlic, capers, thyme, and marjoram. Season with salt and pepper to taste and drizzle over the peppers. Top with the green olives, almonds, and cheese. Sprinkle with the parsley and serve with crusty bread.

notes from our test kitchen

- Cheater's Version: At Whole Foods Market, we bought the wonderful smoky red Spanish pimentón peppers that are roasted and sold in bulk there. (Other places sell them in jars, which makes this approach quite expensive.) Whole Foods also sells toasted Spanish almonds (skip the first step of the recipe) and excellent Manchego. We arranged everything on a big platter, cutting the Manchego into triangles and scattering the little triangles over the peppers. The only real work was mincing the parsley, and frankly, it's not essential.
- To roast red peppers, preheat the oven to 350 degrees. Cut the peppers in half and remove the stems and seeds. Place them skin down on a foil-covered baking sheet and roast for 20 to 30 minutes, until the skins take on some color. You can remove the skins or not, as you like. Don't rinse the peppers, though, since that removes precious flavor.
- There's a lot of imitation Manchego around. Look for the La Mancha designation on the label to get the real thing.

SOURCE: *New York Times*

COOK: Nigella Lawson

ricotta and pine nut salad

SOMEONE WE KNOW refers to salads as "leaf arrangements"—a common enough idea, but one that's increasingly changing as we become more familiar with salads from elsewhere in the world. This one comes from England, and although at its base it's a leaf arrangement, it also affords an entirely fresh look at salad. The many-colored green leaves are arranged on a large platter or in a wide, shallow bowl, lightly dressed with a simple red wine vinaigrette, and then dotted with little hills of herb-flecked ricotta that are dusted with paprika. Toasted pine nuts and fresh basil leaves get scattered around. The result is a completely charming salad that's full of delightful contrasts.

Try it with pasta, roast chicken, ham, cold cuts, or almost anything casual. It's also great with bread and could almost be a meal on its own.

serves 8 to 10

- 2 cups ricotta cheese
- 1/3 cup loosely packed fresh basil leaves, plus more for garnish
- Salt and freshly ground black pepper
- 3/4 cup pine nuts
- 8–10 cups loosely packed mixed salad greens
- 2 heads Belgian endive, torn into pieces
- 1/4 cup extra-virgin olive oil
- 2 tablespoons red wine vinegar
- Paprika for dusting

Place the ricotta in a mixing bowl and break it up with a fork. Tear the basil leaves into pieces and toss with the ricotta. Season with salt and pepper to taste.

Place a small skillet over medium heat and add the pine nuts. Stir constantly until the nuts are darkly golden. Transfer to a small bowl and set aside.

Arrange the salad greens on a large platter and sprinkle with the Belgian endive. In a small bowl, combine the olive oil and vinegar. Add salt and pepper to taste. Sprinkle the mixture over the salad greens and toss. Sprinkle the pine nuts evenly over the greens. Drop small mounds of the ricotta mixture onto the greens. Dust the ricotta with paprika and garnish the platter with basil leaves. Serve immediately.

notes from our test kitchen

- We don't advise using low-fat ricotta here. The creaminess of the real thing is part of the reason it works so well.
- If basil isn't at its best, mint is a fine substitute.

SOURCE: *The New American Chef* by Andrew Dornenburg and Karen Page

COOK: Paula Wolfert

moroccan herb salad

WE'VE NEVER HAD A SALAD QUITE LIKE THIS ONE, and we'll make it again very soon. In Morocco it's used more as a spread or a dip, and it's made with mallow leaves. Paula Wolfert has devised a delicious substitute: a mix of spinach, parsley, celery leaves, and cilantro. When they're steamed together with garlic, they acquire a new personality. The flavors here are extraordinary—not big and bold but subtle, almost ethereal.

The steamed greens are sautéed with the addictive Spanish smoked paprika called Pimentón de la Vera (but that's not a deal breaker; plain old paprika will be fine), a little cumin and cayenne, bits of oil-cured olives, and the mellow garlic that was cooked with the greens. Once the juices are cooked off, the greens get a little more lemon juice and olive oil, as well as preserved lemon, if you have it, and are served at room temperature. The salad is a great partner for a spread of Mediterranean dishes.

It's a bit more like salad if you omit the olives and the preserved lemon rind, more like a spread if you include them.

serves 6

- 1 pound baby spinach
- 4 ounces (2 cups) fresh flat-leaf parsley leaves
- Handful of celery leaves
- 1/2 cup fresh cilantro leaves
- 4 large garlic cloves, peeled
- Extra-virgin olive oil
- 12 oil-cured black olives, pitted, rinsed, and cut into small pieces
- 1 1/4 teaspoons Spanish smoked sweet paprika, or Hungarian sweet paprika
- Pinch cayenne pepper
- Pinch ground cumin
- Salt and freshly ground black pepper
- 1 tablespoon fresh lemon juice, or more to taste
- 1/4 preserved lemon rind, rinsed to remove salt and diced (see notes)

Wash and drain the spinach, parsley, celery leaves, and cilantro. Shred them with a sharp knife. Pour an inch or so of water into a deep kettle and bring to a boil. Set a steamer basket or colander in the pot, add the greens and garlic, cover, and steam for 15 minutes. Remove from the heat and allow to cool, uncovered.

When the greens are cool enough to handle, squeeze out as much moisture as possible. You should have about 2 cups greens. Crush the garlic to a pulp and reserve.

Heat about 1 tablespoon olive oil in a 9-inch skillet over medium heat. Add the garlic, olives, paprika, cayenne, cumin, and salt and pepper to taste and heat for 30 seconds. Add the greens and cook, stirring constantly, until all the moisture has evaporated, about 10 minutes. Let cool to room temperature.

Finely chop the mixture. Blend in the lemon juice and 2 to 3 tablespoons olive oil. Transfer to a serving dish, garnish with the diced preserved lemon rind, and serve.

notes from our test kitchen

- Although it's not the same thing at all, you can substitute the rind from the broiled lemons on page 54 for the preserved lemon rind. Preserved lemons in brine are available at Middle Eastern markets and some gourmet shops. The rind is delicious in this salad but not absolutely essential. You'll love the salad without it, too.
- A pasta pot with a steamer insert works perfectly for steaming the greens. Save the juices in the bottom of the pot for soup; they're full of vitamins and flavor.

SOURCE: *Entertaining for a Veggie Planet* by Didi Emmons

COOK: Didi Emmons

roasted pear, blue cheese, and bibb salad with cranberry vinaigrette

WE'RE ALWAYS ON THE LOOKOUT for a dressy salad that is distinguished enough for holiday entertaining yet doesn't tax our already busy schedules. And this elegant plated one more than qualifies. The various elements—the roasted cranberry vinaigrette, the roasted pears, and the toasted pecans—can all be prepared in advance and then assembled just before serving. In fact, because the dressing is drizzled on and not tossed with the salad, you can plate everything up and let the salads sit for a bit at room temperature before dressing and serving. Ideally, the pears and cheese should be at room temperature anyway.

serves 4

VINAIGRETTE

- 1 1/2 cups cranberries, rinsed and picked over
- 1/2 cup extra-virgin olive oil
- 2 tablespoons balsamic vinegar
- 1 tablespoon honey
- Squeeze of fresh lemon juice
- 1 teaspoon Dijon mustard
- Kosher salt and freshly ground black pepper

SALAD

- 2 Bosc pears (if they're a bit firm, that's fine; see notes)
- 1 small head Bibb lettuce, leaves separated, washed, and thoroughly dried
- 4 ounces Maytag blue or Roquefort cheese
- 1/4 cup chopped pecans, toasted

MAKE THE VINAIGRETTE:

Preheat the oven to 350 degrees. Oil a rimmed baking sheet. Place the cranberries on the baking sheet and roast until they begin to soften and wilt, about 15 minutes. Set aside to cool. Increase the oven temperature to 375 degrees.

Meanwhile, in a medium bowl, combine the olive oil, vinegar, honey, lemon juice, and mustard. Stir in the roasted cranberries and season with salt and pepper to taste. Set aside.

MAKE THE SALAD:

Halve the pears (leave the skins on) and spoon out the seeds. Oil a small baking pan and place the pears cut side down in the pan. Bake for about 30 minutes, until tender and a knife pierces them easily. Let cool.

Arrange the Bibb lettuce leaves on four salad plates. Cut the pear halves lengthwise into thin slices, keeping them in their pear shape. Pick up each pear half with a chef's knife or spatula and place on a salad plate. Crumble the cheese evenly over the salads.

Spoon at least 2 tablespoons of the vinaigrette over each salad (you'll have some left over). Top with the pecans and serve.

notes from our test kitchen

- The pears should be firm-ripe: not so soft that they are hard to handle, but not so firm that they have no flavor.
- A melon baller is a good tool for removing the seeds and cores of the pears.
- Toast the pecans in a 350-degree oven until fragrant, about 5 minutes.
- If you roast the pears in advance, allow them to come to room temperature before serving. (Their flavor is muted by the cold.) The cheese should also be left at room temperature for a while before serving.

SOURCE: *Washington Post*
COOK: James O'Shea after Kevin Thornton
STORY BY: James O'Shea

potato and haricot vert salad

WHO KNOWS MORE THAN THE IRISH ABOUT POTATOES? Even though the Dublin chef Kevin Thornton wouldn't serve this very simple salad to customers at his restaurant, Thornton's, he likes to serve a version of it at home over thinly sliced cured salmon, with a scattering of diced cucumber and a little salmon roe on top. All by itself, though, the salad is delectable, and it has the virtue of working all year long, not just in the summer. The potatoes are lightened by the skinny little haricots verts, and the small hill of chives that goes into it gives it a fresh, lively character.

Because the recipe calls for delicate fingerling potatoes, you don't have to peel them, so you can make this salad more or less on the spur of the moment. Note the Irish technique of cooking the potatoes until just tender, then draining them and returning them to the pot over low heat to steam for a few minutes. Once you taste potatoes made this way, you'll think you haven't had a properly cooked potato before.

serves 6

- 2 pounds fingerling potatoes, scrubbed
- Kosher salt
- 8 ounces haricots verts, trimmed
- 2 bunches fresh chives, thinly sliced
- 1 shallot, finely diced
- 3 tablespoons sherry vinegar
- 1/2 cup extra-virgin olive oil
- Sea salt and freshly ground black pepper

Place the potatoes in a large saucepan. Add 1 tablespoon salt and enough cold water to cover and bring to a boil. Reduce the heat to medium-low and simmer, uncovered, just until tender, 8 to 12 minutes. Drain the water from the pot.

Return the potatoes to low heat, partially cover, and steam for a few minutes. Remove from the heat and set aside to cool. As soon as the potatoes are cool enough to handle, cut them into thin slices and place them in a large bowl.

While the potatoes are cooking, bring another pot of salted water to a boil. Have ready a large bowl of ice water. Add the haricots verts to the pot and cook them until bright green and almost tender, 2 to 5 minutes. Immediately drain the beans, plunge them into the ice water to stop the cooking, and drain again. Cut the beans into ½-inch dice and add them to the potatoes.

In a small bowl, combine the chives, shallot, and vinegar. Whisking constantly, slowly add the oil in a steady stream, whisking until completely emulsified. Season with salt and pepper to taste.

Pour the dressing over the potatoes and beans in a circular motion. Gently mix to coat the vegetables. Taste and adjust the seasonings accordingly. Serve at room temperature or chilled.

notes from our test kitchen

- If you can't find fingerlings, use small red potatoes, peeled, unless they're tiny. If there aren't any haricots verts around, just use the skinniest green beans you can find.
- It's a lot easier to snip chives with kitchen shears than to slice them with a knife.

tip

Here's an even easier way to cook fingerlings, which accents their creaminess. We found this tip in Tom Colicchio's *Craft of Cooking*. Scrub small fingerlings, put them in a pot, and add water to cover. Bring to a boil over low heat, then cover the pot and remove it from the heat. Let the potatoes cool (and finish cooking) in the covered pot for about 25 minutes.

SOURCE: *Redbook*

COOK: Frank Melodia

spinach and tabbouleh salad with feta and olives

THINK OF THIS AS TABBOULEH MEETS GREEK SALAD with a little bit of baby spinach tossed in. The result is an easy-to-make, lively grain salad invigorated with a lemony dressing, briny black olives, creamy bits of crumbled feta, crunchy chunks of cucumber, and silky roasted red pepper strips. With good-quality grape tomatoes and bags of baby spinach available year-round, you can make this in the dead of winter and brighten things up considerably.

serves 6

- 1 cup medium-grain bulgur
- 1 1/2 cups boiling water
- 1/4 cup olive oil
- 1 teaspoon grated lemon zest
- 3 tablespoons fresh lemon juice
- 1/2 teaspoon salt, or to taste
- 1/2 teaspoon freshly ground black pepper, or to taste
- 1 pint grape tomatoes, halved
- 1 cup peeled, seeded, and diced cucumber
- 1/2 cup chopped fresh mint
- 1/2 cup pitted kalamata olives, halved
- 1/2 cup diced red onion
- 1 roasted red pepper, cut into 1/2-x-2-inch strips
- 6 ounces feta cheese, crumbled
- 6 ounces baby spinach

Place the bulgur in a large bowl. Add the boiling water, stir quickly, and cover. Let stand for about 30 minutes, until the bulgur soaks up the water.

Meanwhile, in a small bowl, whisk together the olive oil, lemon zest, lemon juice, salt, and pepper.

When the bulgur has softened, stir in the dressing. Add the tomatoes, cucumber, mint, olives, onion, pepper strips, feta, and spinach. Toss gently to combine. Taste for salt and pepper.

Transfer to a salad bowl or mound on a large platter. Serve immediately or let sit at room temperature for an hour or so.

note from our test kitchen

- If baby spinach leaves are not available, don't substitute the bigger leaves; they won't fold into the salad as nicely. Instead, look for baby arugula or mâche. Either makes a fine substitute.

SOURCE: *Tom's Big Dinners* by Tom Douglas

COOK: Tom Douglas

mac and cheese salad with buttermilk dressing

ALTHOUGH WE'RE USUALLY UNIMPRESSED BY PASTA SALADS, this inspired one from the Seattle chef Tom Douglas caught our attention right away. It's the creamy dressing that's so delicious, and it has an old-fashioned quality that immediately feels right, like a salad you've been eating at family picnics for decades. This is a whole new way to love mac and cheese.

The salad is also almost endlessly flexible. The greens can be mâche (aka corn salad or lamb's lettuce, which is a bit nutty), baby spinach, young pea sprouts, or arugula. In spring, blanched sliced asparagus fits right in, as do blanched fresh peas. The dressing is just as good on chilled, steamed baby red potatoes or shrimp, cucumbers, and Bibb lettuce.

serves 6 to 8

DRESSING

- 1/2 cup mayonnaise
- 1/2 cup sour cream
- 1/2 cup buttermilk
- 1/4 cup thinly sliced fresh chives
- 1 tablespoon chopped fresh dill
- 2 teaspoons minced garlic
- 2 teaspoons minced shallots
- 2 teaspoons fresh lemon juice
- Kosher salt and freshly ground black pepper

SALAD

- 1 pound shaped pasta such as fusilli, farfalle, or cavatappi
- 1/4 cup thinly sliced scallions
- 3 ounces ricotta salata cheese (about 3/4 cup; see notes)
- 3 cups loosely packed mâche or baby spinach

MAKE THE DRESSING:

Whisk together the mayonnaise, sour cream, and buttermilk in a medium bowl. Add the chives, dill, garlic, shallots, and lemon juice and whisk again. Season with salt and pepper to taste.

MAKE THE SALAD:

Bring a large pot of salted water to a boil. Add the pasta and cook until al dente. Drain the pasta and immediately run under cold water until it is completely cool. Drain well.

Put the pasta in a large bowl and, using a rubber spatula, fold in enough dressing to coat it generously. Fold in the scallions, cheese, and mâche or spinach. Mound the salad on a large platter and serve.

notes from our test kitchen

- If you can't find ricotta salata cheese, use pecorino Romano instead.
- You can make both the pasta and the dressing a few hours ahead, then toss them together just before serving. Once the pasta is cooked, run it under cold water, drain, and spread on a lightly oiled baking sheet in a single layer. Cover the pan with plastic wrap and refrigerate.
- Although the salad tastes best served immediately after the dressing and pasta are mixed with the greens, it will keep well for several days if made with baby spinach.

SOURCE: *Food & Wine*
COOKS: Paula Disbrowe and David Norman
STORY BY: Amanda Hesser

sardinian rice salad with tuna, olives, and capers

THIS COLORFUL RICE SALAD, with lots of texture and flavor, makes a fine main course for a luncheon or picnic. We also like to put it on the buffet when the menu needs something fresh-tasting but with a bit of substance. Celery adds great crunch to the mix, but you can substitute shaved radishes or sliced carrots, if you like.

The technique of boiling the rice in plenty of salted water until tender, draining it, and then tossing it with the vinaigrette eliminates the worry that sometimes comes with cooking rice. The grains come out perfectly tender, not sticky, and absorb the lemony flavor of the dressing.

serves 6

- 6 cups water
- 2 cups (14 ounces) Texmati or basmati rice
- 1 teaspoon kosher salt, more to taste
- 1/3 cup fresh lemon juice
- 1/4 cup extra-virgin olive oil
- 8 small scallions, thinly sliced
- 2 large celery ribs, thinly sliced
- 1/3 cup cornichons, thinly sliced
- 1/3 cup pitted kalamata olives, coarsely chopped
- 1/4 cup finely chopped fresh flat-leaf parsley
- 2 tablespoons drained capers
- 1 teaspoon finely grated lemon zest
- 2 6-ounce cans imported tuna packed in olive oil, drained and left in chunks
- 2 large hard-cooked eggs, thinly sliced (see notes)
- Freshly ground black pepper

In a large saucepan, bring the water to a boil. Add the rice and salt and cook over medium-high heat, uncovered, until tender, about 12 minutes. Drain the rice, shaking off the excess water. Let cool slightly.

Meanwhile, in a large bowl, whisk the lemon juice with the olive oil. Stir in the scallions, celery, cornichons, olives, parsley, capers, and lemon zest. Add the rice, tuna, and eggs and toss gently. Season with salt and pepper to taste, transfer to a serving bowl, and serve warm or at room temperature.

notes from our test kitchen

- To hard-cook eggs, place them in a saucepan and cover with cold water. Bring slowly to a boil, cover, and remove from the heat. Let sit for 10 minutes, then shock them under cold tap water. Crack the eggs and peel them, or store, unpeeled, in the refrigerator.
- The salad can be kept at room temperature for up to 3 hours before serving.

SOURCE: *The Apprentice* by Jacques Pépin
COOK: Danny Kaye

chicken salad à la danny kaye

FEW PEOPLE KNOW what an extraordinary cook the comedian and actor Danny Kaye was. Food-world luminaries such as Ruth Reichl, now the editor of *Gourmet,* and Diana Kennedy, the doyenne of Mexican cooking, regularly made pilgrimages to Kaye's kitchen, and so did Jacques Pépin. All of them claim to have learned amazing things from Kaye, especially about Chinese cooking, his specialty.

Pépin learned how to poach the chicken for this zesty salad from the master himself. It's a classic Chinese method, thrifty in the good sense because it spares both cooking energy and flavor. Pépin thinks it's absolutely the best way to poach chicken, leaving the flesh moist, tender, and delicious.

Kaye had a trick of filling the cavity with all kinds of flatware to keep the chicken submerged in the poaching liquid (some Chinese recipes use a large spoon for the same purpose), but Pépin doesn't do that.

serves 4

CHICKEN

- 1 chicken (about 3 1/2 pounds)
- 1 cup sliced onion
- 1/2 cup sliced carrot
- 1 small leek, washed
- 1 celery rib, trimmed
- 1 teaspoon salt
- 1/4 teaspoon black peppercorns
- 2 sprigs fresh thyme
- 2 bay leaves
- About 7 cups tepid water

DRESSING

- 5 tablespoons extra-virgin olive oil
- 1 tablespoon white wine vinegar
- 2 tablespoons Dijon mustard
- 1 teaspoon finely chopped garlic
- 1/2 teaspoon Tabasco sauce
- 1/4 teaspoon salt
- 1/4 teaspoon freshly ground black pepper

- 12 Boston lettuce leaves
- 4 fresh tarragon leaves

PREPARE THE CHICKEN:

Place the chicken, breast side down, in a tall, narrow pot so it fits snugly on the bottom (see note). Add the remaining poaching ingredients. The chicken should be submerged, and the water should reach about 1 inch above it. Bring to a gentle boil, cover, and let boil gently for 10 minutes. Remove the pot from the heat and set aside to allow the chicken to steep for 45 minutes.

Remove the chicken from the pot and place on a platter to cool for a few minutes. (The stock can be strained and frozen for up to 6 months for use in soup.) Pick the meat from the bones, discarding the skin, bones, and fat. Shred the meat with your fingers, following the grain and pulling it into strips. (The meat tastes better shredded than diced with a knife.)

MAKE THE DRESSING:

Mix together all the ingredients in a bowl large enough to hold the chicken.

ASSEMBLE THE SALAD:

Add the chicken shreds to the dressing and toss well.

Arrange the Boston lettuce leaves in a nest around the periphery of a platter. Spoon the room-temperature chicken salad into the center, sprinkle with the tarragon leaves, and serve.

note from our test kitchen

If you don't have a tall, narrow pot, just use the narrowest one you have and put the chicken in it breast down. You will have to add more water to cover the chicken, but it will still cook perfectly.

breakfast and brunch

SOURCE: *The Cheese Board: Collective Works* by the Cheese Board Collective

COOKS: The Cheese Board Collective

killer granola

THOSE EAGER PROSPECTIVE DINERS who can't get into lunch at Chez Panisse in Berkeley often head across the street, where there's usually a line snaking down the sidewalk, to have lunch at the Cheese Board. If Chez Panisse is haute Berkeley, the Cheese Board is Birkenstock Berkeley—good, wholesome vegetarian food turned out by a collective whose members have many a tale to tell.

The pizzas and breads are stars at the Cheese Board, but what caught our eye is this delicious granola and the cookies you can make with it (recipe follows). This cereal is from the dry, flaky school of granola, and it's light—though, as its name indicates, it's not a low-fat choice.

makes 3 cups granola

- 2 tablespoons unsalted butter
- Pinch salt
- 1 cup chopped pecans or other nuts
- 2 teaspoons honey
- 1/4 cup packed light brown sugar
- 1/8 teaspoon pure vanilla extract
- 1 1/4 cups old-fashioned rolled oats
- 1/2 cup unsweetened coconut flakes
- 1/2 cup sunflower seeds
- 1/4 cup sesame seeds

Adjust the rack to the middle and preheat the oven to 325 degrees. Line a baking sheet with parchment paper or a baking mat. In a small saucepan, melt the butter with the salt over low heat. Add the chopped nuts, increase the heat to medium, and cook, stirring frequently, for 5 minutes, until lightly toasted. Add the honey and brown sugar, reduce the heat to low, and stir until melted and combined. Remove from the heat and stir in the vanilla.

In a large bowl, combine the oats, coconut, sunflower seeds, and sesame seeds. Add the sugar mixture and toss until the oats are evenly coated.

Spread the granola evenly on the prepared sheet. Bake for 15 minutes. Remove from the oven and stir to redistribute the granola. Bake for about 10 minutes more, until golden brown.

Let cool completely on the baking sheet before serving. Store in an airtight container for up to a week.

granola cookies

THESE COOKIES ARE EXCELLENT, and they make a good portable breakfast for kids on the go. We love the idea of breakfast cookies, and these are as good with a cup of coffee as they are with a glass of milk.

makes about 36 cookies

- 1 cup (2 sticks) unsalted butter, at room temperature
- 3/4 cup packed light brown sugar
- 2 scant cups all-purpose flour
- 1 1/2 cups Killer Granola
- 1/3 cup chopped pecans
- 1/2 teaspoon kosher salt
- 1 teaspoon pure vanilla extract

TO MIX IN A STAND MIXER:

Cream the butter and brown sugar together in the mixer bowl with the paddle attachment on medium speed for about 4 minutes, until light and fluffy. Add the flour, granola, pecans, salt, and vanilla. Mix just until the ingredients are incorporated.

TO MIX BY HAND:

Cream the butter and sugar together in a large bowl with a wooden spoon until light and fluffy. Add the remaining ingredients and mix just until incorporated.

Transfer the dough to a lightly floured surface and divide into 2 pieces. Using your palms, roll each piece into a log about 4 1/2 inches long and 2 inches wide. Wrap in plastic and refrigerate for at least 2 hours or up to 24 hours.

Adjust two racks just above and below the middle and preheat the oven to 350 degrees. Line two baking sheets with parchment paper or Silpat baking mats. Cut each log into 1/4-inch-thick slices and place the cookies 1 inch apart on the prepared sheets. Bake for about 20 minutes, until the cookies are golden brown. Transfer the cookies to a wire rack and let cool.

note from our test kitchen

Watch the cookies carefully; they may be done before their cooking time is up. "Golden" is the key word here; burned is just another couple of minutes away.

SOURCE: www.dakinfarm.com

COOK: Unknown

baked eggs in maple toast cups

DAKIN FARM IS A FAMILY-RUN COMPANY in northern Vermont that produces a wonderful line of smoked hams and bacon. They also make loads of real maple syrup, which they use in curing their hams and sell by the pint and gallon. We found this recipe posted on their Web site and think it's a fine way to start the day. The little bit of syrup adds a sweet note to the toast cup, and the crumbled bacon inside is a happy surprise.

Depending on whom you're feeding or what you have planned for the day, figure on 1 or 2 cups per person.

serves 3 or 6

- 1½ tablespoons butter, plus more for the muffin cups
- 1½ tablespoons pure maple syrup, plus more for serving (optional)
- 6 slices bread (see notes)
- 3 slices bacon, cooked until crisp and broken into small pieces
- 6 large eggs

Preheat the oven to 400 degrees. Butter 6 muffin cups. In a small saucepan, melt the butter and add the syrup. (You can also do this in a microwave.)

Remove the crusts from the bread. Flatten each slice with a rolling pin. Brush both sides of the bread with the syrup mixture. Pat the bread into the muffin cups and sprinkle the bacon pieces into the bottom of each cup. Break an egg into each cup and bake until the eggs are set; start checking after about 5 minutes. Lift the toast cups from the tin and serve immediately, drizzled with additional syrup, if desired.

notes from our test kitchen

- Use a tight-crumb, relatively thin-sliced white bread for this, such as Pepperidge Farm.
- You can also bake these in individual buttered ramekins. The eggs will take longer to bake, closer to 16 minutes, because the heat is slower to penetrate.

SOURCE: *New York Times Magazine*

COOK: **Julia Reed**

george jones sausage balls

ACCORDING TO MANY, GEORGE JONES IS THE GREATEST country music singer who ever lived. At one point, this larger-than-life legendary bad boy from East Texas was married to Tammy Wynette, and he's dabbled in all sorts of businesses, including the sausage business, for most of his life.

Julia Reed, a terrific food writer from New Orleans, accompanied Jones on an appearance he made at a Kroger supermarket in Tennessee to promote his sausage. The two struck up a friendship, and Reed ended up naming her version of sausage balls for him—and his sausage.

Think of these as sausage and biscuit in one. They're made with just three ingredients, and the only step that takes any time is rolling them into little balls. Fortunately, this can be done a day or more ahead (the balls bake just before serving).

We tend to serve these for brunch, but they also make a fine appetizer or snack. They're a nifty addition to a Super Bowl party, for instance.

makes about 72 balls

- 1 pound spicy bulk sausage (see notes)
- 3 1/2 cups grated sharp cheddar cheese
- 2 cups Bisquick

Preheat the oven to 400 degrees. Combine all the ingredients in a bowl and mix with your hands so there are no dry crumbs. Form into balls about an inch in diameter and place on a baking sheet. Bake until the balls are golden brown, 8 to 10 minutes (a bit longer if they've been refrigerated, and longer still if frozen). Serve hot or warm.

notes from our test kitchen

- George Jones Country Style Sausage (hot or mild) is available at some supermarkets, including Kroger, or can be ordered (in rather large quantities) by contacting the Williams Sausage Company at (800) 844-4242. In its place, use any good spicy country sausage. If you can't find spicy sausage, add a generous amount of freshly ground black pepper and a pinch of cayenne to the mix.
- Lining the baking sheets with parchment paper makes cleanup easier.
- The sausage balls hold their shape better if refrigerated overnight before baking. They can also be frozen and baked directly from the freezer without thawing.

SOURCE: *The Big Book of Breakfast* by Maryana Vollstedt

COOK: Maryana Vollstedt

crunchy breaded bacon

HERE'S A LITTLE TRICK that takes ordinary thick-cut bacon and turns it into something unique—and awfully tasty. The recipe is also convenient when serving a big group, since you don't have to fry endless strips in a skillet. Instead, the bacon bakes in the oven, pretty much unattended except for the breading. These strips stay good and crunchy even as they cool: no soggy bacon for latecomers.

serves 4 to 6

- 12 thick slices bacon
- 1 large egg
- 1 tablespoon water
- 1 teaspoon Dijon mustard
- 1 teaspoon Worcestershire sauce
- 1 cup fine dry bread crumbs

Preheat the oven to 400 degrees. Place the bacon slices in a single layer on a rimmed baking sheet. Bake for 10 minutes. Drain off the fat.

In a large, shallow bowl, whisk the egg with the water. Add the mustard and Worcestershire sauce and mix well. Place the bread crumbs on a piece of wax paper. As soon as the bacon is cool enough to handle, remove it from the baking sheet and coat each slice on both sides with the egg mixture and then with the bread crumbs.

Return the breaded bacon slices to the baking sheet and bake until crisp, about 15 minutes. Drain briefly on paper towels and serve.

notes from our test kitchen

- We like to add a few drops of Tabasco sauce to the egg wash.
- If you want to prepare this in advance, bake the bacon for the first 10 minutes, drain the fat, and set the bacon aside. When it's time for brunch, bread the bacon and finish baking.

SOURCE: *Simple Cooking* newsletter

COOK: John Thorne

grits in the slow-cooker

WE CONFESS TO BEING COMPLETELY SMITTEN with true grits—that is, the very old-fashioned stone-ground milled corn so beloved in the South and Southwest. We hadn't thought of cooking real grits in the slow-cooker, but it's an excellent idea. We actually went out and bought a slow-cooker to try out the recipe, and we're glad we did. The grits take an overnight (or daylong, depending on when you want to eat them) snooze in the cooker, and they come out perfectly cooked and creamy, though a bit looser than traditionally cooked grits.

The only trick here is using first-quality grits (see notes). There's no point in cooking instant or supermarket grits this way.

What really excites us about John Thorne's recipe is his egg drop. He sticks the handle of a wooden spoon into the cooked grits to make holes and plops in a couple of eggs, then cooks them for 20 minutes on low, while the sausage or bacon cooks. This makes a great cold-weather breakfast: no stirring, no worries, just terrific grits.

serves 2

- 2 tablespoons butter
- 1 cup traditional stone-ground white corn grits
- 5 cups water
- 2 teaspoons kosher salt
- 2 large eggs (optional)

Coat the bottom half of the pot with some of the butter to prevent sticking. Add the grits, water, and salt. Stir the mixture and add the rest of the butter. Set the slow-cooker to low, cover, and go to bed.

In the morning, use a spatula to stir in the grits that have stuck to the side of the pot. If you want to serve this with eggs, make a hole in the grits with the handle of a wooden spoon and crack in 1 of the eggs; repeat with the other egg. Spoon the grits over the eggs and cook for 20 minutes on low (see notes). Serve warm in bowls, stirring in the eggs or serving them in the center of the bowl of grits.

notes from our test kitchen

- It's hard to find a slow-cooker that will hold a relatively small amount. The Rival four-quart will cook these grits perfectly, even though the grits are less than the amount recommended by the manufacturer.
- To get good grits, you will probably have to order them by mail and stash them in the refrigerator or freezer (where they keep best). The grits from Logan Turnpike Mill are excellent and are available from www.hoppinjohns.com.
- If the grits are too loose for the wooden handle to leave an impression, just crack the egg onto the surface—the egg will make its own hole. When the white looks cooked (less than 20 minutes), it's done to our taste, which means a slightly runny yolk.
- Turn the slow-cooker off once you've served the grits and let it sit for a while. The "stuck" grits will come right off in a sheet as the crock cools.

SOURCE: *San Francisco Chronicle*
COOK: Kerry Leigh Heffernan
STORY BY: Janet Fletcher

tomato, goat cheese, and focaccia pudding

BREAD PUDDING BECOMES MORE AND MORE POPULAR each year, and the variations run the gamut from savory to sweet and from plain to chock-full of added ingredients. So it shouldn't have surprised us when a Napa Valley chef thought to create a bread pudding using an increasingly beloved bread—focaccia—and spiking it with fresh goat cheese and cherry tomatoes. The chewy, airy texture of focaccia is ideal for absorbing the custard and creating a tender, flavorful dish. Heffernan likes to use green-onion focaccia as an alternative to plain. You might also try it with rosemary-onion or black olive focaccia—whatever sounds good to you.

Since the pudding needs to sit overnight, it's ideal for a big weekend breakfast or brunch. We also like to serve it for dinner alongside a roast chicken or juicy steak. Leftover slices make a great snack.

serves 6

- 8 ounces plain or green onion focaccia (see notes)
- 2 tablespoons extra-virgin olive oil, plus more for the baking dish
- 5 ounces fresh goat cheese, without any rind
- 8 ounces cherry tomatoes, halved
- 6 large eggs
- 2 cups whole milk
- 3/4 teaspoon salt (see notes)
- Freshly ground black pepper
- 1/4 cup freshly grated Parmesan cheese

Rub the bottom and sides of a 9-x-13-inch baking dish with olive oil. Cut the focaccia into 1-inch cubes and place in a large bowl. Toss with the olive oil, then arrange half the focaccia in the prepared dish. Dot with the goat cheese, then scatter the tomatoes over the cheese. Top with the remaining focaccia.

In a large bowl, whisk the eggs well. Add the milk, salt, and several grinds of pepper and whisk until well blended. Pour over the focaccia. With the back of a fork, lightly tamp down the cubes so they soak up some of the liquid. Sprinkle the surface evenly with the Parmesan. Cover the dish tightly with foil and refrigerate overnight.

Remove the dish from the refrigerator and place it, covered, in the cold oven. Set the oven to 350 degrees and bake for 35 minutes. Uncover and continue baking until the pudding is puffed and golden, 25 to 30 minutes. Cool for 20 minutes before slicing. Serve warm.

notes from our test kitchen

- Green onions and scallions are the same thing. Easterners call them scallions.
- Taste the goat cheese before adding it to the pudding. If it is mild and not very salty, increase the amount of salt in the recipe to 1 teaspoon.
- If the oven is already on, simply reduce the initial baking time by 10 minutes.

SOURCE: *The Cape Cod Table* by Lora Brody
COOK: Joanna Keeley

cottage street bakery dirt bombs

AT THE COTTAGE STREET BAKERY in Orleans on Cape Cod, these retro treats are famous. We've also seen them at the Ferry Plaza Farmers Market in San Francisco, at the Downtown Bakery booth, where they're called doughnut muffins. They are, in fact, exactly like a cross between a cinnamon-sugar doughnut and a muffin, with a buttery-sugary exterior that you won't be able to stop eating. And we love the touch of cardamom in this version.

It's a huge fuss to prepare doughnuts from scratch, but making these is no harder than mixing up a batch of muffins, then rolling them in cinnamon sugar. You can serve them warm or at room temperature (we vote for warm).

makes 12 doughnut muffins

DOUGHNUT MUFFINS

Butter for muffin tin
3 cups all-purpose flour
1 tablespoon baking powder
1/2 teaspoon salt
1/2 teaspoon ground nutmeg
1/4 teaspoon ground cardamom
12 tablespoons (1 1/2 sticks) unsalted butter, at room temperature
1 cup sugar
2 large eggs
1 cup whole milk

TOPPING

12 tablespoons (1 1/2 sticks) unsalted butter, melted
1/2 cup sugar
1 1/2 teaspoons ground cinnamon

MAKE THE MUFFINS:

Adjust the rack to the middle and preheat the oven to 400 degrees. Generously coat a 12-cup standard muffin tin with butter, greasing the flat part of the tin as well.

Sift the flour, baking powder, salt, nutmeg, and cardamom into a medium bowl. In a large bowl, either by hand or with an electric mixer, cream the butter and sugar until light and fluffy. Mix in the eggs.

Add the dry ingredients and the milk alternately to the butter mixture in 2 additions, mixing gently by hand to incorporate all the ingredients. Scrape down the bowl to be sure to incorporate all the flour. The batter will be on the stiff side but airy. Don't overmix or beat the batter, as this will make the muffins tough.

Scrape and spoon the batter into the prepared muffin tin without smoothing the tops. Bake for about 25 minutes, until the tops are golden brown and a toothpick or cake tester inserted in the center comes out clean and dry. As soon as the muffins are cool enough to handle, turn them out onto a wire rack.

MAKE THE TOPPING:

Pour the melted butter into a shallow bowl. Mix the sugar and cinnamon together in a separate bowl. Dip the muffins (tops, sides, and bottoms) in the butter, using a pastry brush, if necessary, to cover areas not buttered by dipping. Immediately roll the muffins in the cinnamon-sugar mixture. Serve warm or at room temperature.

note from our test kitchen

Like so many other muffins, these don't keep very well and taste best shortly after they're baked.

for good measure

It's sad but true: most measuring cups are not accurate. The Good Housekeeping Institute tested every brand it could find and discovered that only two brands, Oxo and Michael Graves (sold at Target), were accurate.

The proper measuring cup might mean the difference between success and failure in baking. If you're using several sets of measuring cups in making a single recipe, as we often do, the quantities could be off by as much as 2 tablespoons, says Good Housekeeping. That could present serious problems if you're making a cake or another unforgiving recipe requiring exact measurements. The solution: use only one set, so that at least your proportions are consistent, or use only the two recommended brands.

SOURCE: *Food & Wine*
COOK: Marcy Goldman

iced cinnamon bun scones

WHAT A GREAT IDEA to combine two favorite breakfast treats in one—the icing of a cinnamon bun with the buttery tenderness of a cream scone. This charming idea comes from Marcy Goldman, an inventive and talented pastry chef from Montreal.

The dough is streaked with a brown sugar–cinnamon mixture that melts into the scones as they bake to create wonderful little caramelized patches. When the scones are glazed warm from the oven, the simple cream cheese icing is delightfully melty, but it's also good to know that they may be made ahead and stored in an airtight container for up to 2 days.

makes 8 large scones

SCONES

- 2/3 cup packed light brown sugar
- 2 tablespoons unsalted butter, at room temperature
- 1 1/4 teaspoons ground cinnamon
- 3 cups all-purpose flour, plus more for dusting
- 1/3 cup sugar
- 1 tablespoon baking powder
- 1/2 teaspoon salt
- 8 tablespoons (1 stick) cold unsalted butter, cut into 1/2-inch dice
- 1 cup heavy cream
- 1 large egg
- 1 teaspoon pure vanilla extract

GLAZE

- 1/4 cup cream cheese, at room temperature
- 1 teaspoon fresh lemon juice
- 2 cups confectioners' sugar

MAKE THE SCONES:

Adjust the rack to the middle and preheat the oven to 425 degrees. Line a large, heavy baking sheet with parchment paper. In a food processor, pulse the brown sugar with the room-temperature butter and 1 teaspoon of the cinnamon until soft crumbs form. Transfer the mixture to a medium bowl.

In the processor, combine the 3 cups flour, sugar, baking powder, salt, and remaining 1/4 teaspoon cinnamon and pulse to blend. Add the cold diced butter and pulse until the butter is the size of small peas. Transfer the mixture to a large bowl and make a well in the center.

Add the cream, egg, and vanilla to the well and stir to combine. Using a wooden spoon, gradually stir until a firm dough forms. Crumble the brown sugar mixture over the dough and knead, leaving some brown sugar streaks in the dough.

Lightly dust a work surface with flour. Turn the dough out onto the surface and knead 3 times. Pat or roll the dough into an 8-inch round about 1 inch thick. Cut into 8 wedges, then transfer the edges to the baking sheet and refrigerate for 10 minutes.

Bake for 18 to 20 minutes, until browned. Let cool slightly on the baking sheet, then transfer to a wire rack.

MAKE THE GLAZE:

In a medium bowl, beat the cream cheese with the lemon juice until smooth. Beat in the confectioners' sugar until smooth. Spread the icing over the warm scones and serve.

notes from our test kitchen

- You can make the glaze the day before. Just pull it out of the refrigerator and let it come to room temperature while you make the scones.
- Some of our tasters found these scones a bit too large for one serving. If you prefer more modest-size pastries, divide the dough into 10 or 12 smaller scones. The smaller pastries will take less time to bake.

SOURCE: *Saveur*

COOK: Myron Sikora

cinna-myron caramel sweet rolls

EVERY SUMMER, SOME TEN THOUSAND CYCLISTS from all over the world come together to ride five hundred miles across Iowa in a weeklong event aptly named the Annual Great Bike Ride Across Iowa. The ride is famous for the incredible array of food vendors who set up along the route.

One year, Myron Sikora baked more than three hundred of these amazing sweet rolls before the bikers rode past his sister's house. He sold them all. Tender, golden, rich, cinnamony, and dripping with sticky caramel, they are everything you want a breakfast bun to be. Happily, we now have the recipe and don't have to spend a week on a bicycle seat to get one.

makes 12 rolls

ROLLS

- 1 1/2 cups milk
- 6 tablespoons water
- 7 tablespoons unsalted butter, at room temperature
- 6 tablespoons sugar
- 1/4 cup cornmeal
- 1 1/2 teaspoons salt
- 5 1/4 cups all-purpose flour, plus more for dusting
- 2 1/4-ounce packets active dry yeast
- 2 large eggs, beaten

CARAMEL

- 2 cups packed brown sugar
- 1/2 cup milk
- 9 tablespoons unsalted butter, at room temperature
- 3/4 cup pecans, chopped (optional)

CINNAMON-BUTTER FILLING

- 7 tablespoons unsalted butter, at room temperature
- 6 tablespoons sugar
- 1 1/2 teaspoons ground cinnamon

MAKE THE ROLLS:

Combine the milk, water, 6 tablespoons of the butter, the sugar, cornmeal, and salt in a medium saucepan. Cook over medium-high heat, stirring constantly, until thick, 8 to 10 minutes. Remove from the heat and set aside until the cornmeal mixture is just warm.

Grease a large bowl with the remaining 1 tablespoon butter and set aside. Combine 1 1/4 cups of the flour and the yeast in another large bowl. Using a wooden spoon, beat in the eggs and the cornmeal mixture, then gradually beat in the remaining 4 cups flour. Turn the dough out onto a well-floured surface and knead until smooth and elastic, 12 to 15 minutes. Transfer the dough to the greased bowl, cover with plastic wrap, and set aside in a warm place to rise until doubled in bulk, 1½ to 2 hours.

MAKE THE CARAMEL:

Combine the brown sugar, milk, and 8 tablespoons of the butter in a medium saucepan. Cook over medium heat, stirring constantly, until the butter melts, 5 to 8 minutes. Grease two 7-x-11-inch glass baking dishes with the remaining 1 tablespoon butter. Divide the caramel and pecans (if using) between the dishes; set aside.

MAKE THE FILLING:

Using a wooden spoon, beat the butter, sugar, and cinnamon together in a small bowl and set aside.

ASSEMBLE THE ROLLS:

Turn the dough out onto a floured surface, divide in half, and roll out to make two 12-x-15-inch rectangles. Position 1 rectangle with the long edge parallel to the edge of the work surface. Spread half of the filling along the lower third of the dough. Roll the dough up to form a long cylinder and pinch the seam to seal. Repeat the process with the remaining rectangle and filling. Cut each cylinder crosswise into 6 equal pieces. Place 6 pieces cut side up in each prepared dish, arranging them about 2 inches apart. Cover with plastic wrap and set aside to rise until doubled in bulk, about 1 hour.

Adjust the rack to the lower third and preheat the oven to 350 degrees. Uncover the rolls and bake until they are a deep golden brown and cooked through, 45 to 50 minutes. Remove from the oven, set aside for 1 minute, and very carefully invert the rolls onto baking sheets. Serve warm.

note from our test kitchen

To prepare these rolls ahead, refrigerate them in the baking dishes. In the morning, let them rise for about 1 hour at room temperature while the oven preheats and you brew a big pot of rich coffee.

SOURCE: *Brown Sugar* by Joyce White

COOK: Patricia Stinson

cardamom swirl coffee cake

THIS IS ONE OF THOSE RICH, moist, irresistible coffee cakes that needs no glaze, whipped cream, or other embellishment. It's flavored with a big swirl of heady, sweet cardamom. If you crush your own cardamom seeds, as Joyce White begs you to do, the cake will be even more delectable. But even if you don't, it's just fine.

The cake is almost endlessly adaptable. White sometimes makes it with cinnamon instead of cardamom and raisins instead of walnuts, or with a tablespoon of grated lemon and orange zest and pistachios instead of walnuts. They're all good, and no doubt you'll think of more ways to play with the formula. Part of this cake's flexibility is that it doesn't have to be made first thing in the morning. It's such a good keeper that you can prepare it a day ahead and just slice it for breakfast as soon as the coffee is ready.

serves 8

- 2 tablespoons unsalted butter, plus more for the pan
- 1½–2 teaspoons cardamom seeds, to taste (see notes)
- 1 cup coarsely chopped walnuts
- 1½ cups sugar
- 2 cups all-purpose flour, plus more for dusting
- 1 teaspoon baking powder
- 1 teaspoon baking soda
- ⅛ teaspoon salt
- 8 tablespoons (1 stick) unsalted butter, at room temperature
- 2 large eggs, at room temperature
- 1 teaspoon pure vanilla extract
- 1 cup sour cream, at room temperature
- ½ cup warm water

Adjust the rack to the middle and preheat the oven to 350 degrees. Generously butter a 7-cup fluted tube pan or ring; a 9-inch-round, 2-inch-deep cake pan; or an 8½-inch-round, 2½-inch-deep springform pan. Dust the pan with flour and shake out any excess.

Put the cardamom seeds in a small, heavy skillet over low heat and toast, swirling the pan a couple of times, until lightly browned, about 5 minutes. Remove from the heat and grind the seeds in a spice or coffee grinder or crush with a mortar and pestle. Or wrap the seeds in a tea towel and crush them with a rolling pin. They should be completely pulverized and powdery (see note).

Melt the 2 tablespoons butter in a small skillet or saucepan and remove immediately from the heat. Stir in the cardamom, walnuts, and 1/2 cup of the sugar and mix well. Set aside to use for the filling and topping.

Sift together the flour, baking powder, baking soda, and salt in a medium bowl and set aside.

Combine the remaining 1 cup sugar and 8 tablespoons butter in the bowl of a stand mixer fitted with the paddle attachment, or use a large mixing bowl and a hand-held electric mixer. Beat on medium-high speed for 3 to 5 minutes, scraping the bowl with a rubber spatula 2 or 3 times. Add the eggs and beat for 1 minute. Stir in the vanilla.

Stir together the sour cream and water in a small bowl. Set the mixer on low speed. Add the flour and the sour cream mixture alternately to the butter mixture, mixing for only a few seconds until blended. After the last addition, beat on low speed for 1 minute, scraping the bowl as needed.

Spoon or pour a little less than half of the batter into the prepared pan. Scatter half of the cardamom mixture over the batter in the pan. Add the remaining batter, using a butter knife to swirl it. Top with the remaining cardamom mixture, pressing the topping lightly into the batter with the back of a spoon.

Shake the pan gently to level the batter. Bake for 45 to 50 minutes, until golden brown and puffy and a toothpick inserted in the center comes out clean.

Remove the cake from the oven, place on a wire rack, and let cool in the pan for 10 minutes. Run a metal spatula around the cake, invert the pan onto the rack, tap gently, and remove the pan. Place the cake top side up on the rack and let cool completely before serving.

note from our test kitchen

To get the seeds out of a cardamom pod, lightly crush the pod with your fingers or with the back of a spoon. Then loosen the seeds with your fingers and discard the husk. You will need a small handful of pods to get 1 to 1 1/2 tablespoon seeds. You may need to add 1 tablespoon sugar to the seeds to grind them finely enough.

main dishes

cremini mushrooms with chive pasta

IT WAS HARD TO LIMIT OURSELVES TO JUST ONE RECIPE from Waldy Malouf's very inventive cookbook, but once we tasted this pasta, we knew this was it. At once earthy and fresh, it's easy to make, easy to serve, and easy to love. If you're going to be grilling something else, you can grill the mushrooms, or you can just roast them in the oven. The sauce is instant—a *lot* of chives blended with olive oil, salt, and pepper—and that's it.

More things to love about it: you can serve it hot or at room temperature. It can sit on a buffet for a couple of hours with no loss of flavor, unlike almost any other pasta we can think of. Oh, and it's vegetarian, too.

serves 4 or more

- Coarse sea salt or kosher salt
- 1 pound cremini mushrooms, trimmed
- 1/2 cup plus 2 tablespoons extra-virgin olive oil
- Freshly ground black pepper
- 1 cup roughly snipped fresh chives (2–3 bunches)
- 1 pound spaghettini or angel hair pasta
- Freshly grated pecorino Romano cheese for serving

Light the grill or preheat the oven to 500 degrees. Bring a large pot of salted water to a boil for the pasta. Toss the mushrooms in a bowl with 2 tablespoons of the olive oil and generous pinches of salt and pepper.

TO COOK ON THE GRILL:

Place the mushrooms in a grill basket. Grill, turning once, until tender and browned, about 8 minutes. When cool enough to handle, cut the mushrooms into quarters.

TO COOK IN THE OVEN:

Spread the mushrooms in a single layer on a rimmed baking sheet. Roast, turning once, until tender and browned, about 10 minutes. When they are cool enough to handle, cut the mushrooms into quarters.

In a food processor or blender, combine the remaining 1/2 cup olive oil, the chives, and generous pinches of salt and pepper. Process until pureed.

Cook the pasta until al dente. Drain, reserving 2 tablespoons of the cooking water if you plan to serve the pasta hot. In a large serving bowl, toss the pasta with the mushrooms and chive oil. If serving immediately, toss with 1 to 2 tablespoons of the reserved cooking water. Otherwise, let the pasta cool to room temperature. Serve with the cheese on the side.

notes from our test kitchen

- This pasta is so simple and pure that it pays to use really good ingredients: imported pasta, estate-bottled olive oil, and a good pecorino, such as Fulvi.
- You can substitute scallions for the chives if you must, but the flavor won't be as delicate.

SOURCE: *Everyday Food*
COOK: **Russell Bellanca**

three-ingredient fettuccine alfredo

Most recipes for fettuccine Alfredo contain butter, Parmesan cheese, and cream, but the original dish, created in Rome in the early twentieth century, was said to contain only creamy sweet butter and top-quality Parmesan. So we were more than delighted when we found this recipe from Russell Bellanca, the owner of Alfredo of Rome in New York City, a restaurant that has long held to the claim that it uses the original Roman formula. We should warn you up-front that this recipe is over the top—way over the top. It is rich and creamy beyond belief, but we firmly believe that there are times and occasions that merit such indulgence.

In addition to being entirely delectable, this fettuccine is one of the easiest pasta dishes you'll ever make. The butter and cheese are beaten together with an electric mixer and then quickly tossed onto the hot pasta. Presto! You have a near-instant restaurant-quality meal.

serves 4

1 cup (2 sticks) unsalted butter, at room temperature (see notes)
8 ounces Parmigiano-Reggiano cheese, grated, plus more for serving (optional)
Salt
1 pound dried fettuccine

Using an electric mixer, beat the butter and cheese in a large bowl until creamy.

Bring a large pot of salted water to a boil and cook the fettuccine until al dente, about 12 minutes. Reserve about 1/2 cup of the cooking water; drain the pasta.

Return the fettuccine to the warm pot. Toss with 1/2 teaspoon salt, the cheese mixture, and 1/4 cup of the reserved pasta cooking water. Toss to combine and coat the noodles. Add more pasta cooking water as needed. Serve immediately in warm pasta bowls. Top with additional cheese, if desired.

notes from our test kitchen

- Since there are so few ingredients here, choosing good-quality butter and cheese really makes a big difference. Use only unsalted butter, and if you can find one of the European-style cultured butters (see tip), buy it. For the cheese, only real, freshly grated Parmigiano-Reggiano will do.
- The butter should be soft, but don't leave it out long enough to become oily.
- You can beat the butter and cheese together with a big wooden spoon. It will take a little more muscle.

tip

Bon Appétit featured an article by Ken Haedrich on European-style butters, which are richer and higher in fat than ordinary butter and produce superior sauces, flakier pastries, and superlative fettuccine Alfredo. These upscale butters are increasingly available at specialty stores and some supermarkets. Look for Plugrá (82 percent butterfat), Challenge European Style Butter (83 percent butterfat), Land O' Lakes Ultra Creamy Butter (83 percent butterfat), Organic Valley Family of Farms European Style Cultured Butter (84 percent butterfat), Straus Family Creamery European-Style Sweet Butter (85 percent butterfat), and Vermont Butter & Cheese Company Vermont Cultured Butter (86 percent butterfat).

SOURCE: *Fine Cooking*

COOK: **Robert Del Grande**

tex-mex macaroni and cheese with green chiles

LEAVE IT TO A TEXAN to elevate homey macaroni and cheese to a blockbuster dish with a serious kick. Robert Del Grande, the chef at Cafe Annie and Cafe Express in Houston, explains that comfort food in Texas means cheese and chiles. It also means corn tortillas. So his version of macaroni and cheese combines roasted poblanos, toasted white corn tortillas, fresh cilantro, and, of course, elbow macaroni. And to provide the right amount of creaminess, the casserole is bound together with a savory custard of eggs and half-and-half.

Del Grande warns us that poblanos can vary in heat level; smaller, darker ones can sometimes be spicier. If your nose stings when you handle the chiles, or if the raw chile tastes wildly spicy when you bite into it, use fewer.

serves 4 to 6

- Softened butter for the baking dish
- 1 pound poblano chiles (4–6 chiles)
- Olive oil
- 6 white corn tortillas
- 1 cup fresh cilantro leaves
- 2 cups half-and-half
- 3 large eggs
- Kosher salt and freshly ground black pepper
- 8 ounces elbow macaroni
- 8 ounces Monterey jack cheese, grated
- 8 ounces sharp cheddar cheese, grated

Put a large pot of water on to boil. Butter a shallow 2- to 3-quart baking dish. Preheat the broiler. Rub the poblanos lightly with olive oil and arrange them on a baking sheet lined with foil. Broil the peppers as close to the element as possible, turning as needed, until the skins are blackened all over. Transfer to a bowl, cover with plastic wrap, and let cool to room temperature. Turn off the broiler and preheat the oven to 350 degrees.

Remove and discard the charred poblano skins along with the stems and seeds. Chop the chiles coarsely and put them in a food processor. In a hot, dry skillet over medium-high heat, lightly toast the tortillas until they're just softened and give off a toasted-corn aroma, 30 to 60 seconds per side (don't let them become crisp). Coarsely chop the tortillas and add them to the chiles in the food processor. Add the cilantro leaves and pulse until finely chopped but not pureed.

In a large bowl, whisk together the half-and-half, eggs, and salt and pepper to taste until well combined. Stir in the chopped chile mixture.

When the water boils, salt it generously and cook the macaroni until al dente. Drain well, shaking to eliminate any excess water. Add the pasta to the egg mixture along with two thirds of the grated cheeses. Stir to combine. Pour the mixture into the buttered dish. Scatter the remaining cheeses evenly over the macaroni. (If baking in a 2-quart dish, set it on a baking sheet to catch any drips.)

Bake until browned and bubbling, about 40 minutes. If you want to brown the center more, flash it briefly under the broiler. Let sit for 10 minutes before serving.

note from our test kitchen

This also makes a great side dish for big cowboy steaks, roast pork, or roast chicken. You'll get 8 to 10 side-dish servings.

SOURCE: *Fine Cooking's Quick and Delicious Recipes*
COOK: Isabelle Alexandre

sear-roasted salmon fillets with lemon-ginger butter

THIS RECIPE FIRST APPEARED in *Fine Cooking* about five years ago, and we immediately added it to our repertoire. So we were thrilled—and not the least bit astonished—to see it reappear this year as part of the magazine's 101 favorite quick recipes. Sear-roasting is one of those great restaurant tricks that actually works well at home. You quickly brown the fish on one side in a skillet on the stove and then slide it into the oven to finish cooking. The initial searing produces a delicate crust on the outside, and the enveloping blast of high heat from the oven cooks the fish through without drying it out or creating a heavy crust. The fish comes out perfectly done—crisp and golden on the outside, moist on the inside.

The accompanying compound butter melts onto the warm fish, making an instant lemon-ginger sauce. We sometimes play around with this formula, substituting orange juice for the lemon, shallots for the ginger, and fresh thyme for the chives. Feel free to create your own salmon-friendly combinations.

serves 4

- 6 tablespoons (3/4 stick) unsalted butter, at room temperature
- 2 tablespoons fresh lemon juice, warmed slightly (see notes)
- 2 tablespoons minced fresh ginger
- 2 tablespoons snipped fresh chives
- Olive oil
- 4 salmon fillets (5 ounces each), skinned if you like, patted dry
- Kosher salt and freshly ground black pepper

In a small bowl, stir together the butter, lemon juice, ginger, and chives until well blended. Set aside at room temperature.

Preheat the oven to 500 degrees. Set a large ovenproof skillet over medium-high heat and add just enough oil to make a light film. Sprinkle the salmon lightly with salt and pepper. When the oil is very hot, add the salmon, skin side up, and cook until nicely browned, about 1 minute. Flip the fish over and immediately put the skillet in the oven. Roast for 2 minutes for medium-rare, 4 minutes for medium–well done. Check for doneness with the tip of a knife.

To serve, remove the pan from the oven, transfer the fish to serving plates, and top the salmon with a dab of lemon-ginger butter.

notes from our test kitchen

- Warming the lemon juice before adding it to the butter makes it easier to mix in, but don't get the liquid boiling hot, or it will melt the butter. A quick blast in the microwave is all you need.
- We like to let the salmon fillets sit at room temperature for 15 to 20 minutes before cooking. They seem to sear better when not ice-cold. Just be sure to pat them dry immediately before searing. Moisture will interfere with the browning.
- Any leftover butter can be wrapped in plastic and kept for days in the refrigerator or for weeks in the freezer.

salmon with yogurt and cardamom

CHEFS WHO COOK AT HOME—and there aren't so many of them—tend to come up with very interesting but simple recipes. Matthew Kenney has a special feeling for Middle Eastern ingredients, and here he's produced a slow-roasted salmon seasoned with olive oil and cardamom, chilled for a few hours under a blanket of yogurt and honey and then sent to the oven. The yogurt gives the fish a silky texture and a delicate, rich sauce. The spicing is sweetly subtle.

Kenney says this is his favorite way to cook salmon at home. There's almost nothing to it, and yet it's sublime.

serves 4

- 4 salmon fillets (6–7 ounces each), skinned
- 2 tablespoons extra-virgin olive oil, plus more for brushing
- 2 teaspoons ground cardamom
- 1 cup plain yogurt
- 2 tablespoons honey
- Kosher salt and freshly ground black pepper

Brush the top of each fillet with olive oil and sprinkle evenly with the cardamom. Place the fillets side by side in a large glass baking dish or a platter.

In a small bowl, mix together the yogurt and honey and spoon liberally over the top of each fillet. Wrap the baking dish tightly in plastic wrap and refrigerate for at least 3 hours or up to 6 hours (any longer and the yogurt will begin to break down the fish).

Preheat the oven to 325 degrees. Unwrap the salmon and brush off the excess yogurt. Season with salt and pepper to taste.

Heat the 2 tablespoons olive oil in a large skillet (preferably nonstick, with an ovenproof handle) over medium-high heat. Sear the salmon on one side until it begins to caramelize, 2 to 3 minutes. (Use two pans, if necessary, to avoid crowding the fillets.) Flip the salmon over and place the pan in the oven for about 6 minutes, until the salmon is pink, translucent, and lightly cooked through, or for about 8 minutes, until it is entirely cooked through, depending on the desired doneness. Place each fillet on a warmed plate and serve.

note from our test kitchen

- By all means, get your fishmonger to skin the salmon.

SOURCE: *Cookoff* by Amy Sutherland
COOK: Kristine Snyder

soy-glazed salmon burgers with ginger-lime aïoli

KRISTINE SNYDER is a free-spirited professional harpist who lives in Hawaii and devotes her spare time to competing in—and sometimes winning—amateur cooking contests. Snyder created these salmon burgers for the Sutter Home Build a Better Burger contest held in Napa Valley each year. Having made them ourselves, we're not the least bit surprised that they won first prize.

Snyder's award-winning conceit is a salmon cake (made from fresh, finely chopped salmon) with an Asian twist. During the grilling, the burgers are basted with a sweet-salty soy glaze.

We're so taken with the taste that we don't necessarily wait until grilling weather to make them. Indeed, we've found that they're also excellent sautéed in a skillet. Either way, this recipe is a clear winner.

serves 4

GINGER-LIME AÏOLI

- 1/2 cup mayonnaise
- 2 tablespoons sour cream
- 2 garlic cloves, minced
- 2 teaspoons minced fresh ginger
- 1 tablespoon fresh lime juice
- 1/4 teaspoon salt

SOY GLAZE

- 1/3 cup soy sauce, preferably low sodium
- 3 tablespoons honey
- 1 tablespoon rice vinegar
- 1 tablespoon cornstarch
- 1 tablespoon dry white wine or water

BURGERS

- 1 large egg yolk
- 2 tablespoons sour cream
- 1 tablespoon fresh lime juice
- 1 teaspoon Asian hot chili sauce or bottled hot sauce
- 1 1/4 pounds skinless salmon fillets, finely chopped
- 2 scallions, thinly sliced
- 2 tablespoons chopped fresh mint
- 2/3 cup bread crumbs, preferably fresh
- 1 teaspoon salt
- Vegetable oil

- 4 sesame buns, split
- 1/2 cucumber, peeled, halved, seeded, and julienned
- Radish or soybean sprouts for garnish (optional)

Prepare a medium-hot grill for direct-heat cooking.

MAKE THE AÏOLI:

Combine all the ingredients in a small bowl. Reserve 2 tablespoons for the burgers and refrigerate the rest until serving time.

MAKE THE GLAZE:

Combine the soy sauce, honey, and rice vinegar in a small, heavy saucepan. In a small bowl, mix the cornstarch and wine or water together until smooth. Add to the soy mixture. Place over medium heat and cook, stirring, until the glaze boils and thickens slightly, about 3 minutes. (You can do this by placing the pan on the grill if you're cooking entirely alfresco.) Set the glaze aside.

MAKE THE BURGERS:

In a large bowl, whisk together the egg yolk, reserved 2 tablespoons aïoli, sour cream, lime juice, and chili sauce or hot sauce. Stir in the salmon, scallions, mint, bread crumbs, and salt and combine. Coat your hands with vegetable oil and form 4 patties. Brush the grill with vegetable oil and grill the patties until browned on the bottom, about 3 minutes. Turn the patties and brush the cooked side with soy glaze. Cook for another 3 minutes, turn, and brush the other side with glaze. Grill just until done, 4 to 6 minutes more, turning and brushing with glaze frequently.

ASSEMBLE THE BURGERS:

During the last few minutes of grilling, toast the buns, cut side down, on the perimeter of the grill. Place some cucumber strips on the bottom half of each bun. Top with a burger and some of the aïoli. Garnish with sprouts, if desired, top with a bun, and serve.

notes from our test kitchen

- We chop the salmon by hand because it keeps the burgers moister. You can also use a food processor, but pulse and stop before the salmon turns to mush.
- Depending on your grill, you may find that the glaze causes the burgers to stick. If so, brush the burgers just once on the grilled side.
- The burgers may be cooked indoors on a grill pan or in a nonstick skillet. If you're using a grill pan, brush well with vegetable oil to prevent the cakes from sticking.

SOURCE: *Bon Appétit*

COOK: La Cantinella

baked snapper with potatoes, oregano, and white wine

WE'RE FOND OF MAIN-DISH RECIPES that incorporate a side dish for two reasons. For one thing, getting two for one generally means less prep time and always means less cleanup. But more important, when the main dish—in this case, red snapper fillets—cooks along with the side dish, potatoes here, the merging of flavors produces something truly greater than the sum of its parts.

This recipe comes from La Cantinella, the only Michelin-starred restaurant in Naples. Despite its pedigree, however, the preparation is extremely relaxed. Russet potatoes are thinly sliced and dressed with a classic Italian quartet of olive oil, garlic, red pepper flakes, and oregano. Then the potatoes are baked until tender, topped with the delicate fish fillets, and baked again just long enough to cook the fish and brown the potatoes. You can also substitute other mild-flavored fillets, such as cod or grouper.

serves 4

- 3 russet potatoes (about 2¼ pounds), peeled and cut into ¼-inch-thick rounds
- ½ cup olive oil
- 3 garlic cloves, minced
- 1½ tablespoons chopped fresh oregano
- Salt
- ¼ teaspoon crushed red pepper flakes
- ¾ cup dry white wine
- ¼ cup water
- 4 ¾-inch-thick red snapper fillets (5–6 ounces each)
- Freshly ground black pepper
- 4 tablespoons chopped fresh parsley

Preheat the oven to 450 degrees. Slightly overlap the potato slices in a 9-x-13-inch baking pan (preferably metal). Mix ¼ cup of the oil, garlic, oregano, 1 teaspoon salt, and crushed red pepper in a small bowl. Pour over the potatoes. Pour the wine and the water on top. Cover with foil and bake for 20 minutes. Uncover and bake until the potatoes are tender, about 35 minutes.

Place the fish fillets atop the potatoes and drizzle with the remaining 1/4 cup oil. Sprinkle with salt and pepper and 2 tablespoons of the parsley. Bake, uncovered, until the fish is opaque in the center, about 18 minutes. Sprinkle with the remaining 2 tablespoons parsley and serve.

notes from our test kitchen

- You can substitute 1 1/2 teaspoons dried oregano for the fresh.
- If the fish fillets are less than 3/4 inch thick, expect them to take less time to cook through. For this reason, be sure that the potatoes are completely tender before you place the fish on top.

SOURCE: *The Tante Marie's Cooking School Cookbook* by Mary Risley

COOKS: Mary Sue Milliken and Susan Feniger

sautéed swordfish with fresh tomato chutney

LONG BEFORE THE BAY AREA was the culinary center of the universe, Mary Risley was teaching the locals how to cook at Tante Marie's Cooking School in San Francisco. Now she's gathered the best of the recipes from decades of Tante Marie's. One of our favorites, and hers, is this sensationally good fish dish. Risley learned it from the owners of the Border Grill in Los Angeles, perhaps better known by their TV moniker, the Two Hot Tamales. But this isn't a Mexican dish; the fish is topped with a classic Indian fresh chutney, and it's sublime.

Obviously, it's terrific in the summer, but it's also almost seasonless, thanks to the very good cherry tomatoes coming to us all year long. The ingredient list may seem long, but the prep time is short.

Swordfish has been overfished, so feel free to substitute another meaty fish, such as shark, marlin, or even salmon. You can broil or grill the fish instead of frying it, which makes the recipe even simpler.

serves 8

FRESH TOMATO CHUTNEY

- 3 pounds ripe Italian plum or cherry tomatoes, cored and cut into 1/2-inch wedges
- 2 bunches scallions, equal parts white and green, cut on the diagonal into 2-inch pieces
- 1 large jalapeño chile or 4 serrano chiles, finely chopped
- 3 tablespoons cumin seeds
- 1 1/2 tablespoons crushed black pepper
- 1 1/2 tablespoons mustard seeds, preferably black (see notes)
- 1 tablespoon ground turmeric
- 1 tablespoon paprika
- 2/3 cup grated fresh ginger
- 10 garlic cloves, minced
- 1 cup vegetable oil
- 1 1/2 cups rice vinegar
- 3/4 cup packed dark brown sugar
- 1/2 teaspoon salt

FISH

- 3/4 cup cornmeal
- 1/2 cup all-purpose flour
- Salt and freshly ground black pepper
- 8 1-inch-thick pieces swordfish (4 ounces each), preferably Pacific, or another meaty fish
- About 4 tablespoons (1/2 stick) butter
- 1/4 cup vegetable oil

Cooked couscous for serving

MAKE THE CHUTNEY:

Combine the tomatoes, scallions, and chile(s) in a large glass or ceramic bowl. In a separate bowl, combine the cumin, pepper, mustard seeds, turmeric, paprika, ginger, and garlic.

Heat the vegetable oil in a medium frying or sauté pan over medium-high heat. When it begins to smoke, add the spice mixture and cook for 2 to 3 minutes. Pour the oil with the spices over the tomato mixture.

Combine the vinegar, brown sugar, and salt in a small saucepan over medium-high heat. When it comes to a boil, pour it over the tomato mixture.

COOK THE FISH:

Mix the cornmeal, flour, and salt and pepper to taste in a shallow dish. Dredge both sides of each piece of fish in the mixture.

Place a large frying or sauté pan over medium-high heat and add enough butter to coat. Add the oil. When the butter and oil are very hot, carefully place a few of the fish pieces in the pan so they are not touching. Don't crowd the pan or push the fish around. Cook until golden on the bottom, 3 to 4 minutes. Turn with a metal spatula and cook on the other side until golden. The fish is cooked through when it is firm when pressed with your finger. Remove and repeat with the remaining fish pieces.

To serve, divide the couscous among eight warmed dinner plates, spooning it into the center of each. Lay a piece of fish at an angle across an edge of the couscous, then spoon plenty of chutney and its juices around the fish and over the other edge of the couscous.

notes from our test kitchen

- To check on the status of wild seafood, go to www.seafoodchoices.com. Pacific swordfish populations are considered to be more stable than Atlantic swordfish, so that species is a better choice.
- Look for black mustard seeds at Indian markets. They're slightly more pungent than brown or yellow mustard seeds, so bear that in mind if you use them.
- Risley notes that you can't keep the chutney for more than 3 days in the refrigerator because the tomatoes will ferment.

SOURCE: *The New York Times Seafood Cookbook* edited by Florence Fabricant

COOKS: Craig Claiborne and Pierre Franey

shrimp baked with tomato sauce and feta cheese

THIS RECIPE IS PROOF that truly good things don't go out of style. Created years ago when Craig Claiborne and Pierre Franey were writing for the *New York Times,* this simple, satisfying dinner comes together quickly enough for a weeknight meal and yet appears dressy enough for a formal dinner party. The two elements—a spicy tomato sauce and the sautéed shrimp—can be prepared ahead. Then all you need to do before you sit down is bake the shrimp in the sauce until heated through.

The authors tell us that the ouzo sprinkled on and flambéed before serving is optional. And we would agree from a purely taste standpoint. But what fun to lower the lights and present these flaming casseroles. You may very well feel as though you've slipped back in time to the 1970s.

If you don't have individual baking dishes, this works just as well in one large dish (see notes). Serve rice or crusty dinner rolls and a green salad on the side.

serves 4

- 1 28-ounce can Italian plum tomatoes, crushed
- 1/4 cup extra-virgin olive oil
- 1 teaspoon finely chopped garlic
- 1/4 cup fish broth or clam juice
- 1 teaspoon dried oregano, preferably Greek
- 1 teaspoon crushed red pepper flakes
- 2 tablespoons drained capers
- Salt and freshly ground black pepper
- 3 tablespoons unsalted butter
- 24 large shrimp (about 1 pound), peeled and deveined (see notes)
- 4 ounces feta cheese, crumbled (see notes)
- 1/4 cup ouzo (optional)

Place the tomatoes in a medium saucepan and simmer, stirring occasionally, until reduced to 2 cups.

Heat the oil in a 3-quart saucepan. Stir in the garlic and cook for 30 seconds. Add the reduced tomatoes, fish broth or clam juice, oregano, red pepper flakes, capers, and salt and pepper to taste.

Preheat the oven to 350 degrees. Melt the butter in a large skillet. Add the shrimp, toss briefly over medium heat just until they turn pink, and remove from the heat.

Divide half of the sauce among four 6-inch individual baking dishes or shallow ramekins. Arrange 6 shrimp in each ramekin, top with the remaining sauce, and scatter the feta over the top. Bake until the sauce is bubbling, about 10 minutes. If desired, sprinkle 1 tablespoon ouzo on each, carefully ignite, and serve.

notes from our test kitchen

- The intended baking dishes here are the shallow round ones meant for individual gratins. Deeper soufflé-style ramekins won't do. If you don't own a set of individual dishes, bake this in a 1½-quart gratin or other shallow casserole dish. The idea is to accommodate the shrimp in a single layer.
- We prefer to remove the tails from the shrimp, since they are buried in the tomato sauce and are unpleasant to bite into.
- Shop for the best feta you can find, preferably Greek, French, or Bulgarian. And whatever you do, don't buy the precrumbled stuff. Its flavor is inferior.

SOURCE: *Wegmans Menu Magazine*

COOK: Staff

chicken saltimbocca with escarole and beans

WE DISCOVERED THIS WONDERFUL RECIPE while grocery shopping at a Wegmans supermarket, a family-owned chain in western New York and Pennsylvania. We were wandering around, marveling at the variety and quality of food available, when we caught a whiff of something delicious. Tracking down the source, we found one of the store chefs preparing chicken saltimbocca and offering samples. One taste and we decided on the spot that we'd be making it ourselves for dinner. Moreover, the recipe came with the promise of taking no more than 30 minutes to make.

Any stickler for authenticity will argue that this bears little resemblance to real saltimbocca—aside from the sage and ham—but it's so good that we don't care. The saucy combination of cannellini beans, wilted escarole, and chicken stock lends a satisfying depth to the dish and helps keep the chicken moist. And with greens, beans, and chicken in one dish, all you need on the side is a loaf of crusty bread and a glass of Italian red.

serves 4 to 6

- 4 boneless, skinless chicken breasts (about 7 ounces each)
- 1 tablespoon fresh sage leaves, cut crosswise into thin slivers
- 4 thin slices prosciutto
- Freshly ground black pepper
- 1/2 cup all-purpose flour or finely milled flour such as Wondra for dredging
- Salt
- 4 tablespoons olive oil
- 3 large garlic cloves, minced
- 1 large bunch escarole (about 1 1/2 pounds), trimmed and coarsely chopped
- 1 15 1/2-ounce can cannellini beans, undrained
- 1 cup chicken stock
- 1 pound broccoli crowns, cut into large pieces, stems attached
- 1/4 cup freshly grated Grana Padano or Parmesan cheese

Place a chicken breast smooth side up in a large, sturdy resealable plastic bag. Sprinkle one quarter of the sage leaves on the chicken and lay 1 slice of prosciutto on top. Pound both sides with a meat-tenderizing mallet (a rolling pin or the base of a small saucepan also will work) to an even thickness of about

1/4 inch. (For best results, start in the center and pound outward.) Remove the chicken (prosciutto attached) from the bag and repeat with the remaining breasts. Season the chicken with pepper to taste. Place the flour on a plate or in a shallow dish and dredge each piece of chicken lightly in flour, shaking gently to discard the excess.

Bring a large pot of salted water to a boil.

Heat 2 tablespoons of the oil in a large skillet over medium-high heat until the oil is just about to smoke. Add the chicken pieces in a single layer. If the pan is too small, do this in 2 batches. When the edges of the chicken begin to turn opaque, flip the chicken and continue cooking until cooked all the way through, 5 to 8 minutes total. (You can check by making a small cut in the thickest part or using an instant-read thermometer to check that it is 165 degrees.) Transfer the chicken to a platter.

Reduce the heat to medium and add the remaining 2 tablespoons olive oil to the pan. Add the garlic and cook, stirring, for 30 seconds. Add the escarole, beans, and chicken stock. Season with salt and pepper to taste. Cover and cook until the escarole is wilted, about 3 minutes. Uncover and cook for 10 minutes, stirring occasionally (it will be soupy).

Meanwhile, blanch the broccoli in the boiling water until crisp-tender, 3 to 4 minutes. Drain and set aside in a warm spot.

Return the chicken, prosciutto side up, to the skillet, placing it on top of the escarole. Let it warm through, 3 to 5 minutes.

Arrange the broccoli on a platter. Top with the escarole-bean mixture and chicken. Sprinkle with the cheese and serve.

notes from our test kitchen

- If you prefer to drain and rinse canned beans, that's fine. Just add an additional 1/4 cup stock or water.
- To make this for a crowd, double the recipe, cooking the chicken in batches, and arrange everything in a large baking dish. (It will hold for a couple of hours at this point.) To serve, cover the dish with foil and place in a 350-degree oven for about 15 minutes, until warmed through.

SOURCE: *Food & Wine*

COOKS: Leonard Schwartz and Michael J. Rosen

fried chicken littles

FRIED CHICKEN WAS EVERYWHERE THIS YEAR, and *Vogue*'s Jeffrey Steingarten fried up some two hundred chickens to determine which method worked best. We tried a number of recipes with the same goal in mind, and this one was the winner.

At Zeke's Smokehouse in Montrose, California, people pack the place waiting for this great fried chicken, which is usually served with all-American potato salad. There are a couple of secret ingredients here. One is the self-rising flour in the batter, which makes for an incredibly crisp and airy piece of fried chicken. Another is harissa, the Moroccan spicy sauce that flavors the very delicious seasoned mayonnaise the chicken is dipped into.

The only trick is finding drumettes, the big joint on the chicken's wing, for this recipe. We've seen them at Stop & Shop, an East Coast supermarket chain, and at some butcher shops. If you can't find them, use whole wings or look for small boneless thighs. Your goal here is to find a succulent little piece of chicken with maximum surface, yielding more crunch.

You can use this same batter system for frying regular chicken parts (we like thighs best). Don't let fear of frying scare you away from this recipe. It's easy, and it will make you famous among your friends. These are about a hundred times better than buffalo wings.

serves 4 to 6

SEASONED MAYONNAISE

- 1 cup mayonnaise
- 1/4 cup fresh lime juice
- 1 tablespoon minced onion
- 1 1/2 teaspoons minced garlic
- 1 tablespoon harissa (see notes)
- 1 tablespoon pure ancho chile powder (see notes)
- 1 1/2 teaspoons salt
- 1 1/2 teaspoons ground white pepper
- 1 1/2 teaspoons paprika
- 1 teaspoon cayenne pepper

CHICKEN

- 1 1/2 cups plus 2 tablespoons all-purpose flour
- 1/2 cup self-rising flour, or 1/2 cup all-purpose flour plus 1/2 teaspoon baking powder and pinch salt
- 1 1/2 teaspoons salt
- 1/2 teaspoon baking powder
- 1 3/4 cups water
- Vegetable oil for frying
- 1 teaspoon ground white pepper
- 1 teaspoon paprika
- 4 pounds chicken drumettes

MAKE THE MAYONNAISE:

In a medium bowl, whisk together the mayonnaise, lime juice, onion, garlic, harissa, and chile powder. Stir in the remaining ingredients. Refrigerate.

COOK THE CHICKEN:

In a medium bowl, combine the flours, 1/2 teaspoon of the salt, and the baking powder. Add the water. Using an electric mixer, beat at medium speed until smooth, about 5 minutes.

In a large saucepan, heat 3 inches of oil to 350 degrees. In a large, sturdy resealable plastic bag, combine the remaining 1 teaspoon salt, the pepper, and paprika. Add 10 of the drumettes, seal the bag, and shake until evenly coated. Dip the drumettes into the batter, letting any excess batter drip back into the bowl. Carefully slide them, one by one, into the hot oil and fry until they are golden and rise to the surface, about 12 minutes. Using a slotted spoon, transfer them to a paper towel–lined wire rack to drain. Coat, dip, and fry the remaining drumettes in batches. Serve with the mayonnaise.

notes from our test kitchen

- We think harissa in cans tastes better than the kind in tubes, so we buy it when we see it, which isn't often. Look for it in Middle Eastern stores and gourmet shops. Place any leftovers in a small jar in the refrigerator. It will keep for weeks or even months.
- Don't confuse ancho chile powder with ordinary chile powder. You can find this pure chile powder in large supermarkets or specialty food shops.

SOURCE: *Ready When You Are* by Martha Rose Shulman

COOK: Martha Rose Shulman

stewed chicken with chipotles and prunes

THIS EXCELLENT DINNER PARTY DISH can be made a day ahead—in fact it improves overnight—so all you have to do is heat it up and make some rice and a salad. It's an inspired combination of roasted vegetables, sweet spices such as cloves and cinnamon, prunes, and the sweet-sour-hot kick of chipotle chiles. Each ingredient is given its own flavor-boosting treatment, in the classic Mexican way: the tomatoes and onion halves are roasted first, the garlic is toasted in a skillet, and some of the prunes get a hot soak. This is how they make chicken stew in Veracruz, and it's a knockout.

serves 6

- 12 pitted prunes
- 2 pounds tomatoes
- 1 large onion, halved crosswise
- 2 large garlic cloves, unpeeled
- 4 black peppercorns
- 1 whole clove
- 2 large garlic cloves, minced or pressed
- 2–3 canned chipotle chiles in adobo (to taste), rinsed, stemmed, and seeded
- 3 tablespoons vegetable or canola oil
- 1 chicken (3½–4½ pounds), cut up and skinned, if desired
- Salt and freshly ground black pepper
- 3 cups chicken stock or water
- 1 3-inch cinnamon stick
- Cooked rice for serving

Place 2 of the prunes in a heatproof bowl and add boiling water to cover. Let sit for 15 minutes and drain.

Preheat the broiler and cover a large baking sheet with foil. Place the tomatoes and onion on the sheet in a single layer and broil about 3 inches from the heat (in batches, if necessary). Turn after 3 to 5 minutes, when the tomatoes have charred on one side, and repeat on the other side. As the tomatoes are done, transfer them, using tongs, to a large bowl. The onion will take longer than the tomatoes and will need to be flipped over several times so that it chars rather than burns; this should take 5 to 10 minutes. Add the onion to the tomatoes. When the tomatoes are cool enough, core and peel them.

Toast the whole garlic cloves in their skins in a dry skillet over medium-high heat, turning them often, until they're blackened in a few spots and smell toasty, about 10 minutes. Remove from the heat and peel.

Grind the peppercorns and clove in a spice grinder or coffee grinder. Transfer the tomatoes and roasted onion, along with any juices from the bowl, to a blender. Add the toasted garlic, minced or pressed garlic, ground pepper and clove, soaked prunes, and chipotles and blend until smooth. Pour through a medium-mesh strainer into a bowl. Push the puree through the strainer with the back of a spoon and tap the strainer against the bowl to get it all through.

Heat 2 tablespoons of the oil in a large, heavy nonstick skillet over medium-high heat. Add the chicken in batches and fry on both sides until golden, about 5 minutes per side. Season both sides with salt and pepper to taste after you flip the chicken over. Transfer to a plate or bowl as the chicken is done. When all of the chicken has been browned, pour off the fat from the pan and discard.

Heat the remaining 1 tablespoon oil in the pan over medium-high heat and add a drop of the tomato puree. If it sizzles loudly, add the rest (wait a minute or two if it doesn't). Cook, stirring, until slightly thickened, about 5 minutes. Stir in 1/2 cup of the chicken stock or water and 1/2 teaspoon salt. Bring to a simmer, turn the heat to low, and simmer, uncovered, stirring often with a long-handled spoon, until the sauce is fragrant and thick, about 20 minutes. (Be careful not to stand too close to the pan when you're not stirring, because the sauce will sputter a lot. Have a damp dishtowel handy for wiping the stove.)

Add the chicken pieces, the remaining 10 prunes, the cinnamon stick, the remaining 2 1/2 cups stock or water, and salt to taste to the sauce. Bring to a simmer, reduce the heat, and simmer for 30 to 40 minutes, until the chicken is tender. Taste and adjust the seasoning. Remove the cinnamon stick and serve hot, with rice.

notes from our test kitchen

- We prefer to use all chicken thighs here; 12 of them will serve 6 people. Look for smaller thighs.
- There will be a lot of liquid in the pan. To reduce it a bit and brown the tops of the chicken pieces, you can do the final simmering in a 325-degree oven, checking from time to time to see that the liquid doesn't evaporate too much.

SOURCE: www.hoppinjohns.com
COOK: John Martin Taylor

country captain

OF ALL THE REDISCOVERED FORGOTTEN DISHES of the year, this classic chicken curry deserves first place. Country Captain is an American variation on a mild northern Indian curry popular in the British Isles. The curry is curry powder, unknown in India but by now a British staple. The historic southern U.S. port cities of Savannah and Charleston were sources of fresh, exotic spices, and Country Captain is especially popular in the Lowcountry.

The food writer Cecily Brownstone made a great study of the dish decades ago, and most versions we found can be traced back to hers, which is based on chicken parts. For this more elegant rendition from the Lowcountry culinary historian John Martin Taylor, you bone the chicken before cooking it in a richly flavorful sauce based on homemade chicken stock.

All serious cooks of Country Captain should note that if you're willing to make your own curry powder, you'll be amazed by the depth and subtlety of the result. It's just a few moments of work, so we urge you to try it.

Like all old-fashioned American curries, Country Captain offers a lot of possibilities for garnishes at the table, making it a great party dish. See the notes for some options.

serves 8

CHICKEN

- 1 3½–4 pound chicken (reserve neck and giblets)
- Salt, freshly ground black pepper, and cayenne pepper, to taste
- 3 quarts water
- 2–3 celery ribs, broken into pieces
- 1 large onion, quartered
- 2 bay leaves
- 2 carrots, broken into pieces
- A few fresh thyme sprigs and other fresh herbs of your choice

CURRY POWDER

- 1 tablespoon coriander seeds
- 2 teaspoons cumin seeds or 1½ teaspoons ground
- 2 teaspoons crushed red pepper flakes or 1 large dried red chile pepper
- 2 teaspoons ground turmeric
- ½ teaspoon cloves (about 12)
- 1 cinnamon stick, broken into pieces
- 1 teaspoon black peppercorns
- ½ teaspoon ground ginger
- 2 bay leaves, crumbled

CURRY SAUCE

- 1/2 cup blanched and slivered almonds
- 3 tablespoons peanut oil or clarified butter or ghee (page 169)
- 2 large onions, chopped (about 3 cups)
- 2 large green bell peppers, chopped
- 2 garlic cloves, minced
- 1 28-ounce can peeled tomatoes with their juice
- 1/2 cup dried currants

RICE AND GARNISHES

- 1 1/2 cups long-grain white rice, preferably basmati
- 1/2 teaspoon salt
- Chopped fresh parsley for garnish
- Reserved roasted almonds for garnish
- Other garnishes: freshly grated coconut, chopped scallions (optional)

PREPARE THE CHICKEN:

Rinse the chicken in cold water and pat dry. Sprinkle it all over with salt, pepper, and cayenne. Put the chicken in a large stockpot and cover with the 3 quarts water. Add the neck and other giblets except the liver. Add the remaining ingredients, bring almost to a boil, reduce the heat, skim any foam that rises to the surface, and simmer until the meat is cooked evenly, about 1 hour.

Remove the chicken with a slotted spoon and let cool. As soon as it's cool enough to handle, remove the skin and discard, then pull the chicken meat from the bird, tearing it into small pieces. Put the meat in a covered dish in the refrigerator. You should have 1 pound meat, about 4 cups. Crack the bones of the carcass with a meat cleaver and return them to the stockpot. Continue simmering the mixture until it has a distinct chicken flavor, 30 minutes to 1 hour more. Strain all of the solids out of the stock. Let cool, then refrigerate the stock. Remove any congealed fat from the surface of the stock before using.

MAKE THE CURRY POWDER:

Toast the whole coriander and cumin seeds in a heavy Dutch oven over medium heat, stirring constantly, until they begin to darken, 2 to 3 minutes. If you are using ground cumin, add it about a minute after the coriander. Transfer to a spice grinder. Add the rest of the dried spices and bay leaves to the spice grinder and grind thoroughly. Dump them out onto a plate; you should have about 1/4 cup curry powder. Set aside 2 tablespoons; store the remainder in a tightly covered jar and store in a cool, dry place. It will keep for several months.

MAKE THE CURRY SAUCE:

Add the almonds to the spice-toasting pot and toast, stirring constantly, until they are browned evenly. Remove and set aside.

Add the oil or butter to the pot. Add the chopped onions, bell peppers, and garlic and cook over medium heat, stirring often, until the onions begin to get transparent, about 10 minutes. Put the tomatoes in a blender or a food processor and puree. Add the tomatoes, the 2 tablespoons curry powder, and 1½ cups of the reserved stock to the onion and bell pepper mixture and simmer, uncovered, stirring every 5 to 10 minutes so that the vegetables do not stick to the bottom of the pot, for 30 to 45 minutes, or until almost all the liquid is cooked out.

Add the reserved chicken meat and the currants, stir all together thoroughly, then cover the pot and turn off the heat.

PREPARE THE RICE AND SERVE:

About 30 minutes before serving, add the rice, 3 cups of the remaining stock, and salt to a stockpot with a tight-fitting lid. Bring to a boil, immediately reduce the heat to a simmer, and cover the pot. Do not stir and do not lift the lid. After 13 minutes, remove from the heat and set aside for 12 more minutes. Meanwhile, reheat the curry sauce. When the 12 minutes are up, fluff the rice with a fork and spread it on a platter. Top with the chicken mixture and sprinkle with the chopped parsley and almonds. Serve with the garnishes, if desired.

notes from our test kitchen

- When making your own curry powder, be careful not to overtoast the spices — they can easily burn and turn bitter.
- If you have a really good curry powder, just use 2 tablespoons of it instead of making some from scratch. If there's an Indian market nearby, look for Bolst's Hot Curry Powder, the one the Indian culinary authority Madhur Jaffrey recommends.
- You leave behind a lot of tomato in the food processor or blender. To get it all out, run the machine with the chicken stock in it before you add the stock to the pot.
- It's a huge amount of fun to offer a lot of small bowls of garnishes at the table. Other possibilities: bits of fried bacon, grated hard-cooked egg, dried currants, and crumbled fried onions or shallots (page 161). Chopped roasted peanuts are also traditional, but omit the almonds or you'll have nut overload.

SOURCE: *Boston* magazine

COOK: Angela Raynor

STORY BY: Kim Atkinson

drunken steak

ANGELA AND SETH RAYNOR OWN TWO POPULAR RESTAURANTS on Nantucket, the Boarding House and the Pearl. Seth is the professional chef, but Andrea also has formal culinary training, and she's the one who does a lot of the cooking for the family. This steak is a favorite at their annual Independence Day cookout on the beach.

The secret is a robust bourbon-soy marinade. The alcohol burns off as the steak grills, but the flavors penetrate the meat, and the sugar produces a crisp mahogany-colored exterior. The recipe can easily be doubled or even tripled for a crowd.

serves 8

- 1 cup soy sauce
- 1/3 cup bourbon
- 1 cup packed light brown sugar
- 1/2 orange, cut into 1/4-inch-thick rounds
- 3 garlic cloves, thinly sliced
- 3 shallots, thinly sliced
- 2 pounds flank steak, preferably Black Angus, trimmed

Place all the ingredients except the steak in a sturdy, gallon-size resealable plastic bag, seal securely, and shake until the sugar dissolves. Add the steak, reseal, and shake to coat. Marinate the steak in the refrigerator for at least 2 hours or overnight.

Remove from the refrigerator and let come to room temperature. Preheat the grill to medium and place the steak on the grate. Cook for 8 to 10 minutes for medium-rare, turning once, or to the desired doneness. Remove from the grill, cover loosely with foil, and let rest for 10 minutes. Slice, transfer to a platter, and serve.

note from our test kitchen

You can broil the steak instead of grilling it, if you prefer.

port-and-soy-glazed beef tenderloin

WHEN YOU RUN A RESTAURANT and a cooking school, as the Pences do in Oregon, Christmas at home means luxuriating in free time with friends and family, not spending all day in the kitchen. But of course the meal still needs to be festive.

The solution for the Pences is one that works for any special occasion when you want to spend a minimum of time in the kitchen. Beef tenderloin steaks, aka filets mignons, are luxurious by definition, but they need careful cooking and a little help in the flavor department to taste their best. The port and soy glaze does wonders for them, and the most time you'll be away from your guests while cooking this big-deal main course is 15 minutes.

serves 6

- 1 tablespoon extra-virgin olive oil
- 6 6-ounce beef tenderloin steaks (filets mignons)
- Freshly ground black pepper
- 2 tablespoons unsalted butter
- 1 cup port
- 1/4 cup soy sauce

Preheat the oven to 400 degrees. Heat the olive oil in a very large ovenproof sauté pan over high heat until smoking hot. Season the steaks heavily with pepper. Place them in the pan and sear well, about 3 minutes per side. Set the pan in the oven and roast until the steaks reach an internal temperature of 130 degrees for medium-rare, about 6 minutes.

Remove the steaks from the pan and keep warm. Set the pan over high heat. Add the butter, port, and soy sauce and cook until the sauce thickens and coats the back of a spoon, about 3 minutes. Return the steaks to the pan, turning them over to coat well with the sauce. Transfer to a serving platter, drizzle with any remaining sauce, and serve hot.

note from our test kitchen

If you have a digital cooking thermometer with a probe, this is a perfect place to use it. Put the probe in a steak when the meat goes into the oven, and you'll know exactly when it's perfectly done. Take the steaks out of the pan and keep warm (under foil) while you make the glaze to avoid overcooking them.

SOURCE: *The Weekend Chef* by Barbara Witt

COOK: Barbara Witt

beef stew with tequila

THIS HOMEY BEEF STEW gets an extra dimension from tequila, which provides a special quality that means you'll want to make it again and again (though it tastes nothing like tequila).

It's worth making a double batch because it freezes so well. On a cold night when you don't want to brave the elements to go out and buy something for dinner, it's bliss to have it waiting in the freezer.

There are a couple of things to know about the ingredient list. The beef chuck strips may be hard to come by unless you have an accommodating butcher. You can always buy a small chuck roast and cut them yourself. Pure chile powder isn't the same thing as the chili powder sold for seasoning chili; it's actually powdered chile from one sort of chile or another. You're likely to find pure ancho chile powder in the spice rack at most supermarkets, but if you live in the Southwest, you'll have many more options, all good.

serves 4

- 1/4 cup olive oil
- 4 thick strips beef chuck (about 2 x 2 x 6 inches)
- Kosher salt and freshly ground black pepper
- 3 celery ribs, chopped
- 1 large onion, chopped
- 4 garlic cloves, chopped
- 1 hot red chile, seeded and slivered
- 1 teaspoon pure chile powder
- 1/4 teaspoon ground cinnamon
- 1/4 teaspoon ground cumin
- 1/4 cup tequila
- 1 cup canned plum tomatoes or diced tomatoes with some of the juice
- 1 1/2 cups beef stock
- 1/4 cup minced fresh cilantro for garnish

Preheat the oven to 350 degrees. Heat the oil in a shallow Dutch oven or a deep ovenproof sauté pan over medium-high heat until shimmering. Add the meat and brown well on all sides. Season with salt and pepper to taste. Remove the meat from the pan and set aside. Pour off all but a couple of tablespoons of the oil and sauté the celery, onion, garlic, and chile until the mixture is soft. Stir in the chile powder, cinnamon, and cumin. Pour in the tequila and simmer for a couple of seconds to evaporate the alcohol and release the flavors of the spices. Add the tomatoes and stock and nestle the meat into the pan. (The level of the liquid should not reach the top of the meat.) Slide the pan, uncovered, into the oven and braise the meat for 2 to 3 hours, until fork-tender. Check the liquid level after 30 minutes to judge how rapidly the meat is cooking. Lower the heat if necessary.

Remove the meat from the sauce and slice it thickly. Reduce the sauce, if necessary. Return the meat to the sauce, spoon it into a serving dish, garnish with the cilantro, and serve.

note from our test kitchen

- You don't need the best 100 percent agave tequila for this dish; gold will work fine.

SOURCE: *Come for Dinner* by Leslie Revsin

COOK: Leslie Revsin

braised beef short ribs chinese style

BEEF SHORT RIBS HAVE BECOME a real darling of chefs and serious home cooks in recent years, and there's no mystery about why. When tucked into a braising pot with a few aromatic ingredients and left to simmer quietly for hours, these meaty ribs emerge lusciously tender. Few dishes deliver such big flavor with so little fuss.

In this version, Leslie Revsin uses a classic Chinese combination—sherry, soy sauce, ginger, scallions, and star anise — to give the ribs an intensely aromatic, slightly sweet character. In addition to penetrating the meat, the soy-based braising liquid gives the ribs an appealingly dark, caramelized appearance. Just one look at them, and you know they'll be good.

Like many slow-cooked dishes, these short ribs benefit from being made ahead and left to sit overnight in the braising liquid (see note). Serve with mashed potatoes, with some of the braising liquid spooned over the top.

serves 6

- 1/2 cup soy sauce
- 1/2 cup fino sherry, dry white wine, or dry vermouth
- 2 tablespoons packed light brown sugar
- 1 1/3 cups drained and coarsely chopped canned plum tomatoes
- 2/3 cup water
- 4 star anise
- 6–6 1/2 pounds beef short ribs on the bone, cut into 3-inch lengths
- Salt and freshly ground black pepper
- 1 1/2 tablespoons vegetable oil, plus more if needed
- 6 garlic cloves, crushed with the side of a knife and peeled
- 6 scallions, cut into 2-inch pieces
- 1 1-inch piece fresh ginger about the diameter of a quarter, cut into 8 slices
- 2 tablespoons thinly sliced scallions (cut on the diagonal) for garnish

Adjust the rack to the middle and preheat the oven to 325 degrees. Stir the soy sauce (or sherry, wine, or vermouth), brown sugar, and tomatoes together in a bowl. Stir in the water and star anise. Set aside.

Dry the ribs with paper towels and season very lightly with salt and generously with pepper. Heat the oil in a large, heavy flameproof casserole over medium-high heat. (The casserole should be large enough to hold all the ribs in no more than two layers.) When the oil is hot, add the ribs in batches (do not crowd) and brown on all sides. Remove them as they're browned, adding more oil, if necessary.

When all the ribs are browned, pour off the fat and reduce the heat to low. Add the garlic, scallion pieces, and ginger, alternately tossing and pressing them against the pot for 1 minute to bring out their flavor. Return the ribs to the pot and pour the soy sauce mixture over them. Bring the liquid to a simmer and cover. Transfer the pot to the oven and braise the ribs, turning occasionally, until extremely tender when pierced with a fork, 2½ to 3 hours.

Transfer the ribs to a serving platter. Discard the ginger and star anise and pour the remaining sauce into a large heatproof glass or measuring cup. Let stand for about 5 minutes, then spoon off and discard any fat that has risen to the surface. Reheat the sauce, season generously with pepper, and pour over the ribs. Garnish with the thinly sliced scallions and serve hot.

note from our test kitchen

Short ribs are easier to degrease if you make them ahead and refrigerate them overnight. When the ribs are done, discard the ginger and star anise. Transfer the ribs to a baking dish or other container that can accommodate them in one layer. Pour the braising liquid over the ribs and refrigerate for up to 5 days or freeze for up to 2 months. Skim off the fat, then reheat the ribs and sauce in a moderate oven.

tip

A similar recipe for short ribs by Leslie Revsin appeared in *Fine Cooking.* There she garnishes the ribs with sautéed leeks instead of chopped scallions. At first we thought it might be overkill, but when we tasted it, we realized what a good idea it was. Cut 3 medium leeks (white and light green parts) into 2-inch-long julienne strips (2 to 2½ cups). Rinse the strips, drain, and dry well. Melt 1 tablespoon unsalted butter in a large skillet. Add the leeks and cook, stirring frequently, until they begin to brown, 3 to 5 minutes. Reduce the heat to medium-low and continue cooking, stirring frequently, until tender, 3 to 5 minutes. Season with salt and pepper to taste. When the ribs are ready, scatter the leeks over the top and serve.

SOURCE: *Annie and Margrit* by Annie Roberts, Margrit Biever Mondavi, and Victoria Wise

COOK: Margrit Biever Mondavi

ticino-style pot roast

MARGRIT BIEVER, now Mrs. Robert Mondavi of the great Napa Valley wine empire, grew up in the Ticino, a Swiss canton on Lake Maggiore. Pot roast is as popular there as it is in America, but the Ticino version is subtly different. It's cooked with celery root, leeks, tomatoes, fresh herbs, and Merlot, the everyday wine in the area.

This very flavorful pot roast is both familiar and new. If a pot roast can be refined and even elegant, this one is. Serve it with boiled new potatoes and lots of Merlot.

serves 6

- 2 tablespoons unsalted butter
- 1 2-pound boneless beef chuck roast
- Kosher salt and freshly ground black pepper
- 1 carrot, peeled and chopped
- 1 leek, white and light green parts, sliced
- 1/4 celery root, peeled and chopped (large dice)
- 2 whole cloves
- 2 medium tomatoes, chopped (see notes)
- 3 garlic cloves, chopped
- 1/2 teaspoon chopped fresh basil
- 1/4 teaspoon fresh rosemary leaves
- 1/4 teaspoon fresh thyme leaves
- 1 cup beef stock
- 1 cup Merlot

Melt the butter in a large pot over medium-high heat. Add the meat, sprinkling liberally with salt and pepper. Brown on both sides, turning once, about 5 minutes total.

Without removing the meat, add the carrot, leek, celery root, and cloves and stir to mix. Reduce the heat to medium and cook until the vegetables begin to wilt, about 2 minutes. Add the remaining ingredients, stir, and bring to a boil over high heat. Decrease the heat to medium-low, cover, and simmer for about 1½ hours, until the meat is fork-tender. Remove from the heat and let rest, partially covered, for 30 minutes.

Transfer the meat to a plate and set aside in a warm place. Strain the liquid through a fine-mesh sieve into a bowl, discarding the solids. Let sit for a few minutes to allow the fat to rise to the top, then skim. Return the skimmed liquid to the pot and cook over high heat until slightly thickened, about 15 minutes.

Cut the meat into 1/4-inch-thick slices and arrange on a serving platter. Pour the reduced liquid over the meat and serve immediately.

notes from our test kitchen

- In winter, when you'll most likely be making this dish, fresh tomatoes can be a problem. Use a 14.5-ounce can of Muir Glen diced organic tomatoes with their juice instead.
- If you don't have fresh herbs available, use about half the amount of dried herbs.

SOURCE: *BBQ USA* by Steven Raichlen

COOK: Jim Budros

millionaire's brisket with coffee and beer mop sauce

THIS SPECTACULAR BRISKET is the work of a high-wheeling investment adviser in Columbus, Ohio, who also happens to be co-owner of City Barbeque in Columbus, where they make this heavenly stuff. It's so good, in fact, that Jim Budros's team won the American Royal Barbecue championship for brisket in 1997.

Like any respectable pit master, Budros barbecues an entire brisket, which is about 14 to 16 pounds. For home cooks, the cookbook author and barbecue meister Steven Raichlen has cut it down to 6 pounds, a reasonable thing to ask for at your local supermarket. You want the fat left on the brisket, to moisten it as it cooks. The key thing, says Budros, is to cook it low and slow, to baste it constantly, and not to add any barbecue sauce until right before you serve it—or, better yet, serve the sauce on the side.

The sauce is what Raichlen calls a doctor sauce. You just pick up a good basic barbecue sauce and fix it up a little. Perfect.

serves 8 to 10

RUB AND BRISKET

- 1/4 cup coarse salt (kosher or sea salt)
- 1/4 cup firmly packed light brown sugar
- 1/4 cup sweet paprika
- 2 tablespoons pure chile powder
- 2 tablespoons freshly ground black pepper
- 1 tablespoon onion powder
- 1 tablespoon garlic powder
- 1/2 teaspoon dried oregano
- 1 center-cut piece beef brisket (5–6 pounds)

MOP (BASTING) SAUCE

- 1 cup beer
- 1 cup apple cider
- 1/3 cup cider vinegar
- 1/3 cup brewed coffee
- 1/3 cup beef or chicken stock (preferably homemade)
- 1/4 cup vegetable oil
- 1/4 cup Worcestershire sauce
- 2 tablespoons Tabasco sauce or other hot sauce
- 2 teaspoons coarse salt (kosher or sea salt), or more to taste
- 1 teaspoon freshly ground black pepper

- 6 slices bacon (optional)
- Jim's Really Easy and Really Good Barbecue Sauce (recipe follows)

MAKE THE RUB AND PREPARE THE BRISKET:

Place the salt, brown sugar, paprika, chile powder, pepper, onion powder, garlic powder, and oregano in a small bowl and stir to mix, preferably with your fingers.

In the unlikely event that your brisket comes covered with a thick layer of fat, trim it to a thickness of 1/4 inch. Place the brisket in a roasting pan and generously sprinkle both sides with the rub, using about 3 tablespoons per side and patting it onto the meat with your fingertip. (You'll have about 3/4 cup more rub than you need for the brisket, but leftovers will keep for several months in a tightly covered jar.) You can cook the brisket right away, but it will be better if you cover it and let it cure in the refrigerator for several hours or even a day.

MAKE THE MOP SAUCE:

Place all the ingredients in a nonreactive bowl and whisk to mix. Taste for seasoning, adding more salt, if necessary.

GRILL THE BRISKET:

Soak 4 to 6 cups wood chips or chunks, preferably apple or hickory, in water to cover for 1 hour; drain. Set up the grill for indirect grilling and preheat to medium-low. If you're using a gas grill, place all the wood chips or chunks in the smoker box or a smoker pouch and run the grill on high until you see smoke, then reduce the heat to medium-low. If you're using a charcoal grill, place a large drip pan in the center, preheat the grill to medium-low, and toss 1 cup of the wood chips or chunks onto the coals.

When ready to cook, place the brisket fat side up in the center of the hot grate, over the drip pan and away from the heat. Drape the bacon slices, if using, over the top of the meat, then cover the grill. Cook the brisket until very tender, 5 to 6 hours, depending on the size of the brisket and the heat of the grill. To test for doneness, use an instant-read thermometer: the internal temperature should be about 190 degrees. Generously mop or baste the meat on both sides with the mop sauce once an hour for the first 5 hours. If the brisket starts to brown too much, generously baste it with the sauce, wrap it in foil, and continue cooking until done. If you're using a charcoal grill, you'll need to add 12 fresh coals and 1/2 cup wood chips or chunks to each side every hour.

Transfer the grilled brisket to a cutting board and let rest for 10 minutes. Thinly slice across the grain, using an electric knife or a sharp carving knife. Transfer the sliced meat to a platter. Spoon the barbecue sauce over the meat or, better yet, serve it on the side.

jim's really easy and really good barbecue sauce

makes about 3 1/2 cups sauce

- 2 cups store-bought barbecue sauce, such as Bull's-Eye or KC Masterpiece
- 1–2 cups store-bought salsa (to taste), mild, medium, or hot
- 1/4 cup cider vinegar, or more to taste
- Coarse salt (kosher or sea salt) and freshly ground black pepper

Combine the barbecue sauce, salsa, and vinegar in a nonreactive saucepan over medium heat. Bring to a simmer and cook until thick and flavorful, 5 to 8 minutes. Season with salt and pepper to taste. The sauce can be served hot or at room temperature. It may be refrigerated, covered, for up to 2 days. Bring to room temperature or reheat before serving.

SOURCE: *The Best of Virginia Farms* by CiCi Williamson

COOK: David Walker

smithfield inn's roasted peanut pork chops

AT THE HISTORIC (1752) SMITHFIELD INN in Smithfield, Virginia (where George Washington really did sleep), the favorite entrée is these terrific peanut-crusted pork chops with a shiitake mushroom–bourbon sauce. The sous chef David Walker has taken some all-star southern ingredients—lean Smithfield pork, peanuts, and bourbon—and made something unique.

This is elegant dinner party food, but it's also so quick and unpretentious that it works for a weeknight dinner as well. The only trick is getting thinly sliced chops. If your knife skills are great, buy a 14-ounce loin and do it yourself or, better yet, ask the butcher to do it for you.

serves 4

- 4 boneless loin pork chops sliced 1/4 inch thick (about 3 1/2 ounces each)
- Salt and freshly ground black pepper
- 1/2 cup chopped unsalted roasted peanuts
- 2 tablespoons butter
- 1/2 cup sliced mushrooms (see note)
- 2 teaspoons sugar
- 2 tablespoons bourbon
- 1/2 cup heavy cream

Preheat the oven to 400 degrees. Spray a shallow baking sheet with vegetable cooking spray. Season the pork chops with salt and pepper, then press some of the peanuts into one side of each. Place the chops peanut side up on the baking sheet and roast for about 4 minutes, until the edges of the pork look done.

Meanwhile, melt the butter in a small skillet. Sauté the mushrooms until almost cooked. Sprinkle with the sugar and toss to caramelize for 15 seconds. Deglaze the pan with the bourbon, scraping up any browned bits. Add the cream and simmer until reduced by half. Pour the sauce over the cooked chops and serve.

note from our test kitchen

For the best flavor, use shiitake mushrooms. Pull off their stems and discard before proceeding.

SOURCE: *New York Times*
COOK: Suzanne Goin
STORY BY: Amanda Hesser

three-way pork burgers

WE'RE ALWAYS THRILLED TO DISCOVER a new Suzanne Goin recipe. Somehow, this high-powered chef/owner of two hot Los Angeles restaurants continually manages to wow us with dishes that resonate with an easy, soulful quality. These burgers—spicy, juicy, and just sloppy enough—are no exception and reveal Goin's ability to combine her formal French training with her Southern Californian sensibility.

serves 6

- 1½ teaspoons cumin seeds
- Olive oil
- ¾ cup diced shallots
- 2 small chiles de árbol (or other small dried chile), cut on the diagonal into thin slices
- Kosher salt
- 3 teaspoons fresh thyme leaves
- 3 cups ground pork (about 1½ pounds)
- 1 cup finely chopped smoked bacon (about ⅓ pound), preferably apple wood smoked
- ½ cup chopped Mexican chorizo (see notes)
- ¼ cup coarsely chopped fresh parsley
- Freshly ground black pepper
- 6 round brioche buns or hamburger buns
- Aïoli and romesco (optional; see notes)
- 12 arugula leaves

Put the cumin seeds in a small skillet and place over medium heat. Cook briefly, swirling, until the seeds become fragrant and begin to toast. Grind coarsely with a mortar and pestle or in a spice grinder.

Cover the bottom of a medium sauté pan with a thick slick of oil. Place over medium-low heat and add the shallots. When the oil begins to sizzle, add the ground cumin and chiles. Stir, then season with salt to taste. Cook until the shallots become translucent. Stir in the thyme and remove from the heat. Let cool.

In a large bowl, combine the pork, bacon, and chorizo. Add the shallot mixture and parsley, then season with salt and pepper to taste. Using your hands, lift and fold the ingredients together until blended. Do not overmix. Form the meat into patties that will fit in the buns (about 3 inches in diameter and 3/4 inch thick); do not make them too thick.

Wash the sauté pan, then cover the bottom with a thin layer of oil. Place over medium-high heat and add the buns, cut side down. Toast until lightly browned and set aside.

Add another thin layer of oil to the pan. When the oil is hot, sauté the burgers until browned on the bottom. Turn them, basting with the fat in the pan. Monitor the heat carefully so the burgers brown but do not burn. When they are browned on both sides, cut a slit in the center to check for doneness; there should be only the faintest trace of pink. Spread the rolls with aïoli, if using. Place a burger on each bottom bun, then top with the romesco (if using) and arugula. Set the top buns in place and serve.

notes from our test kitchen

- Don't substitute the stiffer, drier Spanish chorizo for the Mexican chorizo. The Mexican version, increasingly available at specialty stores, is more like fresh sausage. In fact, if you can't find it, use good country sausage in its place.
- These burgers are equally good grilled outdoors. Use medium or indirect heat so they cook through without burning. You can also cook the burgers in the oven. Once you've seared both sides, place the burgers in a 350-degree oven to finish cooking, about 15 minutes.
- If you're at all nervous about making sure the burgers are cooked through, check the inside with an instant-read thermometer. It should read 160 to 165 degrees.
- Goin spreads aïoli (garlic mayonnaise) on the bottom bun and tops the burgers with romesco (a zesty Spanish sauce typically made from fried bread, ground almonds, paprika, and tomatoes), but they are not required. You can substitute a mayonnaise seasoned with minced garlic and fresh lemon juice for the aioli, if you like. We won't tell if you plop a bit of ketchup on these burgers either.

tip

Goin recommends cooking a little lump of the burger mixture before shaping the patties. It takes a few extra minutes, but it's worth it to get the seasoning just right. Pinch off a grape-size piece of the mixture, shape it into a disk, and sauté it until cooked through. Taste and adjust the seasoning before shaping the burgers.

SOURCE: *Bon Appétit*
COOK: Arlene Weston
STORY BY: Rand Richards Cooper

jerk pork tenderloin

JERK IS FROM JAMAICA, but it owes its existence to a group of former slaves known as Maroons who waged a guerrilla war against the British. Their strongholds were in the Blue Mountains, home of the legendary Jamaican coffee, and that's where they hunted wild boar and came up with jerk seasoning. And that's where, says Cooper, many descendants of the Maroons still live today.

Arlene Weston owns a Manhattan restaurant called Maroons, where she uses this pastelike marinade to season jerk chicken and pork. It's not so fiery that it burns your mouth, as do so many jerk seasonings, and part of the reason is that it's mellowed with coffee.

We love the seasoning and also love the idea of serving jerk pork tenderloins. Don't be intimidated by the number of ingredients; that's just for the seasoning paste, which is a snap to put together. The seasoning goes on the meat a day ahead, so all you have to do is cook it the next day. You can grill the pork or roast it in the oven, which means you can serve it all year long.

serves 6 to 8

- 1 tablespoon espresso coffee beans
- 1 1/4 teaspoons whole allspice
- 3/4 teaspoon mustard seeds
- 3/4 teaspoon ground cinnamon
- 3/4 teaspoon ground nutmeg
- 1 bunch scallions, trimmed and chopped
- 1 cup chopped fresh parsley
- 3 garlic cloves, peeled
- 1 tablespoon chopped fresh oregano
- 2 teaspoons chopped fresh thyme
- 1 teaspoon seeded and chopped habanero chile (see note)
- 1 teaspoon grated lemon zest
- 1/4 cup fresh lime juice
- 1/4 cup fresh lemon juice
- 2 tablespoons olive oil
- 2 1/2 pounds pork tenderloin

Put the coffee beans, allspice, mustard seeds, cinnamon, and nutmeg in a small skillet and stir over medium heat until fragrant, about 30 seconds. Finely grind the mixture in a spice or coffee grinder. Transfer to a food processor and add all the remaining ingredients except the pork. Blend well until you have a wet paste. Place the pork in a large glass baking dish and coat with the paste. Cover and refrigerate overnight.

Preheat the oven to 400 degrees. Transfer the pork to a rimmed baking sheet. Roast until a thermometer inserted in the center registers 150 degrees (for medium), about 35 minutes. Slice and serve.

note from our test kitchen

- If you can't find a habanero chile, use a large serrano or jalapeño chile instead. Or add hot sauce to taste.

SOURCE: *Firehouse Food*
by George Dolese and Steve Siegelman

COOK: Bob Lopez, Truck 9, after his mother

chili verde

SAN FRANCISCO FIREHOUSE GUYS cook all their own food, and their meals represent an amazing melting pot of ethnic influences, as well as the inspiration of the food-obsessed Bay Area. This green chili is a good example. We've eaten some excellent green chili in New Mexico, but this one is different, based on tomatillos and not New Mexico chiles. It's mild and deeply flavorful, and we guarantee that anyone who eats it will ask you for the recipe.

Bob Lopez says that it's best served in a soft taco, with a dollop of sour cream and a sprig or two of cilantro. It's also good over rice, with a side of beans. But it also makes a great soup, thinned with a little chicken or pork broth.

serves 6

- 1 pound fresh tomatillos
- 3 tablespoons canola oil
- 3 pounds boneless pork butt, cut into 1-inch cubes
- 2 jalapeño chiles, stemmed, seeded, and chopped
- 5 garlic cloves, minced
- 1/2 teaspoon salt
- Warm corn tortillas (see notes)
- Sour cream
- Fresh cilantro sprigs

Peel and discard the papery husks from the tomatillos. Rinse under cold water. Heat a very large skillet over high heat and toast the tomatillos until lightly browned, about 5 minutes, shaking the pan occasionally. Transfer to a food processor or blender and puree. Set aside.

Heat the oil in a large, heavy-bottomed soup pot or Dutch oven with a tight-fitting lid. Add the pork in batches and brown it on all sides, removing it to a plate when it is browned. Return all the pork to the pot and stir in the chiles and garlic. Sauté for 3 minutes, then stir in the tomatillo puree and salt.

Bring the mixture to a boil, reduce the heat to low, and cover. Cook at a low simmer for 2 hours, stirring occasionally. Season with additional salt, if needed. Serve hot with tortillas, sour cream, and cilantro sprigs.

notes from our test kitchen

- Pull off any outside fat before you cut up the pork.
- This chili is mild. For extra heat, double the number of jalapeños.
- You can cook the pork in a 325-degree oven if you prefer.
- Skim any visible oil from the surface before serving the chili.
- To warm the tortillas, bring them to room temperature, then heat them on a hot griddle, one by one, for 30 seconds, turning once. You can also wrap a stack of 6 tortillas in foil and heat them in a 325-degree oven for 5 minutes. To warm them in a microwave, wrap 6 tortillas in a lightly damp cloth and place in a covered container. Microwave on high for 30 to 45 seconds, until warmed through.

SOURCE: *New York Times Magazine*
COOK: **Jimmy Bradley**
STORY BY: **Sam Sifton**

sausage and mushroom risotto with raisins

JIMMY BRADLEY IS A VERY COOL MANHATTAN CHEF with restaurants on the West Side (the Red Cat), in TriBeCa (the Harrison), and in the East Village (the Mermaid Inn). He takes a commonplace idea—in this case, his grandmother's risotto, which seemed like a good vehicle for the extra mushrooms he needed to cook—and plays with flavors and textures until he comes up with something that's simultaneously simple and extraordinary. Salty, sweet, earthy, and a little bitter—all the elements in this dish play beautifully off one another. Choose the right rice and a good-quality Parmesan, and everything else will fall into place.

serves 4 to 6

- 1/3 cup golden raisins
- 6 ounces sweet or hot Italian sausage (about 1 1/2 links), casings removed
- 2 small garlic cloves, finely minced
- 3 ounces cremini mushrooms, trimmed and quartered (1 cup)
- 4 1/2 cups lightly salted chicken stock, plus more if needed
- 2 tablespoons butter
- 1 tablespoon olive oil
- 3 tablespoons finely minced onion
- 2 tablespoons finely minced celery
- 1/2 teaspoon kosher salt, or to taste
- 1/4 teaspoon freshly ground black pepper, or to taste
- 1 1/2 cups Arborio rice
- 1/2 cup dry white wine
- 1 small head radicchio (8 ounces), shredded (4 cups)
- 1/3 cup freshly grated Parmigiano-Reggiano cheese
- 1 tablespoon fresh thyme leaves, finely chopped

Place the raisins in a small bowl and cover with hot water. Set aside to plump.

Combine the sausage and garlic in a large skillet over medium-high heat. Cook for 5 minutes, breaking up the sausage, until the meat begins to brown. Reduce the heat and add the mushrooms. Cover and cook, stirring occasionally, for about 10 minutes, until the mushrooms start to exude liquid. Set aside.

Place the stock in a medium saucepan and bring to a simmer.

Heat the butter and oil in an enameled cast-iron casserole over medium heat. Add the onion, celery, salt, and pepper and sauté for 5 minutes, until the vegetables are translucent. Add the rice and cook, stirring, for 1 to 2 minutes, until the edges of the grains are translucent and coated with pan juices. Add the wine and simmer for 3 minutes, stirring continuously, until the wine has almost evaporated. Add 1/2 cup of the hot stock and stir over medium-low heat until the mixture is moist but not runny. Repeat, adding 1/2 cup hot stock at a time, until the rice is al dente and the mixture is creamy, about 20 minutes. Adjust the heat to keep the rice cooking gently and add more hot stock or water, if needed.

Drain the raisins and add to the rice. Add the sausage mixture, radicchio, cheese, and thyme and mix well. Taste and adjust the seasoning, if necessary. Serve immediately.

SOURCE: *Crazy for Casseroles* by James Villas
COOK: James Villas after Paul Prudhomme

creole ham and shrimp jambalaya

NOTHING SAYS "HOMEY" LIKE A CASSEROLE, and yet there are plenty of sophisticated dishes that come to the table inside a casserole dish. Jambalaya is one of them. This famous dish dates back to the eighteenth century in the Louisiana Territory, says the food writer James Villas, and its origins are both Creole and Cajun. It can be made with beef, pork, chicken, kielbasa, shrimp, oysters, crawfish, and any number of other elements, but this one is simple and straightforward: just ham and shrimp.

Villas learned to make jambalaya from Paul Prudhomme back in the 1970s, and this recipe has evolved since then. It's very mild, so those who love their jambalaya fired up should be served some hot sauce at the table. This is one of the easiest dishes in this book. It travels well, it holds on a buffet, and any leftovers are delicious the next day.

serves 10

- 8 ounces sliced lean bacon, cut into 1-inch pieces
- 1 large onion, finely chopped
- 2 medium green bell peppers, halved, seeded, and cut into 1-inch-wide strips
- 1 garlic clove, minced
- 2 cups long-grain white rice
- 1 pound smoked ham, cut into strips
- 1 28-ounce can plum tomatoes, drained and coarsely chopped
- 1 teaspoon dried thyme, crumbled
- Salt and freshly ground black pepper
- 3 cups chicken stock, plus more if needed
- 1½ pounds medium shrimp, peeled and deveined

Preheat the oven to 350 degrees. In a heavy, flameproof 3- to 3½-quart casserole, fry the bacon over medium heat until browned but not crisp. Drain on paper towels. Add the onion, bell pepper, and garlic to the fat in the casserole and cook, stirring, until softened, about 5 minutes. Add the rice and stir until the grains become opaque. Return the bacon to the casserole and add the ham, tomatoes, and thyme. Season with salt and pepper to taste and stir until well blended. Add the stock, bring to a boil, cover, and place in the oven for 15 minutes.

Remove the casserole from the oven and add the shrimp, pushing them down into the rice. Continue to bake until all the broth is absorbed and the rice is tender and still moist, about 15 minutes. If the casserole seems dry during the last bit of cooking, add a little more chicken stock—the rice must remain moist.

notes from our test kitchen

- The easiest way to get the smoked ham is to buy a smoked ham slice.
- If you don't have the right-size casserole, a Dutch oven is a good substitute.
- If you want some heat cooked right into the jambalaya, mince a serrano chile (or three) and add it to the pan along with the bell pepper.

SOURCE: *Bon Appétit*
COOKS: Marilyn Tausend and Ricardo Muñoz Zurita

carnitas

CARNITAS (LITTLE BITS OF MEAT) are one of the glories of Mexican cuisine. They have their home in the heartland of Michoacán, El Bajio, where they're traditionally cooked in vats of lard until very crisp and succulent. For those who don't have giant vats of lard, however, here's a stovetop rendition that will melt the hearts of the diners at your table.

This version brings out the sweetness of the pork with fresh orange juice and a touch of brandy, and the result is a bit like pulled pork. Cooking the *carnitas* couldn't be simpler, and you can do it a day ahead. The accompaniments —warm tortillas, an avocado salsa, a tomato salsa, and possibly some rice and beans—are also a cinch.

serves 8

- 4 pounds boneless country-style pork ribs
- 2 cups plus 2 tablespoons water, plus more if needed
- 1 teaspoon grated orange zest
- 1½ cups fresh orange juice
- 6 garlic cloves, peeled
- 2 teaspoons fine sea salt
- ¼ cup brandy
- Warm corn tortillas (see note, page 145)
- Avocado Salsa (recipe follows)
- Fresh tomato salsa (store-bought is fine)

Cut the pork ribs crosswise into thirds. Cut off any big chunks of fat and reserve; leave small pieces of fat attached to the pork. Combine the pork, reserved fat, 2 cups of the water, orange zest and juice, garlic, and salt in a deep 12-inch skillet with a lid (see notes). Bring to a boil, reduce the heat to low, and cover. Simmer, stirring occasionally, until the pork is tender, about 1¾ hours. Add water if necessary, ¼ cup at a time, to keep the pork partially submerged.

Uncover the skillet and boil until the liquid is reduced by half, about 10 minutes. Stir in the brandy and boil, stirring often, until all the liquid evaporates and the meat browns and begins to get crisp, about 15 minutes. Let cool slightly. Discard any loose pieces of fat and tear the meat into strips. Return the meat to the skillet. (The dish can be covered and refrigerated for up to 1 day at this point.)

Add the remaining 2 tablespoons water to the skillet. Place over medium-low heat, cover, and rewarm, stirring, for about 5 minutes (longer if it's been refrigerated). Season with more salt, if desired. Transfer to a bowl and serve with warm tortillas and the two salsas.

notes from our test kitchen

- We don't own a 12-inch skillet with a lid, so we used a standard Dutch oven. It was perfect, except the meat didn't brown properly. So at the end of the cooking, as the meat was starting to fall apart, we lifted it out of the pot with a slotted spoon (leaving behind most of the fat) and put it in a large, shallow gratin dish (you could also use a shallow baking dish). We then baked it at 375 degrees until it was browned, about 10 minutes. Just before serving, we reheated it in the oven until it was sizzling.
- If you don't have brandy in the house, or have only very expensive brandy, use tequila instead.
- Pickled onions go very well with the *carnitas*. Slice the onions thinly and put them in a small bowl with a bit of mild vinegar and water to cover. Add a little salt and some crumbled dried oregano, if you like. Let the onions sit for 1 hour before draining and serving.

avocado salsa

makes about $2^3/_4$ cups salsa

- 3 large ripe avocados, halved, pitted, peeled, and coarsely chopped
- 8 ounces fresh tomatillos, husked, rinsed, and coarsely chopped
- 2 serrano chiles, seeded and coarsely chopped
- 2 tablespoons chopped white onion
- 2 tablespoons coarsely chopped fresh cilantro
- Salt

Combine all ingredients except the salt in a food processor. Using on/off turns, process until you have a chunky puree (see notes). Transfer to a medium bowl and season with salt to taste. (The salsa can be made up to 4 hours ahead. Just press plastic wrap directly onto the surface and refrigerate.)

notes from our test kitchen

- The avocado salsa is like a glorified guacamole. Don't puree it; as with all good guacamole, you want some chunkiness here. You may want to mash and mix by hand instead of using a food processor.
- The recipe makes a lot, but you won't regret having leftovers the next day. We especially like this salsa with a squeeze of fresh lime juice.

SOURCE: *From My Mexican Kitchen* by Diana Kennedy

COOK: Diana Kennedy

tacos with chorizo and potato filling

GOOD-QUALITY MEXICAN FOOD PRODUCTS are tumbling into our markets today, barely keeping pace with our appetite for them. One we see everywhere now is that delectable rustic sausage called chorizo. What do you do with leftover chorizo? Pair it with some leftover cooked waxy potatoes and a chipotle chile from the fridge (see page 181), and you have an instant authentic filling for either soft (briefly heated tortillas) or fried tacos. You can add some typical taco garnishes—shredded lettuce, grated cheese, diced tomatoes, and cilantro—or not, as you like.

makes enough filling for 4 tacos

About 1 tablespoon lard or vegetable oil
1 Mexican chorizo (about 3 ounces), casing removed
About 1 rounded cup diced, cooked (al dente) waxy potatoes
1 chipotle chile in adobo, chopped (optional)
Sea salt
4 warm tortillas (see note, page 145) or fried tacos

Melt the lard or place the vegetable oil in a small skillet. Crumble the chorizo, add to the pan, and cook over low heat for a few minutes until the fat has been rendered. Add the potatoes and chile (if using) and continue to cook over medium heat, scraping the bottom of the skillet from time to time to prevent sticking, until the potato is well seasoned, about 8 minutes. Season with salt to taste. Set aside to cool a little before using.

note from our test kitchen

Mexican chorizo isn't the same thing as Spanish chorizo, and you can't substitute one for the other.

SOURCE: www.fostersmarket.com

COOK: Sara Foster

grilled butterflied leg of lamb with fresh mint-pepper jelly

WHEN IT COMES TO EASY SUMMER ENTERTAINING, grilled butterflied leg of lamb is a great way to go. For one thing, if you know how to grill a steak, you'll have no problem cooking this cut. But lamb has more cachet than steak; its richer flavor and appealing texture make it somehow dressier. Its other advantage is that the butterflied leg presents more surface area than a whole leg for the wine and herb marinade to soak into and more seared flavor from the grill.

The mint-pepper jelly is a perfect condiment for rosy slices of grilled lamb. Sara Foster uses her own Foster's Seven Pepper Jelly, but we've had great luck with any spicy-sweet hot pepper jelly.

serves 6 to 8

LAMB

- 1 butterflied leg of lamb (4½–5 pounds), trimmed of excess fat and silver skin
- 8 garlic cloves, halved and smashed lightly with the flat side of a knife
- ¼ cup fresh rosemary leaves or 1 heaping tablespoon dried rosemary, or a mixture of rosemary, marjoram, and oregano
- ½ cup Marsala or dry red wine
- 3 tablespoons olive oil, plus more for the grill
- 3 tablespoons chopped fresh mint
- 1 tablespoon freshly ground black pepper
- 1 teaspoon kosher salt

MINT-PEPPER JELLY

- 1 cup hot pepper jelly
- ¼ cup chopped fresh mint
- 3 tablespoons red wine vinegar
- 1 teaspoon freshly ground black pepper

PREPARE THE LAMB:

With a small knife, make about 8 small incisions on the fatty side of the lamb and insert a garlic half and some rosemary into each slit. Rub the lamb on both sides with the Marsala or red wine, olive oil, mint, pepper, salt, and any remaining rosemary and garlic. Place the lamb in a large baking dish and cover with plastic wrap. (You can also put the marinade ingredients in a large resealable plastic bag; see tip.) Let stand at room temperature for 1 hour or refrigerate overnight.

MEANWHILE, MAKE THE JELLY:

Combine all the ingredients in a small bowl and whisk until blended. Cover and refrigerate if marinating the lamb overnight. (The jelly may be made up to a week in advance.) Let the jelly sit at room temperature for 1 hour before serving.

GRILL THE LAMB:

If the lamb has been in the refrigerator, let it come to room temperature. Prepare a hot fire on one side of the grill, leaving the other side free for indirect grilling. Brush the grate with olive oil.

Remove the lamb from the marinade but reserve the marinade. Sear the lamb directly over the coals, basting occasionally with the marinade and turning once, until the meat is nicely seared, about 15 minutes. Move the lamb to the side with no coals and continue to grill, turning once, until the meat registers 130 to 135 degrees for medium-rare or 140 to 145 degrees for medium, 15 to 20 minutes. Transfer to a cutting board, cover lightly, and let rest for 10 minutes. Cut into thin slices and serve with the jelly.

note from our test kitchen

Depending on where you shop, you may have to call ahead to order a butterflied leg of lamb. It's also helpful to tell the butcher that you plan on grilling the lamb. That way, he or she will butterfly it into as even a thickness as possible. If there are any excessively thick parts, slice into them and fold them open like a book, so that the entire piece grills more evenly. You can also take a mallet or heavy skillet and pound the thick parts a bit. Ideally, the whole thing should be 2 to 3 inches thick.

tip

When *Rosie Magazine* ran this recipe, the editors suggested marinating the lamb in a sturdy, gallon-size resealable plastic bag.

side dishes

SOURCE: *The Slow Mediterranean Kitchen* by Paula Wolfert

COOK: Paula Wolfert after Carlos Posadas

asparagus baked in parchment with caper mayonnaise

FOR THIRTY YEARS NOW, PAULA WOLFERT (aka the Queen of the Mediterranean) has been tracking down unusual recipes most of us would never have tasted without her efforts. Finding these gems is just the beginning, however. Wolfert is a great refiner who's not afraid to reinvent even famous chefs' recipes to bring us the most superlative version of a dish.

This way of preparing asparagus, which she learned from Carlos Posadas of the Amparo restaurant in Madrid, is a case in point. Chef Posadas's method of slow-cooking asparagus in its own juices, flavored with just a little tarragon and olive oil, is the basis for Wolfert's dish. Posadas serves his version with mashed potatoes and slices of a Parmesan-like cheese on top, but we think Wolfert's simple caper sauce is an even better idea. Either way, the asparagus tastes intensely of itself and is cooked perfectly, so the tips don't become mushy as they so often do.

serves 2 to 4

- 18–24 thick asparagus spears
- 1/3 cup extra-virgin olive oil
- 1/2 teaspoon sea salt, plus more to taste
- 1/4 teaspoon sugar
- 1 long sprig fresh tarragon
- 12 salted capers (see notes)
- 2 tablespoons mayonnaise
- 2 tablespoons heavy cream

Preheat the oven to 175 degrees. Place a 2-foot-long sheet of parchment paper on a large baking sheet. Arrange the asparagus spears in a single layer on the parchment. Drizzle the olive oil over the asparagus, sprinkle with the salt and sugar, and top with the tarragon sprig. Fold the paper over the spears and tuck the ends underneath to form a tight package. Secure the package with kitchen string.

Bake the asparagus for 1½ to 2 hours, until the spears feel tender when pressed through the parchment.

Meanwhile, soak the capers in water for 1 to 2 hours. Pat dry and chop coarsely. In a small bowl, blend the mayonnaise, heavy cream, and chopped capers. Season with salt if needed.

When the asparagus is cooked, carefully cut the parchment paper open and transfer the asparagus to a platter. Mix any cooking juices into the sauce, pour over the asparagus, and serve warm.

notes from our test kitchen

- You can use bottled capers instead of salted ones, but they still need to be rinsed very well in a small strainer to get rid of the brine.
- We discovered by accident that if you have leftovers, the sauce (warmed gently) is delicious over chicken, steak, or fish.

SOURCE: *Cooking 1-2-3* by Rozanne Gold

COOK: Rozanne Gold

oven-roasted asparagus with fried capers

RUTH REICHL, the esteemed editor in chief of *Gourmet* magazine, thinks this stunning dish is the best that the cookbook author Rozanne Gold has ever created—which is saying something. Over and over, Gold comes through with minimalist dishes that sing with perfect pitch. This time she roasts asparagus at very high heat, then tops them with a surprise: fried capers.

Because the spears are in the oven for such a short time, they emerge with their green still intact, touched with roasty highlights. The final flourish of fried capers is, as Gold points out, startling.

serves 4

- 2 pounds medium-thick asparagus spears
- 1/4 cup extra-virgin olive oil
- Salt
- 1/4 cup large capers, drained
- Freshly ground black pepper

Preheat the oven to 500 degrees. Remove the woody bottoms of the asparagus, then trim the stalks to equal length. Drizzle 2 tablespoons of the olive oil on a rimmed baking sheet. Place the asparagus on the sheet and roll them in the oil. Sprinkle lightly with salt. Roast for 8 minutes, shaking the pan several times during the roasting. Transfer to a warm platter.

Meanwhile, heat the remaining 2 tablespoons oil in a small skillet. Fry the capers over high heat for 1 minute. Top the asparagus with the capers and serve, passing the pepper mill at the table.

notes from our test kitchen

- This dish is delicious hot, warm, or at room temperature, so it's a good choice for a party or the buffet table.
- You can turn this into a brunch or lunch dish by topping it with a gently fried or poached egg and serving Canadian bacon on the side.

SOURCE: *Gourmet*
COOK: Melissa Roberts-Matar

green beans with crisp shallots, chile, and mint

WHO SAYS GREEN BEANS HAVE TO BE ORDINARY? Here's a quick way to transform a commonplace vegetable into something uncommonly good. After blanching the beans in a big pot of salted water, toss them with fried shallot rings, a fiery chile pepper, and a generous dose of fresh mint. The combination hits all the right buttons of crispy, salty, spicy, and fresh. Serve it alongside pork, beef, or chicken.

serves 4

- 1 tablespoon plus 1/2 teaspoon salt
- 1 1/2 pounds green beans, trimmed
- 2/3 cup vegetable oil
- 6 ounces shallots (5 medium), thinly sliced crosswise and separated into rings
- 1 small Thai or serrano chile (2 1/4 inches long; preferably red), thinly sliced into rings
- 1/2 cup chopped fresh mint

Bring a 4- to 5-quart pot of water to a boil. Add 1 tablespoon of the salt and boil the beans, uncovered, until just tender, about 5 minutes. Drain in a colander.

Heat the oil in a heavy 12-inch skillet over medium heat until hot but not smoking. Fry the shallots in 3 batches, stirring frequently, until golden brown, 3 to 5 minutes per batch. (Watch carefully; shallots burn easily.) As the shallots brown, use a slotted spoon to transfer them quickly to paper towels to drain. They will crisp as they cool.

Discard all but 1 tablespoon of the oil in the skillet, then cook the chile over medium heat, stirring often, until softened, about 2 minutes. Add the beans and the remaining 1/2 teaspoon salt and toss with tongs until heated through. Remove from the heat and add the fried shallots and mint. Toss to combine and serve.

notes from our test kitchen

- A fresh red chile is preferable here because it adds color to the dish.

- Peppermint has a fresher, brighter taste than spearmint. It can be recognized by its shiny leaves tinged with dark veins. Spearmint leaves are fuzzier, thicker, and a lighter green.
- When making this recipe, have all the ingredients ready before you start cooking. Once you begin frying the shallots, things move quickly, and you don't want to have to stop to slice the chile or chop the mint.

tip

We found another quick way to turn green beans into a blockbuster side dish, referred to as Dry-Fried Green Beans in a wonderful collection of authentic Sichuan recipes, *Land of Plenty*, by Fuchsia Dunlop. Remove any strings from 10 ounces of haricots verts or skinny green beans and trim the tops and tails. Cut or break the beans into 2-inch pieces. Heat 2 tablespoons peanut oil in a wok over medium heat. Add the beans and stir-fry until they are tender with slightly puckered skins, about 6 minutes (thicker beans may take longer). Remove from the pan and set aside. Add 2 tablespoons more oil to the pan and heat over high. Add 8 small dried chiles (preferably Sichuan; snipped in half) and 1/2 teaspoon Sichuan peppercorns (these are hard to find and therefore optional). Stir-fry very briefly until fragrant. Quickly add 2 scallions (sliced on a sharp angle into 1 1/2-inch pieces) and 3 garlic cloves (thinly sliced) or the equivalent of fresh ginger. Stir-fry until fragrant. Return the beans to the pan, toss, and add salt to taste. Serves 4.

SOURCE: *New York Times*
COOK: Chris Schlesinger
STORY BY: Amanda Hesser

roasted maple-glazed baby carrots with dried grapes

BEFORE WE DISCOVERED THIS SMART RECIPE, we never had much use for the little rounded "baby" carrots that come in 1-pound bags—except to have on hand as a snack. But here's a way to turn them into a stunning side dish for a crowd without having to chop a single vegetable. The two-part recipe is the brainchild of Chris Schlesinger, the ingenious Boston chef known for his intrepid approach to flavor. The first step is to make oven-dried grapes, which takes a couple of hours but can be done a day ahead. Then it's a matter of quickly roasting the carrots, adding the grapes, and tossing the lot in a buttery, sage-infused maple glaze. This is a perfect addition to any big holiday dinner.

serves 6 to 8

- 1 pound small green seedless grapes, stemmed (3 cups)
- Vegetable cooking spray
- 2 pounds baby carrots
- 2 tablespoons butter
- 1 tablespoon chopped fresh sage
- 2 tablespoons pure maple syrup
- 1 tablespoon olive oil
- 1 teaspoon fine sea salt
- 1/2 teaspoon grated lemon zest
- 1/2 teaspoon freshly ground black pepper

Preheat the oven to 250 degrees. Put the grapes in a mixing bowl and spray lightly with vegetable cooking spray (see notes). Toss to coat. Transfer the grapes to a 12-inch, nonstick ovenproof skillet. Dry in the oven, tossing every 20 minutes or so, until the skins shrivel and the grapes are tawny and lightly caramelized, 2 to 2 1/2 hours. Remove from the oven and set aside. (The grapes can be made a day ahead and refrigerated.)

Place the carrots on paper towels to dry. Raise the oven temperature to 500 degrees. Place a broiler pan or heavy roasting pan in the oven. Melt the butter in a small saucepan over low heat, cooking until it turns golden brown (this may take a while, but don't stray too far or it may burn). Add the sage, maple syrup, and dried grapes. Swirl to combine, then turn off the heat, but leave the pan on the burner to keep warm.

Place the carrots, olive oil, and salt in a bowl and toss, rubbing the oil and salt into the carrots. Turn the carrots out onto the hot broiler pan in a single layer. Roast, shaking the pan occasionally, until the carrots have begun to color and are almost tender, about 10 minutes.

Pour the grape mixture over the carrots and toss with a heatproof spatula to coat. Roast until the glaze begins to set and the carrots are tender and spotty brown, about 5 minutes. Remove from the oven and sprinkle with the lemon zest and pepper. Transfer to a warm bowl and serve immediately.

notes from our test kitchen

- We're not big fans of the flavor of vegetable cooking spray. Instead, we use one of those Misto pressurized pump spray bottles and fill it with olive oil. If you do the same, spray the grapes with olive oil instead of vegetable spray. They will taste even better.
- Don't be tempted to skip the step of drying the carrots on paper towels. Most baby carrots emerge from the plastic bag somewhat damp, and even this little bit of moisture will prevent them from browning.

SOURCE: *The Maccioni Family Cookbook*
by Egi Maccioni with Peter Kaminsky
COOK: Egi Maccioni

pan-roasted cauliflower with capers

THE MACCIONI FAMILY is part of restaurant royalty. Sirio Maccioni presides over an empire in New York City that includes Le Cirque. The Maccioni sons also work in the family business, and Egi Maccioni, their mother, participates mostly behind the scenes, contributing her signature Tuscan recipes. She's a superb home cook, unswayed by the gourmet trends of the moment.

When she decided to write her own cookbook, she had a number of favorite dishes in mind, but not this one, which seemed much too simple to her. Then one night she made it for Sirio, who took a second helping and said, "Why don't you put this in your book?"

Thank you, Sirio. From now on, this is our favorite way to fix cauliflower. Cooking the cauliflower whole keeps it from getting watery and overcooked in places, and it's also easier. Then there are the capers. Sweetly delicious as it is, cauliflower needs help, and capers are the ticket.

serves 4

- 1 head cauliflower
- 1/4 cup olive oil
- 4 garlic cloves, minced
- 2 tablespoons capers, rinsed and drained
- Salt and freshly ground black pepper

Place the cauliflower in a large pot and cover with water. Bring to a boil, reduce the heat, and simmer until the base is tender, about 15 minutes (see note). Drain the cauliflower and cut into bite-size chunks when it's cool enough to handle.

Heat the olive oil in a large skillet over medium-high heat. Add the garlic and cook for 1 minute. Add the cauliflower chunks and cook, stirring, for about 5 minutes, until lightly browned. Remove from the heat. Stir in the capers and season with salt and pepper to taste. Serve warm.

note from our test kitchen

If you have a relatively small head of cauliflower, it may take less time to cook. Check the base; if it's tender, it's done, which may happen in 8 to 12 minutes.

SOURCE: *Saveur*

COOK: Staff

corn cooked in milk with chiles and coconut

IMAGINE THE COMFORTING TEXTURE OF CREAMED CORN with the exciting flavors of Indian spices, and you'll understand what makes this dish so good. First the corn simmers in milk for close to an hour, until it's creamy, sweet, and tender. Although you could certainly stop there and serve it as is, it was the next few steps that caught our attention. Quickly sautéing a gang of Indian spices—cumin, chiles, ginger, and turmeric—and adding them to the corn just before serving takes this dish into a whole new realm of wonderful.

serves 4

- 3 cups fresh corn kernels (see notes)
- 2 1/2 cups whole milk
- Salt
- 1 tablespoon ghee or clarified butter (see notes)
- 1/8 teaspoon cumin seeds
- 2 serrano chiles, chopped
- 1 1/2-inch piece fresh ginger, grated
- Pinch ground turmeric
- 2 tablespoons fresh or dried shredded unsweetened coconut
- 6 sprigs fresh cilantro, chopped

Combine the corn and the milk in a medium saucepan and simmer over medium heat, stirring often, until the milk is reduced by three quarters, 40 to 45 minutes. Season with salt to taste.

Heat the ghee or clarified butter in a medium skillet over medium heat and toast the cumin seeds for 10 seconds. Add the chiles, ginger, turmeric, and corn mixture and stir to combine thoroughly. Add the coconut and cilantro, stir, and cook for 1 minute. Adjust the seasonings and serve.

notes from our test kitchen

- We make this in the winter with frozen corn kernels with great success.
- If you can't find ghee in the store, you can use a mixture of butter and peanut oil (or other neutral vegetable oil) or make your own ghee (see opposite page).

making your own ghee

If you have a nearby Indian market, you can buy ghee there, but it's much better to make your own. It's very easy and lends a wonderful aroma to the kitchen. Ghee isn't just clarified butter; the milk solids on the bottom of the pan are actually "toasted," giving the butter a delicious flavor.

Here's how to do it, courtesy of our Bombay-born friend Niloufer Ichaporia King. Put a pound of unsalted butter in a heavy saucepan and set it over medium heat. Once the butter has completely melted, continue to cook over low heat until the milk solids on the bottom of the pan are very lightly browned, but no longer; dark brown will ruin the flavor. Altogether, the time shouldn't be more than an hour, and you don't need to stir the butter—just watch the color.

Remove the pan from the heat and let the ghee cool a bit (but not long enough to solidify, in which case you'd have to reheat it) before straining through a coffee filter or a fine-mesh strainer into a heatproof jar. Let cool completely before covering the jar. Stored out of the light at room temperature, ghee will keep almost forever.

The toasty bits left behind in the strainer are delicious in scrambled eggs or stirred into rice, says King.

SOURCE: *O, The Oprah Magazine*
COOK: Michel Nischan

vanilla "creamed" corn

WONDERFUL AS CORN IS WITH CREAM, something else entirely happens when you use the starch in the corn itself—cornstarch—to make the "cream." It's a very delicate and, in Michel Nischan's version, amazing flavor. Corn and vanilla? Soulmates.

serves 6

- 12 ears sweet corn, husks and silks removed (see notes)
- 1/2 cup whole milk
- 1/2 vanilla bean, split in half lengthwise, or 1/2 teaspoon pure vanilla extract
- Salt and freshly ground black pepper

Using a sharp knife, remove the kernels from the cobs. Puree half the kernels in a food processor, then transfer to a fine-mesh strainer lined with cheesecloth and set over a bowl. Gather up the edges of the cheesecloth and twist to squeeze the corn juice into the bowl. Discard the squeezed-out kernels.

In a large saucepan over medium heat, bring the corn juice, the remaining kernels, the milk, and the vanilla bean or extract to a simmer. Simmer gently, stirring constantly, until the sauce begins to thicken, about 3 minutes. Continue to simmer until the kernels are cooked through, about 3 minutes more. Season with salt and pepper to taste, discard the vanilla bean (if using), and serve.

notes from our test kitchen

- If you use frozen corn, defrost 2 bags of corn kernels before starting the recipe.
- If you scrape down the corncobs a second time using the dull side of the knife (stand them in a shallow bowl), you'll get more juice.
- Confession: we didn't use cheesecloth to strain the corn juice, but we did use the following tip to extract more juice.

tip

In the *Craft of Cooking*, Tom Colicchio adds water to his corn. Add 1/3 cup water to the corn kernels before pureeing (the extra liquid will quickly disappear in the simmering).

SOURCE: *The Breakaway Japanese Kitchen* by Eric Gower

COOK: Eric Gower

greens and oranges

IN HIS EXTRAORDINARY BOOK, the Napa Valley chef Eric Gower builds a bridge between traditional and innovative Japanese cooking and the exciting cuisine of the area just north of San Francisco.

These very simple greens are filled with flavor and yet delicate. The orange and the brown rice vinegar (a mild Japanese vinegar that's slightly sweet) bring out the sweetness hidden in the greens but also give them piquancy. They're easy and quick to prepare and served at room temperature, so they're perfect for a buffet or entertaining. Never mind that they're also good for you.

serves 2 or 3

- 2 bunches greens, such as spinach, kale, or collards
- Several tablespoons extra-virgin olive oil, as needed
- 1–2 tablespoons brown rice vinegar, to taste
- Sea salt and freshly ground black pepper
- Juice of 1/4 orange or other orange citrus, such as tangerine
- Several orange sections, membranes removed
- Zest of 1 orange or other orange citrus, minced

Bring a pot of water to a boil. Meanwhile, rinse and trim the greens. Boil them briefly for several minutes (see note). Drain and rinse with cold water. When slightly cooled, squeeze out as much water as possible (save this, if you wish, for making rice or soup stock).

Place the squeezed greens on a cutting board and coarsely chop. Transfer to a large bowl and add the olive oil, vinegar, and salt and pepper to taste. Mix and adjust the seasoning. Sprinkle the orange juice over the greens, add the orange sections, and sprinkle over the zest. Serve at room temperature.

note from our test kitchen

Cook the greens until they're just tender; spinach will take much less time than collards.

SOURCE: *New York Times Magazine*
COOK: **Unknown**
STORY BY: **Jonathan Reynolds**

armenian chickpeas and spinach

THE PLAYWRIGHT JONATHAN REYNOLDS LIKES TO AMBLE along Bedford Street—eight blocks in New York City's Greenwich Village that seem to encompass the entire world. You can eat almost anything on this stretch, and you can also stop in to have your palm read. An unprepossessing bare-bones place with copper-topped tables called Moustache features the cooking of the pre–World War I Fertile Crescent, along with that of Iran, Tunisia, Algeria, and Morocco. Reynolds thinks it's possibly the best Middle Eastern restaurant in New York City.

Moustache offers this terrific cooked-salad side dish, which is both mellow and bracing. The secret ingredient is harissa, that complex, somewhat fiery condiment that seems to confer magic on any dish. The salad is especially delicious with lamb, as well as a good companion to a group of room-temperature Mediterranean salads.

Although Moustache specifies that the chickpeas must be cooked dried chickpeas, not canned, we think it doesn't make a big difference if you didn't grow up eating this salad. Using canned chickpeas and packaged baby spinach makes this a quick pantry dish.

serves 6 to 8

- 1/2 cup extra-virgin olive oil
- 4 cups chopped Spanish onion
- 2 teaspoons harissa (see page 121)
- 1 1/2 tablespoons minced garlic
- 2 1/2 cups canned plum tomatoes with juice, pureed in a food processor
- 1 1/4 teaspoons salt
- 2 cups cooked or canned chickpeas, drained
- 12 cups coarsely chopped spinach, tough stems removed (about 10 ounces)
- Juice of 1 lemon

Heat the olive oil in a large, deep pot over medium-high heat. Add the onion and cook until golden, 15 to 20 minutes. Add the harissa and garlic and cook for a few more minutes. Add the tomatoes and salt, lower the heat, and simmer, uncovered, for 10 minutes. Add the chickpeas and simmer until some moisture has evaporated and the mixture is thick, about 15 minutes. Stir in the spinach and cook until it has released its liquid. Simmer until the mixture is no longer soupy, about 5 minutes.

Transfer to a serving dish and serve warm or at room temperature, with lemon juice squeezed over the top.

notes from our test kitchen

- For the 2½ cups canned tomatoes, you'll need just slightly less than one 28-ounce can.
- Cooking your own chickpeas in a slow-cooker is a snap. Rinse dried chickpeas and put them in the slow-cooker, adding a pinch of sugar, a little salt, and a bay leaf. Cover with water. Set the temperature to high until the chickpeas come to a boil, then reduce it to low and cook until tender but not mushy, 3 to 4 hours, depending on the chickpeas.

SOURCE: *Bistro Cooking at Home*
by Gordon Hamersley with Joanne McAllister Smart

COOK: Gordon Hamersley

braised fennel

AS MUCH AS WE ENJOY the distinct flavor and refreshing crunch of raw fennel, we're even more enamored with what happens when it's braised. Gently cooking wedges of fennel in a mixture of wine, stock, and seasonings brings out this vegetable's inherent sweetness and leaves it tender and delectable. In fact, even if you don't enjoy the assertive taste of raw fennel, we're betting that you'll fall for the mellow flavor and silky texture of this dish.

Chef Gordon Hamersley, the owner of Boston's Hamersley's Bistro, tells us that he likes to serve braised fennel when he throws a dinner party at home. When the fennel comes out of the oven, he whisks a bit of butter into the reduced braising liquid to create a deliciously concentrated sauce to drizzle over it. It's a small detail—and yes, it's an added step—but the flavor return is enormous.

Braised fennel complements fish and chicken dishes especially well.

serves 4

- 2 fennel bulbs (see notes)
- 1 tablespoon olive oil
- 2 tablespoons unsalted butter
- 1/2 small onion, thinly sliced
- Kosher salt and freshly ground black pepper
- 1/4 teaspoon fennel seeds
- Pinch crushed red pepper flakes
- Pinch herbes de Provence (see notes)
- 3/4 cup chicken stock
- 1/2 cup dry white wine
- 1 tablespoon anisette or Pernod (optional)

Preheat the oven to 325 degrees. Remove a few of the feathery fronds from the fennel and reserve. Trim the stalk off the fennel bulbs and remove and discard any tough outer layers. Cut the fennel lengthwise into quarters.

Heat the olive oil and 1 tablespoon of the butter in a large ovenproof sauté pan over medium-high heat (see notes). Add the fennel and onion and season with salt and pepper to taste. Brown the fennel on all sides, about 8 minutes. Add the fennel seeds, red pepper flakes, and herbes de Provence and cook for 1 minute.

Add the chicken stock, white wine, and anisette or Pernod (if using) and bring to a boil. Transfer to the oven and braise until the fennel is tender when pierced with the tip of a small knife, about 45 minutes.

Lift the fennel out of the pan with tongs and arrange on a platter. Chop the reserved fennel fronds and add them to the pan. Cook the liquid over medium-high heat until reduced by half. Add the remaining 1 tablespoon butter and whisk until combined. Taste and season with more salt and pepper, if necessary. Spoon the onion and juices over the fennel and serve.

notes from our test kitchen

- Choose medium fennel bulbs (12 to 14 ounces each). Larger ones will certainly work, but you'll want to cut them into sixths (not quarters) and expect that you'll have enough to serve 6 people.
- Herbes de Provence is a mixture of dried herbs and spices used in southern France. It's sold with the herbs and spices in many supermarkets, but if you can't find any, use tiny pinches of dried thyme and rosemary. The dish will lack some perfume, but it will still be wonderful.
- For best results, choose a skillet that is large enough to just hold all the fennel wedges in a single layer.
- When browning the fennel in the butter and oil, don't expect it to brown evenly. Instead, it will develop more of a speckled bronzed appearance.
- If the braising liquid evaporates before the fennel is tender, add about 1/4 cup stock or water to the pan and continue braising. Likewise, if the pan appears dry when you remove the fennel from the oven, add a few tablespoons stock or water and stir to dissolve the pan drippings, then whisk in the butter as directed to finish the sauce.

SOURCE: *Washington Post*
COOK: Renee Schettler

parsnip crisps

YOU'VE PROBABLY SEEN LITTLE CRISP WISPS of this sweet root vegetable served as a garnish at trendy restaurants for years. But now the home cook can produce these tasty morsels, too. You can fry them, roast them in the oven, or even sauté them. Fried parsnip crisps have more crunch and the appeal of all fried foods, but you do have to fry them in batches. Roasted parsnip crisps couldn't be easier, so they're a good choice if you're serving more than just a few people.

The secret of crisping them with just a brief cooking is to shave them thin with a vegetable peeler. (For once, a mandoline won't do a better job.) Cut this way, parsnips have an earthy-nutty taste, with none of the bitterness that chunkier, quickly cooked parsnips can develop. They make great nibbles to have with drinks, and they're also a fine side dish.

serves 6

8 ounces parsnips, peeled
Mild olive oil
Coarse sea salt

Use a vegetable peeler to shave wisps of the parsnips into a bowl. Have ready a plate lined with paper towels.

TO ROAST THE CRISPS:

Preheat the oven to 350 degrees. Line one or two baking sheets with foil.

Drizzle the parsnip wisps with 2 to 3 tablespoons oil and, using your hands, toss gently to coat each wisp. Scatter the parsnips on the sheets and spread into a single layer. Roast, stirring and checking every few minutes, until evenly and lightly browned and crisp, 8 to 12 minutes.

TO FRY THE CRISPS:

In a deep skillet or pot over medium heat, heat about 1/2 inch oil until hot but not smoking. Toss a small handful of parsnip wisps into the oil, using your thumb and forefinger to separate them as they fall from your hand. Do not crowd the pan. Fry, stirring and checking as necessary, until evenly and lightly browned and crisp, 3 to 4 minutes.

TO SERVE THE CRISPS:

Transfer the crisps to paper towels, season generously with salt, and serve hot or at room temperature.

notes from our test kitchen

- We discovered by accident that parsnip peels are delicious, too. Just scrub the parsnips well and shave the entire parsnip into wisps, peel and all. Roast or fry the peels along with the rest.
- Avoid the woody center of the parsnips; the outer circle is what you want.

tip

In Alton Brown's *Gear for Your Kitchen*, we found this fascinating bit of information: if you keep your root vegetables —carrots, turnips, beets, parsnips—in play sand in the vegetable crisper, they'll keep much better and longer. You can find play sand at the hardware store. Brown keeps a sack of it in his refrigerator—his own modern-day root cellar. (This doesn't work for potatoes and garlic, however, since they should never be refrigerated.)

SOURCE: *Bon Appétit*

COOK: Betty Rosbottom

roasted sugar snap peas with fleur de sel

ROASTING A SWEET LITTLE SUGAR SNAP PEA under the broiler seems counterintuitive, but it's actually a fine idea. The peas stay crisp but get a little tender, as well as taking on some appealing bronze highlights—all in only 2 minutes. A sprinkling of chives and a little *fleur de sel* lifts them out of the ordinary.

Fleur de sel is a very delicate French sea salt that's especially wonderful on tomatoes. It's also very expensive. If *fleur de sel* isn't in your pantry or on your shopping list, just use good sea salt.

serves 6

1 pound sugar snap peas
1 tablespoon olive oil
Fleur de sel or good sea salt
2 tablespoons chopped fresh chives

Preheat the broiler with the rack 4 to 6 inches from the heat. Line a large baking sheet with foil. Toss the peas with the olive oil on the baking sheet. Arrange them in a single layer and broil, stirring once with a spatula, until just crisp-tender and beginning to brown in spots, about 2 minutes. Transfer to a bowl. Sprinkle with the *fleur de sel* or sea salt, then the chives, and serve.

SOURCE: www.cincypost.com

COOK: Sarah Leah Chase for Butterball

glazed pearl onions with mustard and brown sugar

OLD-FASHIONED CREAMED ONIONS ARE A CLASSIC—especially at Thanksgiving—but let's face it, they take forever to make, they're excessively rich, and they're often disappointing. Here's the perfect solution. Caramelized in butter and brown sugar with a little Dijon to liven them up, these onions are so easy to make and so good that they belong in your regular repertoire. They make a fine side dish for everything from pork chops to roast chicken to meat loaf.

serves 6 (see notes)

- 2 tablespoons unsalted butter
- 1 16-ounce package frozen small whole onions, thawed (see notes)
- 2½ tablespoons light brown sugar
- 1 tablespoon Dijon mustard
- 2 tablespoons minced fresh parsley
- Salt and freshly ground black pepper to taste

Melt the butter in a large skillet over medium heat. Add the thawed onions and cook, stirring occasionally, until they begin to brown on all sides, 10 to 12 minutes. Sprinkle with brown sugar and gently stir in the mustard to make a smooth coating for the onions. Cook for 2 minutes more. Season with salt and pepper. Sprinkle with the parsley; serve hot or warm.

notes from our test kitchen

- This recipe makes 6 small servings, which is plenty if there are a lot of other side dishes on the table. If not, figure on 4 servings.
- Thaw the onions in a strainer to drain off the water they release. If you don't have time to wait for them to thaw (or you forget), pour them into a pie plate and zap in the microwave on high until just barely warmed through, about 5 minutes. As long as the onions aren't frozen solid, they will work fine.
- We also make this with regular small white onions. Start by dropping the onions (unpeeled) in boiling water for 3 minutes. Drain and slip off their peels. Combine the onions with the butter, sugar, mustard, and salt and pepper. Place the onions in a small buttered baking dish, and bake at 350 degrees until browned and heated through, about 30 minutes. Garnish with the fresh parsley before serving.

SOURCE: *Bon Appétit*

COOK: Jeanne Thiel Kelley

mashed potatoes with sage and white cheddar cheese

WHEN THE HOLIDAYS ARRIVE, we look high and low for make-ahead recipes that can serve a crowd and that everyone will love. We've learned from experience not to stray too far from the classics, but we can't resist those with a twist or some surprise element to make a truly memorable feast. Here's one such recipe.

Regular mashed potatoes get a boost from sage-infused browned butter and grated sharp cheddar cheese. By using white cheddar—not the bright orange stuff—the potatoes don't look different, but one taste will tell you that they are deliciously so.

serves 10

- 4 pounds russet potatoes, peeled and cut into 1 1/2-inch cubes
- Salt
- 4 tablespoons (1/2 stick) unsalted butter
- 2 tablespoons plus 1 teaspoon minced fresh sage
- 3/4 cup whipping cream
- 3/4 cup whole milk
- 2 1/4 cups coarsely grated sharp white cheddar cheese (about 9 ounces)
- Freshly ground black pepper

Butter an 8- to 10-cup baking dish. Cook the potatoes in a large pot of boiling salted water until tender, about 12 minutes.

Meanwhile, melt the butter in a medium saucepan over medium-high heat. Add 2 tablespoons of the sage and stir until the butter begins to brown, about 3 minutes. Add the cream and milk and bring to a simmer.

Drain the potatoes and return to the pot. Stir over medium heat until the excess moisture evaporates. Begin to mash the potatoes with a hand masher. Add the cream mixture and continue mashing until the potatoes are as lump-free as you like. Stir in 1 3/4 cups of the cheese. Season with salt and pepper to taste and transfer to the prepared dish. Sprinkle with the remaining 1/2 cup cheese and the remaining 1 teaspoon sage. (The potatoes can be made up to 2 days ahead, covered with plastic wrap, and refrigerated.)

Preheat the oven to 375 degrees. Bake the potatoes, uncovered, until heated through and golden brown, about 45 minutes. Serve hot.

notes from our test kitchen

- For best results in boiling the potatoes, start them in cold water and bring them to a gentle boil over medium-high heat. Dropping them into already boiling water will cause them to cook unevenly.
- Don't rush when you're browning the butter and sage. If the butter's not really browned, it won't have the same depth of flavor.
- For entirely lump-free, fluffy potatoes, use a ricer to mash them after you've dried them over the heat and before adding the cream mixture.
- The potatoes will take less time to bake if they haven't been refrigerated, a bit more if they've been chilled overnight.

SOURCE: *Gourmet*

COOK: Lori W. Powell

roasted potatoes with anchovies and lemon

IT'S HARD TO IMAGINE IMPROVING on perfect roasted potatoes—browned and crisp on the outside and creamy inside—but we think this recipe manages to do just that. The combination of garlic, anchovies, and lemon juice adds an irresistible zip to these potatoes. Whenever we make them, which is often, we can't stop eating them.

These zesty potatoes are especially good served alongside roast chicken.

serves 4 to 6

- 2 pounds small (2-inch) white boiling potatoes, quartered
- 1/2 teaspoon salt, or more to taste
- 1/4 teaspoon freshly ground black pepper, or more to taste
- 3 tablespoons extra-virgin olive oil
- 1 1/2 tablespoons minced anchovy fillets
- 1 1/2 tablespoons fresh lemon juice
- 1 1/2 tablespoons finely chopped garlic (3 large cloves)
- 1/3 cup chopped fresh flat-leaf parsley

Adjust the rack to the lower third and preheat the oven to 450 degrees. Toss the potatoes with the salt, pepper, and 2 tablespoons of the oil in a large, shallow baking pan (1 inch deep). Roast, without turning or stirring, until the undersides are golden brown, about 20 minutes.

Meanwhile, in a small bowl, whisk together the anchovies, lemon juice, and remaining 1 tablespoon oil.

Turn the potatoes over with a spatula and roast for 10 more minutes. Toss with the garlic and roast for 5 minutes longer. Transfer to a bowl and stir in the anchovy mixture, parsley, and salt and pepper to taste. Serve hot.

note from our test kitchen

If you don't have a shallow roasting pan, a rimmed baking sheet will do fine. Avoid using a deep pan, since the sides would prevent the potatoes from browning evenly.

SOURCE: *Gourmet*

COOK: **Staff after Bobby Flay**

whipped chipotle sweet potatoes

SMOKY, SPICY CHIPOTLE CHILES are born partners for sweet potatoes. At his Manhattan restaurant, Mesa Grill, Bobby Flay serves a more complicated version of this dish, adding a little cinnamon, crème fraîche, and maple syrup. This minimalist adaptation is dynamite. Once you've tasted it, all other sweet potato dishes will seem wimpy.

You can prepare the dish a day ahead, then bake it on the day you serve it. It's also wonderful with ham and roast pork.

serves 8 to 10

- 5½ pounds sweet potatoes, scrubbed
- 1 tablespoon (1½–2 chiles) minced chipotle chiles in adobo, or to taste, mashed to a paste (see notes)
- 3 tablespoons unsalted butter, cut into tablespoon-size pieces, at room temperature
- 1 teaspoon salt

Adjust the rack to the middle and preheat the oven to 450 degrees. Line a baking sheet with foil and butter a shallow 2-quart glass or ceramic baking dish.

Pierce each potato several times with a fork, place on the baking sheet, and bake until very soft, 1 to 1½ hours. Remove the potatoes from the oven and reduce the oven temperature to 350 degrees.

When the potatoes are cool enough to handle, halve them and scoop the flesh into a bowl. Beat the potatoes, chile paste, butter, and salt with an electric mixer on medium speed just until smooth. Spread in the prepared baking dish. Bake until hot, 20 to 25 minutes. Serve immediately.

notes from our test kitchen

- Small cans of chipotle chiles in adobo are found in some supermarkets and many ethnic markets. The easiest way to use them is to puree the contents in a food processor. Keep any leftover puree in a small glass jar in the refrigerator. It's great stirred into mayonnaise for a dip or sandwich spread, used in marinades, or added to soups that need livening up.
- Bobby Flay uses a little more chile paste than this recipe specifies, but if your guests aren't wild for spicy foods, keep it under control.

SOURCE: *The New Great American Writers Cookbook* edited by Dean Faulkner Wells

COOK: John T. Edge

ginger ale–spiked sweet potatoes

WE ALWAYS PRICK UP OUR EARS and listen when John T. Edge, a leading southern culinary historian, says something about food. This idiotically simple recipe relies on Blenheim ginger ale, which you probably haven't tasted unless you live in the Deep South. Blenheim's comes in two styles—hot and not as hot. The hot version can take your head off, and even the less hot one is a force to contend with, but it's that fiery ginger spice that makes this dish so tasty. If you can't find real Blenheim's, try making this with ginger beer, a milder potion but also delicious. We've also tried it with ginger beer infused with a little grated fresh ginger for about 10 minutes—startling. Even made with regular old ginger ale, the sweet potatoes are memorable.

serves 4

- 2 sweet potatoes, peeled and cut into 1/4-inch-thick slices
- Salt and freshly ground black pepper
- 1 12-ounce bottle Blenheim ginger ale (see note)

Preheat the oven to 350 degrees. Dot the bottom of a small casserole dish or deep pie plate with butter. Layer the sweet potato slices so that they overlap. Sprinkle in a bit of salt and a grind or three of pepper. Pour the ginger ale over the top. Bake for about 1 hour, until the potatoes are browned and the sauce is caramelized. Serve hot.

note from our test kitchen

You can order a case of Blenheim ginger ale—Hot or Not as Hot, by calling (800) 270-9344. Otherwise, try one of the variations described above.

SOURCE: *New York Times Magazine*
COOK: **Julia Reed after her mother**

spinach and artichoke casserole

HERE IT IS, THE FIFTIES CASSEROLE SIDE DISH MADE with ingredients that are almost unspeakable in the age of Julia Child and Alice Waters —frozen spinach, cream cheese, canned artichoke hearts, and Ritz crackers. It's also the dish that's the hit of our holiday dinner parties. The fact is, you don't have to serve this with a Crown Roast of Franks—it's fine food, all on its own. Julia Reed's mother, a southern cook with an excellent palate, has served it to diplomats, famous Manhattan hostesses, and other nabobs with the usual great success.

Reed confesses that once, in a fit of high-mindedness, she made all the ingredients from scratch, using some basic recipes from Julia Child's first book. It wasn't better, and it took forever, whereas this little gem takes only about 10 minutes and is highly portable. We can't rave about it enough.

serves 6 to 8

- 1 tablespoon butter, for greasing the dish
- 2 10-ounce packages frozen chopped spinach
- 9 tablespoons butter, melted
- 1 8-ounce package cream cheese, at room temperature
- 1 teaspoon fresh lemon juice
- 1 14-ounce can artichoke hearts, drained and quartered
- 1/2 cup coarse Ritz cracker crumbs (about 10 crackers)

Adjust the rack to the middle and preheat the oven to 350 degrees. Butter a shallow 2-quart casserole. Cook the spinach according to the package directions, drain well, and place in a mixing bowl. Add all but 1 tablespoon of melted butter, the cream cheese, and lemon juice and blend well with a fork.

Scatter the artichoke quarters evenly over the bottom of the casserole. Cover with the spinach mixture and smooth the top. Sprinkle with the cracker crumbs and drizzle with the remaining 1 tablespoon melted butter. Bake until bubbling in the center and lightly browned on the top, about 25 minutes. Let cool for about 5 minutes and serve.

SOURCE: *Celebrate!*
by Sheila Lukins with Peter Kaminsky
COOK: Sheila Lukins after Riad Aamar

roasted tomatoes and onions

SHEILA LUKINS (OF *SILVER PALATE* FAME) found this unusual dish at Oliva, a restaurant in northwestern Connecticut, where the Middle Eastern chef Riad Aamar serves it in the summer. It's halfway between a salad and a side dish—a big platter loaded with roasted tomatoes, sweet roasted onions, lots of olive oil, a little hill of ricotta cheese, and slivers of basil scattered over the whole thing. It's important to serve this with plenty of crusty rustic bread to catch all the intense juices. There's nothing fancy here, just pure flavors, so be sure you have great tomatoes, good olive oil, and very good fresh cheese.

You make this dish in the oven, so it's as good for a rainy day as a sunny one. You can even prepare it a couple of hours ahead, since it's served at room temperature (see note). It seems born to go with grilled leg of lamb or lamb chops.

serves 8

- 8 medium onions, cut into 1/4-inch-thick slices
- 1 cup extra-virgin olive oil
- 16 small ripe plum or heirloom tomatoes, halved lengthwise
- 1 pound fresh ricotta or goat cheese
- Salt and freshly ground black pepper
- 1 cup slivered fresh basil leaves
- Crusty peasant bread for serving

Preheat the oven to 425 degrees. Arrange the onion slices in one layer on two to four baking sheets and brush both sides with olive oil.

Place the tomatoes cut side up in one or two small, shallow pans and brush the tops with olive oil.

Roast the onions for about 25 minutes, turning them after 15 minutes. When they are done, they will be a deep golden brown. Remove and set aside. Roast the tomatoes until the centers are soft and the skins are charred, about 25 minutes.

To serve, spoon the ricotta or goat cheese in the center of a platter. Separate the onion slices into rings and place them in four even piles around the ricotta on the platter. Arrange the tomatoes between the onions. Season with salt and pepper to taste and sprinkle with the basil. Drizzle with any remaining olive oil, if desired. Serve with bread to soak up the juices and oil.

note from our test kitchen

- You can roast the vegetables a couple of hours ahead of time. When done, cover the pans loosely with foil and keep at room temperature.

SOURCE: *Everyday Greens* by Annie Somerville
COOK: Annie Somerville

butternut squash rounds with sage

THIS SIMPLE DISH from the famous San Francisco vegetarian restaurant Greens is unusual, easy, delicious, and gorgeous. Served on a rustic platter, as Somerville suggests, the intensely orange squash rounds are especially beautiful.

But they're not just another pretty face: the squash, brushed with a little garlic oil, caramelizes as it roasts, becoming savory and just a bit sweet. The sage pulls it all together into what seems to be the essence of fall.

serves 6

- 2 butternut squash with long necks
- 1 tablespoon garlic oil (see notes)
- 10–15 fresh sage leaves (to taste), chopped
- Salt and freshly ground black pepper

Preheat the oven to 400 degrees. Cut each squash at the base of the neck, reserving the bulbous part with the seeds for another dish. Remove the stem and skin of the neck and cut into 3/4-inch-thick rounds. You should have about 12 slices.

Lay the squash slices on a baking sheet. Brush both sides with the garlic oil and sprinkle with the sage and a little salt and pepper. Roast for 15 minutes, then use a spatula to loosen the rounds, but don't turn them—they will brown on the bottom all by themselves. Cook for another 5 minutes, until the squash is tender and the color is vibrant. Serve warm.

notes from our test kitchen

- Keep an eye out in the fall for butternut squash with very long necks. Sometimes you'll find one that's nearly all neck, which is convenient for making the squash rounds. Since butternut squash keeps well, you can acquire yours weeks ahead of when you plan to cook it. Save the bulbous part of the squash for soup, which you can garnish with the toasted seeds.
- You can buy garlic oil, or you can make your own on the spot. Smack a garlic clove with the side of a chef's knife so it breaks open and let it sit in olive oil for 30 minutes. Remove the garlic and use the oil. Refrigerate any leftover oil for 1 to 2 days.

SOURCE: *At Blanchard's Table*
by Melinda Blanchard and Robert Blanchard

COOK: Melinda Blanchard

island rice with cumin and coconut

MELINDA AND ROBERT BLANCHARD lead the kind of lives many of us dream about. They run a restaurant in the Caribbean in the winter and spend their summers in Vermont, where they operate a salad dressing company, Blanchard & Blanchard. And if the picture they paint in their books is at all accurate, they appear to have found happiness in the bargain.

Melinda is the chef, and her cooking reflects a brazen approach to ingredients. For instance, here's a simple way to transform ordinary rice from a mere backdrop into a bold side dish. It's basically a rice pilaf to which Melinda adds shredded coconut, raisins, and a generous dose of ground cumin. The result is slightly sweet and very flavorful—a fine accompaniment to grilled seafood, roasted chicken, and almost any pork dish.

serves 4

- 1 tablespoon unsalted butter
- 2 shallots, minced
- 1 cup long-grain white rice
- 2 teaspoons ground cumin (see notes)
- Salt and freshly ground black pepper
- 1/4 cup shredded unsweetened coconut
- 1/4 cup raisins (see notes)
- 1 3/4 cups chicken stock
- 2 tablespoons chopped fresh parsley

Melt the butter in a medium saucepan over medium heat. Add the shallots and cook for a few minutes until soft. Add the rice, cumin, and salt and pepper to taste and cook for 2 minutes. Add the coconut, raisins, and stock and bring to a boil. Cover and cook over low heat until all the liquid is absorbed, 12 to 15 minutes. Fluff with a fork, add the parsley, and taste for salt and pepper. Serve hot.

notes from our test kitchen

- Golden raisins complement the tropical flavor of the rice. Dark raisins are fine, too.
- This rice tends to be a little wet after cooking. To eliminate some of the excess moisture, remove the lid when the rice is done and fluff it with a fork. Then drape a clean dishtowel over the pot and secure the lid in place. Let stand for 8 to 12 minutes before serving.

SOURCE: *The New Great American Writers Cookbook* edited by Dean Faulkner Wells

COOK: Louise Erdrich

wild rice for lots of people

THE NATIONAL BOOK CRITICS CIRCLE Award–winning novelist (*Love Medicine*) and poet Louise Erdrich knows her way around the kitchen. She lives in Minnesota, the source of the country's best wild rice, and has a deep respect for it.

Her appealingly crunchy side dish does indeed serve a lot of people, who will be delighted by its Mediterranean touches, sun-dried tomatoes in olive oil, and optional chopped basil.

If you have leftovers, the rice reheats very well.

serves 12 to 16

1 pound wild rice (see tip)
Water or stock, as needed (see notes)
3 garlic cloves, peeled, or more to taste
1 tablespoon olive oil
2 yellow onions, chopped
8 ounces sunflower seeds
1 small jar chopped sun-dried tomatoes in olive oil
Chopped fresh basil (optional)

Wash the rice until the water comes clean. Remove any bits of hull that float to the top. Dump the rice in a Dutch oven and fill with water or stock (bouillon cubes are okay) to just above the level of the rice. Test by touching the top of the rice with the tip of your thumb; the water should be at the level of your first knuckle.

Bring to a boil, cover, lower the heat, and simmer for 30 to 35 minutes, until the rice is cracked open. Add the garlic to the pot while the rice cooks. Gradually turn down the heat and let it stand, covered, for 10 minutes.

Meanwhile, heat the olive oil in a skillet, add the onions, and cook until soft. Set aside. Toast the sunflower seeds in a cast-iron skillet, stirring, until fragrant, just a few minutes.

Once the rice is fluffy, add the seeds, onions, and tomatoes and their oil and stir it all around. Add some chopped basil, if you like. Done! Serve hot.

notes from our test kitchen

- You'll need about 3 cups stock or water to start, but you may need to add more, 1/4 cup at a time, as the rice cooks. Chicken stock or vegetable stock is a good choice.
- For a different flavor that's good for the holidays, skip the tomatoes (and basil) and use 1 cup dried cranberries instead.
- To save yourself from washing an extra pot, you may want to cook your onions in the Dutch oven before cooking the rice, then set them aside.
- It's a bit easier to toast so many sunflower seeds in the oven. Scatter them on a baking sheet and toast them at 350 degrees until they begin to smell good.
- The cooking time may be as long as 55 minutes, depending on the rice. If it dries out before it's done, add 3/4 cup water.

tip

The source of wild rice is important—there's a lot of bad rice out there. Louise Erdrich recommends the wild rice harvested by Ojibway Indians, available from White Earth Land Reclamation, P.O. Box 327, White Earth, MN 56591.

SOURCE: *The Texas Cowboy Kitchen* by Grady Spears
COOK: Grady Spears

green chile–cheese grits

THIS ULTIMATE COMFORT-FOOD DISH comes from the cowboy chef Grady Spears, a guy who knows his grits and knows how to create stunningly good food. You can make these Texas-style grits with the regular supermarket variety, but if you can find the real thing—traditional stone-ground corn grits—you'll be in heaven (see page 87).

We know about grits made with cheese, eggs, and butter, but we hadn't thought of adding roasted green chiles, roasted garlic, cilantro, and jalapeños. This casserole, with its zesty flavors, makes great party food. You can put it together ahead of time and just reheat it—and your guests will go wild.

serve 8 to 10

- 12 tablespoons (1 1/2 sticks) butter, plus 1 tablespoon more for the dish
- 2 roasted green chiles, seeded and chopped (see notes)
- 1 large garlic head, roasted (see notes)
- 3/4 cup chopped fresh cilantro
- 1–2 jalapeño chiles (to taste), stemmed, seeded, and minced
- 6 cups water
- 1 1/3 cups hominy grits
- 3 large eggs, beaten
- 1 cup grated sharp cheddar cheese
- 1 cup grated caciotta or Monterey jack cheese (see notes)
- Kosher salt and ground white pepper

Preheat the oven to 350 degrees. Use 1 tablespoon of the butter to grease a 9-x-13-inch casserole and set aside. Combine the chiles, garlic, cilantro, and jalapeños in a blender or food processor. Process until smooth and set aside.

Bring the water to a boil in a large pot. Add the grits and stir well. Reduce the heat to low and stir while the grits thicken, anywhere from 25 minutes to an hour. When the mixture is thick, remove from the heat. Stir in the eggs, adding them slowly, followed by the remaining 12 tablespoons butter, the cheeses, and the chile mixture. Add salt and pepper to taste. Pour the mixture into the prepared casserole and bake for about 45 minutes, until set. Serve hot.

notes from our test kitchen

- If you're living outside the Chile Belt, you can use a small can of green chiles (about 4 ounces).
- To roast a head of garlic, preheat the oven to 375 degrees. Slice the very top off the head to expose the cloves, being careful not to cut off too much. Place the garlic on a large square of heavy-duty foil. Drizzle with olive oil and wrap to make a tight pouch. Roast until the garlic feels tender when you push on the outside of the foil, about 1 hour. Carefully open the foil to release the heat and let the garlic cool. When cool enough to handle, squeeze each clove to extract the roasted garlic.
- Caciotta is a buttery, mild, semisoft cheese, similar to Bel Paese. In Tuscany it is made from sheep's milk. Grady Spears no doubt uses the Texas version—a mellow cow's milk cheese made by the Mozzarella Company (www.mozzco.com). Monterey jack is a fine substitute.

tip

If you have leftovers, grilled grits are a revelation. Use the information in Steven Raichlen's *BBQ USA:* Form the cold grits (they need to chill for at least 6 hours) into small cakes about 3/4 inch thick and grill them on a well-oiled grate, turning once, for 2 to 4 minutes per side. If you like, you can brush the tops with melted butter after you turn them and the other side once they come off the fire. Serve right away.

SOURCE: *America's Best Chefs Cook with Jeremiah Tower* by Jeremiah Tower

COOK: Charlie Trotter

crisp arugula-polenta cakes

ALTHOUGH HE'S FAMOUS for his spectacular, complicated dishes that mere mortals can only aspire to in the kitchen, Charlie Trotter also appreciates simple food. These polenta cakes are unusual because of the chopped arugula that's folded in just after the polenta is cooked. It gives the comforting polenta an extra little bite, as well as some fresh flavor.

Trotter is flexible about using regular polenta or instant, and he suggests making the polenta and refrigerating it a day ahead so it sets very firmly.

The polenta cakes are delicious with roast beef, lamb, ham, or almost anything grilled or braised.

serves 6

- 6 cups water
- 1 tablespoon salt, plus more to taste
- 2 tablespoons extra-virgin olive oil, plus more for frying
- 2 cups coarse-grain or instant polenta (see notes)
- 8 tablespoons (1 stick) butter, plus more for frying
- 1 cup arugula leaves, coarsely chopped
- Ground white pepper

Bring the water, 1 tablespoon salt, and the olive oil to a boil. Transfer 2 cups to a heatproof glass measuring cup. With the remaining water still boiling, gradually sprinkle in the polenta, stirring constantly. Keep adding and stirring, paying particular attention to the corners of the pan so no polenta sticks there and burns. When all the polenta has been added, reduce the heat to a simmer and cook, stirring every 5 minutes, until soft, creamy, and tender, 30 to 40 minutes (10 minutes for instant). If the polenta becomes too thick (it should be like porridge), add some of the reserved hot water.

While the polenta is cooking, use 1 tablespoon of the butter to grease a large baking sheet (see notes). Place in the refrigerator.

When the polenta is cooked, stir in the chopped arugula and 6 tablespoons of the butter. Season with salt and white pepper to taste. Pour the polenta onto the chilled baking sheet and spread it evenly. Smear the remaining 1 tablespoon butter over the surface. Let cool, then cover the sheet with plastic wrap and refrigerate until firm. Cut into squares or rounds. In a large skillet, heat about 1/4 inch olive oil or butter (or a combination) over medium-high heat. Add the polenta cakes and fry, turning once, for a few minutes per side, until browned and crisp. You can also crisp them in the oven (see notes). Serve immediately.

notes from our test kitchen

- You can use regular coarse-ground cornmeal instead of polenta—it's the same thing.
- We like the polenta best with 1/2 cup freshly grated Parmigiano-Reggiano cheese folded in along with the butter at the end of the cooking. If you do that, leave out 2 tablespoons of the butter.
- If you use a full-size baking sheet, the polenta will be spread too thin. A half sheet will be the right size.
- You don't need to make the polenta a day ahead, but it does need to chill for at least 5 hours. You can start it off in the freezer for about 15 minutes, then move it to a cold place in the refrigerator for the rest of the chilling time.
- Use a large glass to cut rounds of polenta if you don't have a large round cookie cutter.
- We sometimes cook these on a buttered baking sheet in a 375-degree oven instead of frying. They don't get as crisp, but they are still excellent and much easier to manage.

tip

We learned from Jeremiah Tower that you can turn the firm, chilled polenta right back into creamy soft polenta if you want to. Just add enough hot water to thin it to the desired consistency. Kept in a double boiler over hot water, this born-again polenta will stay soft for hours, never to harden again, says Tower.

SOURCE: *Cider* by Annie Proulx and Lew Nichols

COOK: Annie Proulx after Jehane Benoit

baked beans in cider

BEFORE SHE WAS WRITING NOVELS, ANNIE PROULX collaborated on a book about cider, which was reissued this year. Among the recipes is this very good Quebecois way of baking beans.

There's nothing unusual here except the cider, and that's what makes these beans so good. Finding fresh apple cider isn't difficult if you live in an apple-growing region. Sweet bottled cider from the supermarket is really just apple juice and will give you a much more sugary result.

Baked beans aren't hard to make, but they're a bit of a commitment, best reserved for a weekend unless you're home anyway. The amazing thing about this recipe is that it also does wonders for canned white beans: just rinse 4 cans of beans, add them to the flavoring ingredients (skip the soaking and boiling steps), and bake for the same amount of time.

serves 10 to 12

4 cups dried beans (see notes)
8 ounces salt pork
1 quart fresh apple cider
1 large onion, peeled
Dry mustard to taste
1/2 cup molasses
1 tablespoon salt

Pick over and wash the beans. Soak in cold water to cover for 12 hours.

Rinse the salt pork in cold water and slice off two or three 1/4-inch-thick strips. Chop the rest into 1/2-inch cubes. Set aside.

Add the cider to the drained beans, bring to a boil, and boil for 30 minutes.

Preheat the oven to 275 degrees. Cover the bottom of an earthenware bean pot (see notes) with cubes of salt pork, reserving the strips for the top. Turn the beans and the cider liquid into the bean pot. Roll the onion in dry mustard and bury it in the middle of the beans. Pour the molasses over all. Place the strips of salt pork on top of the beans and add enough hot water to cover. Add the salt and cover the bean pot.

Bake until the beans are tender and have absorbed much of their liquid, 4 to 6 hours. An hour before the beans are done, uncover the pot and add water if the beans seem too dry. Serve hot or warm.

notes from our test kitchen

- The right beans are pea beans, navy beans, or white beans.
- If you don't have an earthenware pot, use a Dutch oven.

breads

easy biscuits

THERE'S SOMETHING THRILLING about a two-ingredient recipe that really delivers. This one appears in a church cookbook called *The Pantry Shelf,* published by members of the Indianapolis Christian School, and that's where the anthologist Lari Robling found it.

Sure, you could use Bisquick or another store-bought mix, but these terrific little biscuits, as Robling points out, are lighter and tenderer and lack the acrid baking powder taste. They also have an excellent texture that we can only describe as "bitey"—a slightly elastic quality that makes you want to take another bite and then another.

As it stands, the recipe makes small, dainty rounds that are excellent for hors d'oeuvres. As Robling suggests, you can scatter some herbs, grated cheese, or spices on top before they go in the oven for savory biscuits to go with soups or salads. Or cut bigger biscuits and make shortcakes.

makes about 12 small biscuits

- 1 cup self-rising flour
- 1 cup sour cream

Adjust the rack to the upper third and preheat the oven to 425 degrees. Grease a baking sheet. Blend the flour and sour cream with a fork until the dough just comes together.

On a well-floured board, roll out the dough to a 3/4-inch thickness. Using a floured 1-inch biscuit cutter, cut out 12 rounds, reworking the dough as little as possible.

Place the biscuits on the sheet and bake for 12 to 15 minutes, until lightly browned. Serve right away.

note from our test kitchen

It takes a little work to bring the dough together, but don't worry—you're not doing anything wrong, and it will come together soon. As with all biscuits, barely mix the elements together and try not to handle the dough more than you absolutely have to.

SOURCE: *Bon Appétit*
COOKS: Elizabeth and Susan Allen

popovers with sage butter

THESE POPOVERS ARE SOME OF THE BEST WE'VE EVER HAD. Buttery, tender, fragrant, and light—they have the right balance of crusty exterior and eggy, pull-apart center. The addition of sage butter, both in the batter and to spread on the warm popovers, makes them ideal for Thanksgiving.

Popovers are most impressive when they first emerge from the oven—tall and golden—so wait until the very last minute to bake them. The best plan of action is to make the sage butter in advance, then, just before the turkey is ready, whip up the batter. When the turkey comes out, crank up the oven and bake the popovers. By the time the turkey is carved and your guests find their seats, the popovers will be ready.

makes 12 popovers

- 1 cup (2 sticks) unsalted butter, at room temperature
- 1 tablespoon chopped fresh sage
- Salt and freshly ground black pepper
- 2 cups all-purpose flour
- 2 1/2 cups cold whole milk
- 4 large eggs

Stir the butter and sage together in a small bowl. Season with salt and pepper to taste and stir to mix. Heat 5 tablespoons of the sage butter in a small saucepan. Transfer the remaining sage butter to a small dish.

Adjust the rack to the lower third and preheat the oven to 450 degrees. Using 3 tablespoons of the melted sage butter, brush each cup of a 12-cup muffin tin (see notes).

Whisk together the flour and 1 teaspoon salt in a large bowl. Whisk together the milk, eggs, and remaining 2 tablespoons melted sage butter in a medium bowl. Pour the egg mixture over the dry ingredients and whisk until the batter is smooth. Divide among the muffin cups.

Bake for 15 minutes without opening the oven door. Reduce the temperature to 350 degrees and bake until the popovers are puffed and brown, about 20 minutes longer. Transfer the warm popovers to a platter. Serve immediately with the unmelted sage butter.

notes from our test kitchen

- A standard muffin cup should hold about 1/2 cup. Check yours by filling it with water if you're not sure.
- Keeping the oven door closed during the initial baking is essential so that the popovers "pop." Resist the temptation to peek until close to the time you expect them to be done.
- Popovers do collapse and wilt as they cool. They also will stick to the muffin tin if you let them cool there.

tip

If you make only a half batch of popovers, here's a helpful tip from Rose Levy Beranbaum in *The Bread Bible:* Fill any empty muffin cups with water. This creates steam, which will help the popovers rise.

SOURCE: *Boston Herald*
COOK: Jay Murray
STORY BY: Mat Schaffer

stuffin' muffins

THE STORY GOES THAT JAY MURRAY, the chef at Grill 23 & Bar, one of Boston's premier steakhouses, was trying to come up with a bread pudding to serve at Thanksgiving in place of the traditional turkey stuffing. Somewhere along the way, he became charmed by the rhyming sound of stuffin' muffin and whipped these up instead. Having made these several times ourselves, we can tell you that we're very glad Murray followed his inner poet.

The first step in making these golden beauties is to sauté what Murray calls "goodies"—a mixture of bacon, onion, celery, and thyme that is folded into a savory batter to give the muffins their stuffing-like flavor. The finished muffins are moist and eggy—almost popover-like—a perfect accompaniment to roast turkey or just about any other roast meat. If there's gravy on the table, cut a hole in the top of each muffin and pour in some warm gravy. We promise, no one will whine about not having the standard bread stuffing.

makes 24 muffins

"GOODIES"

- 4 tablespoons (1/2 stick) unsalted butter
- 4 ounces smoked bacon, diced small
- 4 celery ribs, diced small
- 1 large onion, diced small
- 2 tablespoons dried thyme (see notes)
- 1 teaspoon kosher salt, or to taste
- Freshly ground black pepper

MUFFINS

- Vegetable oil for the muffin tin
- 4 cups all-purpose flour
- 1/4 cup sugar
- 2 tablespoons baking powder
- 2 teaspoons Old Bay seasoning
- 2 large eggs
- 2 cups milk
- 1/2 cup vegetable oil or, ideally, rendered chicken fat

MAKE THE GOODIES:

Melt the butter in a large sauté pan over medium heat. Add the bacon and sauté, stirring often, until golden, about 3 minutes. Add the celery, onion, thyme, salt, and a few grinds of pepper. Cover, reduce the heat to low, and cook, stirring occasionally, until the vegetables have softened, about 15 minutes. Remove the goodies from the pan and let cool to room temperature.

MAKE THE MUFFINS:

Adjust the rack to the middle and preheat the oven to 400 degrees. Oil two standard 12-cup muffin tins. Mix the flour, sugar, baking powder, and Old Bay seasoning together in a large bowl. Make a well in the center. In another bowl, lightly beat the eggs, then stir in the milk and oil or rendered chicken fat. Pour the wet mixture into the well in the dry ingredients. Mix together quickly and gently until the dough is just moistened. Gently fold in the cooled goodies. Pour the batter into the prepared muffin tins. Bake until golden and a skewer inserted in the center of a muffin comes out clean, about 25 minutes. Transfer the muffins to a platter and serve warm.

notes from our test kitchen

- The amount of dried thyme in the recipe may seem like a lot, but it's important for the stuffing-like flavor. You may want to cut it back, and that's fine, too. If you substitute fresh thyme, this is one instance where you can use the same amount as dried.
- The muffins can be made up to 2 days ahead and reheated with the turkey. Keep them tightly wrapped in a cool, dry place, and warm them wrapped in foil in a 350-degree oven.

SOURCE: *New York Times*
COOK: Marjorie Cronin
STORY BY: Joan Nathan

cranberry cornbread

MARJORIE CRONIN grew up in Plymouth, Massachusetts, and knows a thing or two about how to celebrate Thanksgiving. The Cronin family gatherings included more than fifty people—all relatives—and inspired days of cooking and baking in preparation. Although the numbers may have dwindled, Cronin, now in her seventies, and her sisters still cook up a storm in their eighteenth-century kitchen.

Every year Cronin drives over to the Jenney Grist Mill, built in 1636, to purchase some stone-ground grits, and then on to Bog Hollow Farm for fresh cranberries, so she can make her cranberry cornbread to serve for breakfast on Thanksgiving morning. Few of us are situated so neatly between a gristmill and a cranberry bog, but we can still make this wonderful little cornbread, a fine choice for breakfast as well as for the holiday table.

serves 12

- Butter for the pan
- 1 cup cranberries, rinsed and picked over
- 1/2 cup confectioners' sugar
- 1 cup all-purpose flour
- 3/4 cup stone-ground cornmeal
- 1/2 cup sugar
- 1 tablespoon baking powder
- 3/4 teaspoon salt
- 1 cup milk (see notes)
- 1 large egg
- 2 tablespoons unsalted butter, melted

Adjust the rack to the middle and preheat the oven to 400 degrees. Butter an 8-inch square baking pan. Cut each cranberry in half (see notes), place in a large bowl with the confectioners' sugar, and toss to coat. Sift in the flour, cornmeal, sugar, baking powder, and salt and mix together. In a small bowl, whisk together the milk, egg, and melted butter. Pour over the cornmeal mixture and fold together gently but thoroughly. Pour the batter into the prepared pan and bake until golden and a toothpick inserted in the center comes out clean, 20 to 35 minutes.

Cut into squares and serve warm, or let cool in the pan on a wire rack.

notes from our test kitchen

- Don't cheat by chopping the berries in a food processor—it will whir the berries to oblivion and not give the same results.
- Warming the milk slightly before mixing it with the egg and butter prevents the melted butter from hardening. A quick zap in the microwave is all it takes; you don't want it hot enough to cook the egg.
- Sift the dry ingredients through a coarse sifter or regular-mesh sieve. Anything too fine will sift out the good parts of the stone-ground cornmeal.
- This cornbread keeps well and can be made a day ahead.

SOURCE: *Bernard Clayton's Complete Book of Breads*
by Bernard Clayton, Jr.

COOK: Bernard Clayton, Jr.

cheese shortbread

As the bread-making expert Bernard Clayton points out, this cheese shortbread looks exactly like ordinary pie crust—something you'd never give a second glance. That would be a big mistake. This is a simply superb bit of rich, cheesy pastry—crumbly, crispy, and just about irresistible.

Clayton suggests serving it with coffee or tea, which is fine, but it also goes well with soups and salads. Delectable as it is, it's also fragile. Don't worry if it falls into crumbs and little crisp bits as you bite into it—you'll relish every morsel.

makes 12 wedges

- 7 tablespoons butter, at room temperature, plus more for the pan
- 4 ounces Swiss cheese, grated (1 cup), at room temperature
- 1½ cups bread flour or all-purpose flour
- ¼ teaspoon salt
- 1 teaspoon cold water, if needed

Adjust the rack to the middle and preheat the oven to 400 degrees. Butter a 9-inch cake pan or flan ring (placed on a buttered baking sheet).

TO MIX IN A STAND MIXER OR BY HAND:

In a medium bowl or mixer bowl, combine the cheese, butter, flour, and salt. Work the mixture with your hands until it forms a soft ball. If it's too sticky, add a bit more flour; if it's too stiff, add the cold water. This may be done with a paddle mixer, but the dough may be too heavy for the paddle to blend the ingredients thoroughly.

TO MIX IN A FOOD PROCESSOR:

Place all the ingredients (except the water) in a processor fitted with a steel blade and process 3 or 4 times until you have a soft ball.

With a rolling pin, roll out the dough between two lengths of wax or parchment paper until it is slightly larger than the bottom of the pan or ring. Peel back the paper with care, quickly invert the dough over the pan, and let it drop in. Press the dough snugly into the bottom of the pan.

Neatly trim around the dough, because shortly you will be giving it a new edge. Fashion the scraps into a long, thin roll—long enough to go around the inside of the pan. Press the new edge onto the pastry, pressing with your fingertips so it adheres.

With a knife or pastry wheel, cut the shortbread 6 times across to make 12 wedges. If you're using a flan ring, remove it and space the wedges 1/2 inch apart on the baking sheet underneath. Whether the wedges are separated or not, the demarcations will remain and make the shortbread easier to cut after it comes out of the oven.

Bake the shortbread until it is only faintly browned, about 14 minutes. Don't overbake; it burns easily. Remove from the oven and let cool slightly. If you're using a pan, cut along the lines and remove the wedges from the pan. Serve warm or at room temperature.

tip

In *Real Simple* magazine, we learned that oiling the holes of the grater will minimize the amount of cheese sticking to it.

SOURCE: *The Bread Bible* by Rose Levy Beranbaum

COOK: Rose Levy Beranbaum after Noel Comess

tom cat rosemary matzoh

IN THE SAME THOUGHTFUL AND THOROUGH MANNER that Rose Levy Beranbaum tackled cakes and pies in her previous bibles, she has crammed her treatise on bread with techniques, tips, scientific explanations, and every manner of bread recipe. We'll admit that we had some trouble choosing—until we landed on this recipe.

Beranbaum borrowed the idea for homemade matzoh from Noel Comess, co-owner of the Tom Cat Bakery, one of New York's best bread bakeries. Unlike the store-bought kind, these matzohs are crisp and delicate, with a sweet taste of olive oil and the faintly resinous perfume of rosemary.

You'll need a pizza stone to bake these—otherwise, they won't bubble up as nicely. A pizza peel helps, too, but is not necessary. In the end, you'll be rewarded with an impressive basket of large, crisp, paper-thin crackers dotted with golden bubbles. Everyone will marvel that you made them yourself.

Serve these plain with drinks—Beranbaum recommends champagne—as an elegant snack before a big meal. They also make fine crackers for a dip or hummus.

makes six 11-inch round matzohs

- 2 3/4 cups unbleached all-purpose flour, plus more for dusting
- 1/4 cup whole wheat flour, preferably finely ground
- 1 1/8 teaspoons salt
- 1 cup water, at room temperature
- 1/4 cup olive oil, plus more for oiling the dough
- 1/2 tablespoon finely chopped fresh rosemary
- Cornmeal for dusting (optional)

TO MIX IN A STAND MIXER:

Combine the flours and salt in the bowl of the mixer. Make a well in the center and pour in all but 1 tablespoon of the water, the olive oil, and the rosemary. With the paddle attachment, mix on medium speed (#4 if using a KitchenAid) until the dough cleans the side of the bowl. If the dough does not come together after 1 minute, add the remaining 1 tablespoon water, 1/2 teaspoon at a time. If the dough seems sticky, you can add more flour as necessary without destroying the texture. Transfer the dough to a work surface and knead lightly for 1 to 2 minutes, until smooth and satiny. (It will be a round ball that flattens after relaxing.)

TO MIX BY HAND:

Place the flours on a work surface or in a large bowl and sprinkle with the salt. Make a well in the center and add the olive oil and rosemary. Add all but 1 tablespoon of the water in 3 or 4 additions, using your fingers and a bench scraper or spatula to work the flour into the liquid until you can form a ball. If necessary, add the remaining 1 tablespoon water. Knead the dough until it is very smooth and elastic and feels like satin, about 5 minutes, adding extra flour only if it is still very sticky after kneading for a few minutes.

TO ROLL OUT AND BAKE:

Pour about 1 teaspoon olive oil on a small plate and turn the dough in it so that it is coated all over. Leave the dough on the plate, cover with plastic wrap, and let sit at room temperature for at least 30 minutes, or refrigerate overnight.

About 1 hour before baking, adjust the rack to the middle, place a baking stone on it, and preheat the oven to 450 degrees. Lightly dust a pizza peel or baking sheet with flour or cornmeal.

Cut the dough into 6 equal parts and shape them into balls. Flatten them into disks, cover, and let sit for about 10 minutes.

Work with 1 piece of dough at a time, keeping the rest covered. Place the disk on a floured surface and dust with flour. Roll it into a rough circle 12 to 13 inches in diameter. As you roll, lift the dough and slide it on the surface at regular intervals, flouring as necessary to prevent sticking.

Slide the dough onto the prepared peel or baking sheet. If using a peel, slide the dough onto the hot stone by jiggling the peel as you gradually pull it forward. If using a baking sheet, set the baking sheet directly on the stone.

Bake for 1 minute; then, with a fork or the tip of a knife, poke any big air bubbles that may have formed. Continue baking for 2 minutes. Hold a clean potholder in one hand and use a large pancake turner to lift the matzoh and flip it over onto the potholder. Slide the matzoh back onto the stone and bake for another 2 to 3 minutes, or until the raised bubbles are lightly browned.

With a pancake turner, remove the matzoh from the oven and set it on a wire rack to cool completely while you shape and bake the remaining dough. If the matzoh isn't crisp after cooling, return it briefly to the oven. If desired, gently brush any flour from the surface with a soft brush.

notes from our test kitchen

- When the first matzoh is baking, roll out and shape the second. Once you get the hang of it, you should be able to shape one in the short time it takes for another one to bake. If the dough becomes hard to roll, cover and let rest for a few minutes.
- The matzohs are best served the day they're baked, but they'll keep in an airtight container for a few days.

popcorn focaccia

DESCRIBED AS A LOVE STORY with recipes, *The Cornbread Book* has to be one of the most charming books we've read this year. When we spied this recipe using ground-up popcorn for some of the flour in focaccia dough, we were dubious. But Jeremy Jackson says it's the best one in the book, and boy, are we glad we tried it. The popcorn flour, which is basically popcorn ground up in a food processor, doesn't dramatically alter the taste of the focaccia, but instead gives it a subtle sweetness and a tender but still chewy texture, with big airy pockets. The little bits of kernel fleck the bread, adding a nice textural contrast.

While this focaccia is fantastic as is, its mild character also makes a great base for all sorts of toppings and flavorings. You can either sprinkle on or knead in any of the usual focaccia or pizza toppings: cheese, herbs, olives, onions, and so forth.

makes 2 small to medium focaccias or pizzas

- 1 1/4-ounce packet (2 1/2 teaspoons) active dry or instant yeast
- 1 1/4 cups lukewarm water (110 degrees)
- 2 1/2 cups unbleached all-purpose flour, plus more as needed
- 1 cup Popcorn Flour (recipe follows)
- 1 1/2 teaspoons salt
- 2 tablespoons olive oil, plus more for the bowl
- Cornmeal for sprinkling

Dissolve the yeast in the water in a mixing bowl. Add 2 cups of the all-purpose flour, the popcorn flour, the salt, and the oil and stir vigorously for 3 minutes. Stir in the remaining 1/2 cup all-purpose flour a little at a time, just until you have a soft but kneadable dough.

Turn the dough out onto a floured work surface and knead until smooth and elastic, about 5 minutes, adding only as much flour as needed to keep it from sticking (about 1/4 cup). Drizzle olive oil into a medium bowl and then turn the dough in the bowl to coat. Let rise, covered, until doubled in bulk, at least 1 hour. Punch the dough down, turn, cover, and let rise again until doubled in bulk, 30 to 35 minutes.

Divide the dough into 2 equal pieces and put each piece on a cornmeal-sprinkled pizza peel, a largish cutting board, or the back of a baking sheet (the focaccia needs to slide off easily onto the baking stone). Gently poke each piece of dough with the tips of your fingers to flatten it a bit and press some of the air out. Adjust the rack to the middle and preheat the baking stone and the oven to 450 degrees. Let the dough rest for 10 minutes.

Shape the dough into 2 rough rectangles by poking at it with your fingertips and tugging at it gently, if necessary, until it is about 1/2 inch thick. If you have a very sharp knife or razor blade, slash the top of each focaccia with 4 to 6 slashes in a grid pattern—a dull knife will tear the fragile dough. Cover and let rise until puffy, about 30 minutes.

In one swift motion, slide one focaccia onto the hot baking stone and bake for 10 to 15 minutes, until lightly browned, stiff, and hollow-sounding when tapped on the bottom. Remove and bake the second focaccia.

Serve warm, sliced into long, narrow breadsticks. This bread also freezes nicely. Rewarm before serving.

popcorn flour

About 2 cups unseasoned popped popcorn, cooled (about 2 heaping tablespoons unpopped corn)

Working with 1 cup at a time, put the popcorn in a blender or food processor and pulse until it resembles very coarse meal, like instant tapioca powder. Freeze any leftover popcorn flour in an airtight container.

notes from our test kitchen

- We recommend making a large batch of popcorn flour and keeping it in your freezer, since you will certainly want to make this bread again once you've tried it.

Jeremy Jackson suggests cutting back the salt to 1 to 1¼ teaspoons if you plan to use this as a pizza dough (a great notion).

tip

Jeremy Jackson offers the following as a foolproof way to pop corn, leaving you with no "old maids" and not a single burnt kernel. Put 2 tablespoons canola oil and 3 unpopped kernels in a 3- to 4-quart stockpot, cover, and heat over medium-high heat, or slightly lower, until the first kernel pops. Immediately add ⅓ cup kernels to the pot and wait. When the kernels begin popping, shake the pot frequently and listen until the popping stops.

desserts

desserts

SOURCE: *Food & Wine*

COOK: Greg Patent

fresh apricot-berry crumble

WE FIRST NOTICED THIS APPEALING RECIPE a year ago, so we were thrilled when we saw that *Food & Wine* had selected it as one of their top twenty-five recipes *ever* and smartly substituted almonds for the apricot kernels that the cookbook author Greg Patent had originally used in the topping. Although the almond flavor in an actual almond is less intense than that of the apricot kernels, we don't find this crumble lacking in any way. And we're very relieved not to have to haul out the hammer to crack open the apricot kernels.

Fresh apricot season is painfully brief for most of us, which may explain why there are so few recipes for such an amazingly delicious fruit. But when you do find ripe apricots, there is no better way to honor them than to bake them in this summer crumble with its toasty oat topping.

serves 8

- 2 pounds firm ripe apricots, halved and pitted
- 8 whole almonds
- 1 cup packed light brown sugar
- Finely grated zest of 1 lemon
- 1½ cups raspberries
- 1½ cups blueberries
- 2 tablespoons fresh lemon juice
- 1 cup all-purpose flour
- ¾ cup old-fashioned or quick-cooking (not instant) rolled oats
- 1 teaspoon ground cinnamon
- ¼ teaspoon salt
- 10 tablespoons (1¼ sticks) cold unsalted butter, cut into tablespoon-size pieces

Adjust the rack to the lower third and preheat the oven to 375 degrees. Place the apricots in a shallow 2½-quart baking dish, such as a 10-inch deep-dish pie plate.

In a food processor, grind the almonds with ¼ cup of the brown sugar until fine, about 30 seconds. Add the lemon zest and process for 5 to 10 seconds. Scrape the sugar mixture over the apricots and toss. Scatter the raspberries and blueberries over the apricots and drizzle with the lemon juice.

In the food processor, combine the flour, oats, cinnamon, salt, and remaining 3/4 cup brown sugar. Process for 10 seconds. Add the butter and pulse just until the mixture resembles coarse crumbs. Sprinkle the topping evenly over the fruit and bake for about 55 minutes, until the topping is browned and the filling is bubbling. Let the crumble cool on a wire rack and serve.

notes from our test kitchen

- If you're game for smashing open the apricot pits, by all means substitute 8 apricot kernels for the almonds. They may be smaller, but they pack a bigger wallop. Don't use more, or the filling will taste bitter.
- There's no need to clean the food processor bowl between grinding up the almonds and making the oat topping.

SOURCE: *Bon Appétit*

COOK: American Bounty Restaurant at the Culinary Institute of America

apple and dried fig cobbler

WE ALWAYS PAY ATTENTION to the recipes requested by readers in magazines and newspapers. If a dish is memorable enough for someone to write away for the recipe, that's a very good sign. This comforting cobbler was served at an innovative restaurant at the Culinary Institute of America in Hyde Park, New York. Now that we've made it, we can see why someone went to the trouble to track down the recipe.

Combining fresh apples with dried figs creates a reliably delicious fruit dessert that you can make year-round. The figs are first poached in red wine, port, and warm spices, including cinnamon and star anise—a step that gives them an intoxicating flavor and ensures that the cobbler bubbles with tasty juices. Serve this warm with a scoop of vanilla ice cream. For an added treat, reduce the fig poaching liquid to a syrup and drizzle it over the ice cream.

serves 8 to 10

FRUIT

- 1 cup ruby port
- 1 cup dry red wine
- 1 cup water
- 2 tablespoons fresh lemon juice
- 3/4 cup sugar
- 1 orange, thinly sliced into rounds
- 18 black peppercorns
- 1 cinnamon stick
- 2 cloves
- 1 star anise
- 1 pound dried figs, hard stems removed and quartered
- 4 tablespoons (1/2 stick) unsalted butter, plus more for the dish
- 1/2 cup store-bought apple butter
- 3 1/4 pounds Granny Smith apples (5 or 6), peeled, cored, and cut into wedges (see notes)
- 1/2 cup packed light brown sugar
- 1 teaspoon ground cinnamon
- 1/4 teaspoon ground nutmeg

TOPPING

- 2 1/4 cups all-purpose flour
- 6 tablespoons sugar
- 2 tablespoons packed light brown sugar
- 1 tablespoon baking powder
- 1 teaspoon salt
- 5 tablespoons cold unsalted butter, cut into pieces
- 1 cup half-and-half
- 1/2 teaspoon almond extract

PREPARE THE FRUIT:

In a large, heavy saucepan, combine the port, red wine, water, lemon juice, sugar, orange slices, and spices. Simmer over medium heat for 20 minutes to infuse. Strain the liquid through a fine-mesh sieve. Discard the solids and return the liquid to the saucepan. Add the figs to the liquid. Simmer over medium heat until tender, about 20 minutes. Drain, reserving the liquid for another use (see notes).

Adjust the rack to the middle and preheat the oven to 350 degrees. Butter a 9-x-13-inch baking dish. Spread the apple butter over the bottom of the dish. Melt the butter in a large, heavy skillet over medium heat. Add the apples and sauté until just tender, about 10 minutes. Add the brown sugar, cinnamon, and nutmeg and toss gently to combine. Gently stir in the drained figs. Spoon the mixture over the apple butter.

MAKE THE TOPPING:

Combine the flour, sugar, brown sugar, baking powder, and salt in a large bowl. Add the butter and rub it in with your fingertips until the mixture resembles coarse meal. Add the half-and-half and almond extract, stirring with a fork to form a moist dough. Drop by tablespoonfuls onto the fruit. Bake until the fruit is tender and the topping is golden brown, about 25 minutes. Serve hot.

notes from our test kitchen

- Depending on the size of the apples, cut them into 6 or 8 wedges each, about 3/4 inch thick.
- We like to dress up the topping a bit by quickly brushing it with a little egg wash, dusting it with sugar (preferably coarse sugar), and sprinkling it with sliced almonds before baking.
- If you're planning on serving this cobbler with vanilla ice cream (which we highly recommend), heat the leftover fig poaching syrup to a simmer and reduce it to a thick glaze while the cobbler bakes. To serve, drizzle the warm, sweet glaze over the ice cream. You can also save the syrup for another day—it's quite delightful spooned over pancakes or a bowl of ice cream on its own.

SOURCE: *Fine Cooking*

COOK: **Leslie Revsin**

pear and hazelnut gratin

WE HEARD RAVES ABOUT THIS RECIPE from a friend who received the gratin from a neighbor as a get-well gift. Unfortunately, the neighbor wasn't sure where she'd found the recipe. Then suddenly it surfaced, hidden in plain sight in a magazine we'd both read cover to cover.

Although it may seem unprepossessing, don't make the mistake of overlooking it as we did. The pears and hazelnuts are great partners, and the ginger preserves bring them together beautifully. A touch of grated orange zest —where you might expect lemon—makes for a surprise. This is an easy, homey, consoling dish, served warm with cream. You probably won't have leftovers, but if you do, they're great the next day.

serves 6

- 6 tablespoons (3/4 stick) cold unsalted butter, cut into cubes, plus more for the dish
- 1/4 cup plus 1 tablespoon sugar
- 1/4 cup ginger preserves, at room temperature (see notes)
- 1 1/4 teaspoons finely grated orange zest
- Pinch salt
- 1/2 cup whole unblanched hazelnuts
- 1/2 cup fresh white bread crumbs
- 1 tablespoon fresh lemon juice
- 2 pounds firm ripe Bosc pears (about 4)
- 3/4 cup light or heavy cream for serving

Adjust the rack to the lower third and preheat the oven to 400 degrees. Butter the bottom and sides of six 6-inch (8-ounce) gratin dishes or a shallow 1 1/2-quart gratin dish or baking pan. In a small bowl, combine 1 tablespoon of the sugar, the ginger preserves, orange zest, and salt. Stir well and set aside.

Put the hazelnuts in a food processor and process until coarsely chopped. Add the bread crumbs and the remaining 1/4 cup sugar and pulse 4 or 5 times to combine. Add the butter and pulse until the mixture barely comes together, about 30 seconds; it should be chunky and crumbly. (To do this by hand, coarsely chop the hazelnuts and combine them with the bread crumbs and sugar in a small bowl. Cut in the butter with a pastry cutter or two knives until chunky and crumbly but combined.)

Put the lemon juice in a large bowl. Peel the pears, cut them in half lengthwise, and spoon out the core (a melon baller works well). Cut them lengthwise into 1/4-inch-thick slices, put them in the bowl, and toss gently with the lemon juice. Add the ginger mixture and toss again to coat.

Transfer the pears and juices to the prepared gratin dishes and distribute evenly. Scatter the hazelnut mixture evenly on top. Bake the gratins until the tops are browned, the juices are bubbling, and the pears are still intact but tender when pierced with a fork, 30 to 35 minutes for individual gratins, 40 to 50 minutes for a large one. Let cool for 10 to 15 minutes before serving. Pass the cream separately in a pitcher for guests to drizzle over each serving.

notes from our test kitchen

- Ginger preserves are available in most supermarkets. Look for them with the high-end jams and jellies.
- Leslie Revsin notes that if you're reheating the gratin, you should let it come to room temperature first, then place in a 350-degree oven for a few minutes to warm through.

SOURCE: *Williams-Sonoma Christmas* by Carolyn Miller

COOK: Carolyn Miller

citrus compote

SOMETIMES THE ONSLAUGHT OF RICH FOOD during the holidays becomes almost unbearable. That's when you need this refreshing, clean-tasting compote, which can also sit on a buffet table looking gorgeous.

Blood oranges are the centerpiece, but they're not essential—and indeed, last year their season was so late that they weren't even available. You can use navel oranges or tangelos instead. Cassis and pomegranate seeds brighten things up considerably, and a scattering of mint freshens the entire dish.

serves 8 to 10

- 12 large blood oranges, navel oranges, or tangelos, or a mixture (about 4 pounds; see notes)
- 1/4 cup crème de cassis or cassis syrup
- 2 tablespoons fresh lemon juice (see notes)
- 3 tablespoons minced fresh mint
- Pomegranate seeds (optional)
- Fresh mint sprigs for garnish

Remove the zest from 1 orange with a zester (see notes) and set aside. Using a large chef's knife, cut off the top and bottom of an orange down to the flesh. Stand the orange upright and slice off the peel in vertical strips, following the contour of the fruit; discard the peel. Repeat with the remaining oranges. (If you're using tangelos, just peel them by hand.) Slice all the oranges crosswise into 1/4-inch-thick rounds. Remove the hard white center and any seeds. Put the orange slices in a large nonaluminum bowl.

Pour the cassis and lemon juice over the oranges and stir to blend. Cover and refrigerate for 30 to 60 minutes.

To serve, transfer the oranges to a serving dish and sprinkle with the minced mint, orange zest, and pomegranate seeds (if using). Garnish with mint sprigs and serve.

notes from our test kitchen

- Taste the oranges. If they're very tart, you may not need the lemon juice, or you may not need as much.
- If you don't have a citrus zester, remove the zest with a sharp vegetable peeler or paring knife, being careful to take away only the orange zest and none of the white pith. Once you've removed the zest, slice it into ultra-thin strips or chop it finely.
- If you remove the orange peels earlier in the day, it's a cinch to slice the oranges into rounds, mix in the lemon juice and cassis, and have everything else ready for when the oranges are finished macerating.
- The compote looks prettiest made with half blood oranges and half navel oranges or tangelos and served in a glass bowl. Go easy on the pomegranate seeds—they can be overwhelming.

SOURCE: *Granita Magic* by Nadia Roden

COOK: Nadia Roden

grapefruit and star anise granita

ONE OF THE MOST ORIGINAL BOOKS of the year was a little book about granita, the flavored Italian ice. The author, Nadia Roden, is the daughter of the legendary cookbook author Claudia Roden. Nadia is an accomplished artist and designer, as evidenced by the charming illustrations throughout the book. She's also a clever cook.

One of the best things about granita, besides its sparkling crystalline texture, is that it doesn't require any sort of machine or special freezer to make and it takes hardly any effort. Frozen in a regular freezer and stirred with a fork as it freezes, it emerges like colorful, glittery, flavorful snow.

We'll admit that we had a hard time choosing from Roden's appealing combinations. In the end, the winner was this delightfully refreshing pairing of fresh grapefruit juice with the exotic taste of star anise. Roden suggests passing around Pernod or another anise-flavored liqueur for anyone looking to spike his or her dessert.

serves 4 to 6

- 2/3 cup water
- 1/2 cup sugar
- 1 teaspoon finely grated grapefruit zest
- 6 star anise
- Juice of 4 large white grapefruit (about 4 cups)

Put the water, sugar, grapefruit zest, and star anise in a saucepan and simmer for 5 minutes. Remove from the heat and let cool completely. Remove the star anise (save them to decorate the granitas at the table), or leave them if you prefer a stronger flavor. Mix in the grapefruit juice. Pour the mixture into a wide, shallow container (a 9-x-13-inch baking dish works well; see notes) and cover with a lid, foil, or plastic wrap. Freeze for an hour or two, until it has frozen around the edges.

Remove container from the freezer and scrape the ice with a fork, mixing it from the edges into the center. Repeat this scraping and mixing process every 30 minutes or so (at least 3 times), until the entire mixture has turned into small, sequined ice flakes.

It is best to serve the granita at once, but if you leave it in the freezer overnight or longer, let it sit for about 10 minutes, until it softens a little, and then scrape it with a fork to lighten the texture.

notes from our test kitchen

- The shallower the container, the quicker your granita will freeze. A container that is about 3/4 inch deep is ideal.
- Stainless steel conducts cold faster than plastic, so a wide, shallow stainless steel container works best. Whatever you use, make certain it is nonreactive.
- Refrigerating the mixture and the container before freezing will help the granita freeze more quickly.

tip

Charlie Apt, president of the Manhattan gelato and sorbet company Ciao Bella, recommends slightly overripe fruit for making sorbet (the same applies to granita) because it has more flavor. Also, if you're using fresh herbs such as mint, leave it in the syrup for a full 24 hours to infuse fully. A touch of wine or vodka adds a little extra flavor and softens the texture of frozen confections by lowering the temperature at which they freeze. Serve in a chilled glass so the sorbet (or granita) doesn't melt when it's scooped in. (From *New York* magazine)

SOURCE: *Zingerman's Guide to Good Eating* by Ari Weinzweig

COOK: Julie Stanley

food dance café's double-chocolate pudding

A PERFECT CHOCOLATE PUDDING offers a delicate balance of smooth, creamy texture and rich, dark chocolate flavor. It shouldn't be airy like a mousse or thick like a ganache. Getting it right may seem like a simple matter, but after tasting our way through countless disappointments, we can attest that it's not. Thus we were thrilled when this recipe turned up.

It comes from the Food Dance Café, a happy spot along I-94 between Detroit and Chicago. The use of cocoa powder and bittersweet chocolate gives the pudding its intensity. The incredibly smooth and surprisingly light texture comes from using milk (not cream), a bit of flour (not cornstarch), and eggs. This pudding may be why they invented the word "mmmmm."

serves 8

- 1 vanilla bean (see notes)
- 4 1/2 cups whole milk
- 1 cup sugar
- 1/3 cup unsweetened cocoa powder, sifted (see notes)
- 1/4 cup all-purpose flour
- 1/8 teaspoon fine sea salt
- 2 large eggs
- 4 large egg yolks
- 10 ounces bittersweet chocolate, broken into small pieces
- 4 tablespoons (1/2 stick) unsalted butter
- 1/2 cup cacao nibs, toasted (optional; see notes)

Split the vanilla bean lengthwise with a small, sharp knife. Combine 4 cups of the milk and 1/2 cup of the sugar in a medium saucepan. With the tip of the knife, scrape the seeds out of the bean and into the saucepan. Add the seedless pod, too. Heat over low heat, stirring. When the mixture starts to simmer, remove from the heat. Let stand for 10 minutes, then discard the bean.

Meanwhile, combine the remaining 1/2 cup sugar, the cocoa powder, flour, and salt in a medium bowl. Whisk in the remaining 1/2 cup milk until you have a smooth paste.

Whisk 1/4 cup of the warm vanilla-milk mixture into the cocoa paste until well blended. Return to the saucepan and whisk well to combine. Bring to a simmer over low heat and cook, stirring frequently, until fairly thick, about 5 minutes.

Meanwhile, whisk the eggs and yolks together in a small bowl until well blended. Very slowly whisk about a cup of the warm chocolate mixture into the eggs until combined and smooth. Slowly stir this mixture back into the saucepan, whisking constantly until it thickens, 3 to 5 minutes. Do not allow it to boil.

Remove from the heat and place the saucepan on a wooden cutting board or other stable, heatproof surface. Add the chocolate and butter and whisk until smooth.

Pour the pudding into eight custard cups or small bowls. Refrigerate for 2 to 3 hours, until the pudding is set. For added chocolate intensity and textural contrast, serve the pudding garnished with the cacao nibs, if you like.

notes from our test kitchen

- You can substitute 1 teaspoon pure vanilla extract for the vanilla bean.
- For the best pudding, use top-quality cocoa powder and chocolate, such as Scharffen Berger or Valrhona.
- *Dutch-processed,* or *dutched,* cocoa powder is typically darker in color than *natural* cocoa powder. Although the flavor is not necessarily richer, the color will be. You can use either here.
- Cacao nibs are the crunchy, intensely flavored, roasted nutmeats of cacao beans (from which all chocolate is made). If you like bitter chocolate with complex nuances, you might enjoy adding these. You can find them in specialty stores.

tip

We're also head over heels for an insanely simple and completely decadent mocha pudding that *Food & Wine* selected as one of its best recipes ever. The recipe comes from Jan Newberry, who says the original idea came from Ann Hodgman, who says she got it off a Nestlé's package. Combine 1/2 cup heavy cream and 2 teaspoons instant espresso powder in a small saucepan. Bring to a boil over high heat. Meanwhile, in a food processor, combine 6 ounces bittersweet chocolate (coarsely chopped) with 1/2 cup sugar. Pulse until the chocolate is very finely ground. Add 1 large egg (at room temperature), 1 teaspoon pure vanilla extract, and a pinch of salt. Pulse again to form a paste. With the machine on, add the hot cream in a steady stream and blend until smooth, about 1 minute. Transfer the pudding to small (6-ounce) ramekins and refrigerate for at least 1 hour or overnight. (If you're in a hurry, freeze for 20 minutes.) Garnish, if you like, with lightly sweetened whipped cream and chocolate curls. Serves 4.

SOURCE: *HMCo Cooks*

COOK: **Dorie Greenspan**

chunky peanut butter and oatmeal chocolate chipsters

WE FOUND THIS RECIPE in our publisher's cookbook newsletter, and it called to us. It won't appear in Dorie Greenspan's *Baking: From My Home to Yours* for a while yet, but once we tried it, we had to share it.

When we divvy up extra portions of desserts with friends, these cookies are always the first to go—everyone wants them, young and old alike. We also could make a case for their being healthy — they're full of old-fashioned oats, peanut butter, and newly good-for-you chocolate. But the fact is, they're just irresistibly tasty, so it's a good thing the recipe yields a lot. Bake these for bake sales, after-school snacks, long car trips, cookie swaps, or anytime you want to make people very happy.

makes about 60 cookies

- 3 cups old-fashioned rolled oats (not steel-cut Irish oats)
- 1 cup all-purpose flour
- 2 teaspoons ground cinnamon
- 1/4 teaspoon freshly grated nutmeg
- 1 teaspoon baking soda
- 1/4 teaspoon salt
- 1 cup (2 sticks) unsalted butter, at room temperature
- 1 cup peanut butter, chunky or smooth (Dorie prefers chunky)
- 1 cup packed light brown sugar
- 1 cup sugar
- 2 large eggs
- 1 teaspoon pure vanilla extract
- 1 1/2 cups chocolate chips or chunks

Adjust the racks to divide the oven into thirds and preheat to 350 degrees. Line two baking sheets with parchment paper, Silpat baking mats, or foil. In a large bowl, stir together the oats, flour, spices, baking soda, and salt just to blend.

With an electric mixer (preferably a stand mixer fitted with a paddle), beat the butter, peanut butter, brown sugar, and sugar on medium speed until smooth and creamy. Add the eggs, one at a time, and beat in the vanilla. Reduce the mixer speed to low and add the dry ingredients slowly, beating only until blended. Stir in the chocolate chips or chunks. (At this point, the dough can be covered and refrigerated for up to 1 day.)

If the dough is at room temperature, drop rounded tablespoonfuls 2 inches apart onto the prepared baking sheets. If the dough has been refrigerated, scoop it out by rounded teaspoonfuls and roll the balls between your palms. Place them 2 inches apart on the sheets. Press the balls gently with the heel of your hand until they are about 1/2 inch thick. Bake for 13 to 15 minutes, until the cookies are golden and just firm around the edges. Lift the cookies onto wire racks with a wide metal spatula—they'll firm as they cool. Repeat until all the dough has been used.

note from our test kitchen

- These cookies are definitely sweet. If you like a less sweet cookie, cut back the sugar a bit.

SOURCE: *Home Baking*
by Jeffrey Alford and Naomi Duguid

COOK: Martha's mother

martha's mother's cookies

THE CANADIAN COOKBOOK DUO Jeffrey Alford and Naomi Duguid are best known for traipsing all over the world in search of recipes, but here's a gem from close to home. These terrific little cookies come from the mother of a childhood neighbor named Martha. The thing that makes them special is their flaky, layered texture, which is achieved by a quick rolling and folding of the dough. They are surprisingly easy to make and not at all too sweet. Martha's mother's original version features orange or lemon zest, but Alford and Duguid prefer them with no extra flavoring. Your choice.

The cookies need to chill a bit before being rolled out, but that's all to the good. You can make the dough as much as 2 days ahead and have it ready to roll out when you want to bake them. Because they are so delicate, the cookies are especially good with fruit desserts or sorbet. But at Martha's mother's house, they were known simply as "the cookies"—the ones you make for any occasion.

makes about 30 cookies

- 1-inch strip orange or lemon zest (optional)
- 1 cup (2 sticks) unsalted butter, at room temperature
- 1 8-ounce package cream cheese, at room temperature
- Scant 2 cups all-purpose flour
- Pinch salt
- 1 large egg, separated
- 1/4 cup sugar, plus more if needed

If using the zest, heat a heavy skillet over medium heat. Add the zest and turn it over and over on the hot surface for several minutes to dry it out a little without browning or burning. Turn out onto a cutting board, mince, and set aside.

In a food processor, combine the butter, cream cheese, flour, salt, egg yolk, and zest (if using). Process until smooth. Transfer to a sturdy resealable plastic bag and flatten into a square about 6 inches across with the palms of your hands. Seal the bag and chill for 1 to 3 hours, or up to 2 days. (Refrigerate the reserved egg white in a sealed container until you are ready to bake the cookies.)

Turn the dough out onto a very lightly floured surface. Rolling from the center outward, and without rolling over the edges of the dough, roll out to a rectangle measuring about 8 x 12 inches. Fold into thirds, like a business letter. Lightly dust the rolling pin with flour and roll the dough out again, to about 8 x 16 inches. Again fold into thirds, using a dough scraper, if necessary, to detach the dough from the work surface. Repeat rolling out and folding one more time, then roll out to about 10 x 16 or 17 inches. Refrigerate the dough for 1/2 hour.

Adjust two racks just above and below the middle and preheat the oven to 350 degrees. Line two baking sheets with parchment paper or wax paper. Place the egg white in a wide bowl and beat with a fork until frothy. Place the sugar in a shallow bowl. Remove the dough from the refrigerator and, leaving it on the baking sheet, cut out 2-inch (or 2 1/2-inch) round cookies using a cookie cutter or a fine-rimmed glass—you want a good clean cut (see notes). Brush the rounds with the egg white. Place each round face-down in the sugar, then transfer to a prepared baking sheet, sugar side up. Leave 1/4 inch between cookies.

Bake until shiny and risen, 18 to 20 minutes. After the first 10 minutes, rotate the sheets to ensure even baking. After the cookies come out of the oven, wait about 2 minutes, then use a spatula to transfer them gently to fine-meshed wire racks to cool. (The dough scraps can be pulled together, rolled out, and cut into squares. Brush them with egg white, dip in sugar, and bake as above.)

notes from our test kitchen

- If you roll out the cookies on a baking mat, you'll hardly have to flour the dough at all. You can also bake the cookies on the mat instead of parchment paper.
- Alford and Duguid note that you can cut squares instead of rounds, which avoids the problem of extra dough scraps. It's also easier. Using a pizza wheel or a sharp knife, cut the dough into squares, brush the whole sheet of cut dough with the egg white, and sprinkle sugar generously on top. Use a spatula to transfer the squares to the baking sheets, leaving 1/4 inch between them. Bake as directed.

SOURCE: *Dallas Morning News*

COOK: Coretta Williams

coffee-walnut pinwheels

THIS RECIPE, FROM CORETTA WILLIAMS of Mesquite, Texas, took home first prize at the annual *Dallas Morning News* Holiday Cookie Contest, and we concur with the judges 100 percent—except we don't wait until the holidays to make these cookies. The delicate filling has an enchanting flavor that combines caramelized sugar, toasted walnuts, and rich coffee. The dough, a tender, unsweetened cream cheese pastry, strikes a perfect balance with the candylike filling. As you might guess, these pinwheels are wonderful served with mugs of strong coffee, but we also like them after dinner with a wee glass of brandy. They work at midnight, too, with a glass of cold milk.

makes 24 cookies

- 1 cup (2 sticks) butter, at room temperature
- 1 8-ounce package cream cheese, at room temperature
- 2 cups all-purpose flour
- 2 cups finely chopped walnuts (see notes)
- 1 cup sugar
- 1/4 cup strong brewed coffee, cooled, plus more if needed

Cream the butter and cream cheese together in a large mixing bowl. Gradually add the flour and mix until a smooth dough forms. Shape into a ball, cover, and refrigerate overnight.

Stir together the walnuts and sugar in a medium bowl. Gradually add the coffee until the mixture is lightly moistened; set aside.

On a lightly floured surface, roll the dough out into a long rectangle 1/4 inch thick. Sprinkle the walnut mixture over the dough to within 1 inch of the edge. Carefully roll up the dough, jellyroll style, starting at the long edge of the rectangle. Pinch the edges to seal. Wrap the roll in plastic and refrigerate for 1 to 4 hours.

Adjust the rack to the middle and preheat the oven to 350 degrees. Using unflavored dental floss, slice the dough into 1/2-inch-thick rounds. Bake on an ungreased baking sheet until just barely golden, 23 to 27 minutes. Let cool on a wire rack.

notes from our test kitchen

- If you use unsalted butter, add a pinch of salt to the dough.
- The walnuts should be very finely chopped, not ground. We find it easiest to drop them into a food processor along with the sugar and process just until they are finely chopped. The sugar prevents the nuts from turning into a paste in the processor.
- Be sure to roll the dough into a rectangle longer than it is wide. This ensures that the pinwheels won't be too large.
- The coffee-walnut filling caramelizes as the cookies bake and can stick to the baking sheet. Lining the baking sheet with parchment paper or a Silpat baking mat will help with cleanup.
- Don't worry if some of the filling oozes out as the cookies bake. It will harden as it cools, adding a delicious candy-crunch to the cookies.
- The pinwheels are best eaten the day they are made, but they can be stored for a few days in a tightly covered container.

SOURCE: *Prevention*

COOK: **Julie Van Rosendaal**

linzer cookies

WE'RE TOUGH CRITICS when it comes to low-fat recipes. But occasionally we find one that's all about flavor, and these cookies are exactly that.

Crisper and lighter than a traditional linzer cookie, they delight everyone we serve them to — and they are among the first to fly off the cookie plate. Instead of being made with a dough of ground nuts, they are topped with a little halo of sliced almonds and confectioners' sugar. They have some nutty crunch but are not at all heavy or oily. In fact, the one drawback might be that they are so tasty, it's hard to stop at one . . . or two.

makes about 2 dozen cookies

- 4 tablespoons (1/2 stick) unsalted butter
- 1 tablespoon vegetable oil
- 3/4 cup sugar
- Grated zest of 1 lemon
- 1 large egg
- 1 teaspoon pure vanilla extract
- 1 2/3 cups all-purpose flour (see notes)
- 1 teaspoon baking powder
- 1/4 teaspoon salt
- Vegetable cooking spray
- 1/4 cup sliced almonds
- 1/3 cup raspberry jam (see notes)
- Confectioners' sugar

Beat the butter, oil, sugar, and lemon zest until light in a stand mixer or in a medium bowl with a hand-held electric mixer. Beat in the egg and vanilla until smooth.

In another medium bowl, combine the flour, baking powder, and salt. Add the flour mixture to the butter mixture and stir by hand just until the dough is soft. Divide the dough in half and shape each half into a disk. Wrap in plastic and refrigerate for about 1 hour, until well chilled (see notes).

Adjust the rack to the middle and preheat the oven to 350 degrees. Butter a baking sheet or spray with vegetable cooking spray. On a lightly floured surface, roll out 1 disk 1/4 inch thick. Using a 1 1/2- to 2-inch cookie cutter or glass, cut out the cookies. Using a 1/2-inch round or shaped cutter, cut centers out of half the cookies.

Place the cookies 2 to 3 inches apart on the baking sheet. Sprinkle the cut-out cookies with the almonds, pressing gently to help them adhere (see notes).

Bake for 10 to 12 minutes, until light golden around the edges. Let cool on a wire rack. Spread the solid cookies with jam and sprinkle the cut-out cookies lightly with confectioners' sugar. Top each jam-covered cookie with a cut-out cookie.

notes from our test kitchen

- Measure the flour carefully for this recipe. Any extra can make the dough too crumbly to handle.
- Seedless raspberry jam spreads more easily than jam with seeds.
- It's best not to chill the dough for more than an hour. Doing so can make it difficult to roll out.
- Brushing the cut-out cookies with beaten egg white before pressing on the almonds helps ensure that they will adhere.
- These cookies are not good keepers; that's partly because they're so lean. They do, however, freeze well. Just wait to fill and assemble them until after they've thawed to room temperature.

SOURCE: *El Mundo de Frontera* (Frontera Grill newsletter)

COOK: Rick Bayless

chocolate pecan pie bars

EVERYONE SEEMED TO BE PUTTING bittersweet chocolate in pecan pie this year, but Rick Bayless, the chef-owner of the Frontera Grill and Topolobampo in Chicago, goes one step further: he turns the pie into bars and skips the pastry. These have all the joy of pecan pie without the overwhelming gooeyness. And they're also especially easy on the cook, because you make the entire recipe in the food processor.

Bayless uses Mexican chocolate—a robust, semisweet chocolate often flavored with cinnamon, almonds, and vanilla. Don't worry if you can't find it; just substitute regular semisweet chocolate and add a pinch of cinnamon.

makes 24 bars

- 2 1/2 cups (about 10 ounces) pecan halves
- 1 cup finely chopped Mexican chocolate, such as the widely available Ibarra brand (about 6 ounces), or see above
- 6 ounces (6–8 slices) fresh white bread, preferably cakey sandwich bread, such as Pepperidge Farm, broken into large pieces
- 1 cup (2 sticks) butter, melted, plus more for the pan
- Generous 3/4 teaspoon salt
- 5 ounces semisweet or bittersweet chocolate, chopped into pieces not larger than 1/4 inch
- 3 tablespoons all-purpose flour
- 4 large eggs
- 1 cup packed dark brown sugar
- 1 cup corn syrup, preferably dark, or a mixture of corn syrup and molasses, sorghum, Steen's cane syrup, or most any of the other rich-flavored syrups that are on the market
- 2 teaspoons pure vanilla extract
- Confectioners' sugar for dusting

Adjust the rack to the middle and preheat the oven to 325 degrees. Spread the pecans on a baking sheet and bake until richly browned and toasty-smelling, about 10 minutes. Let cool, then scoop into the food processor and coarsely chop by pulsing. Remove about 1 1/2 cups of the nuts and put in a large bowl to use in the filling. Add half of the Mexican chocolate to the food processor and pulse to mix. Add the bread slices and process to achieve fairly fine crumbs. Add 1/3 cup of the melted butter and 1/4 teaspoon of the salt. Process just to moisten everything. Liberally butter a 9-x-13-inch baking pan, then evenly pat in the crumb mixture. Refrigerate while you make the filling.

Add the remaining Mexican chocolate, the semisweet or bittersweet chocolate, and the flour to the bowl with the pecans. In the food processor (don't bother cleaning it), mix the eggs and brown sugar until well combined. Add the syrup and pulse a couple of times. Add the remaining 2/3 cup melted butter, the remaining 1/2 teaspoon salt, and the vanilla. Process to combine thoroughly, then pour over the pecan mixture. Stir well and scrape everything into the crumb crust.

Bake for 40 to 50 minutes, until the bars have pulled away slightly from the sides of the pan. Let cool to room temperature before cutting into 2-inch squares and dusting with confectioners' sugar.

note from our test kitchen

Bayless suggests lining the pan with a carefully flattened piece of heavy-duty foil to help lift the bars out (let it extend over two sides of the pan). Chilling the bars will make them easier to cut. We recommend doing both.

SOURCE: *Saveur*

COOK: **Monica Sharpe**

apricot and oat squares

THERE'S NOT MUCH TO THIS RECIPE, but one small bite was all it took for us to realize that simple can translate into memorable. The recipe comes from a cheerful little café in a small town south of Queenstown, New Zealand. Run by brother and sister Toby and Monica Sharpe, the Glenorchy Café specializes in home-baked goodies, and these old-fashioned treats are one of their bestsellers.

With a generous layer of softened apricots sandwiched between two crunchy layers of brown sugar–sweetened, butter-enriched oats, these squares are rich and filling.

makes 12 large squares

- 2 cups (12–14 ounces) dried apricots, coarsely chopped
- 2 cups (4 sticks) unsalted butter, at room temperature
- 4 cups all-purpose flour
- 3 1/2 cups old-fashioned or quick-cooking (not instant) rolled oats
- 2 cups packed light brown sugar
- 4 teaspoons baking soda
- 1/2 teaspoon salt

Adjust the rack to the middle and preheat the oven to 350 degrees. Put the apricots in a medium saucepan and cover with water. Bring to a boil over medium-high heat. Remove from the heat and set aside until the apricots are swollen and soft, about 5 minutes. Drain well and set aside. Grease a 9-x-13-inch pan with 1 teaspoon of the butter.

Mix the flour, oats, brown sugar, baking soda, and salt together in a large bowl. Using a pastry cutter or two table knives, cut the remaining butter into the flour mixture until it resembles coarse meal. Using your hands, press half of the flour mixture into the prepared pan in an even layer. Scatter the apricots in an even layer on top, then scatter the remaining flour mixture evenly over the apricots.

Bake until golden brown, about 50 minutes. Let cool on a wire rack. Using a sharp knife, cut into 12 squares (see notes).

notes from our test kitchen

- Be sure to let cool completely before cutting into squares. The bars will be crumbly, but they should hold together just fine. The crumbs are the cook's treat.
- We like to cut these into smaller squares, in which case the recipe makes closer to 24.
- These keep well, sealed in a cookie tin.

SOURCE: *Cooking from the Heart* by Michael J. Rosen
COOK: Deborah Madison after her grandmother

deborah madison's grandmother's raisin squares

ONCE EVERY WINTER, WHEN DEBORAH MADISON was growing up in California, a large box packed with layers of these little confections would arrive from her grandmother back East. Because of their sturdy, moist filling, they survived the cross-country voyage intact and tasted fresh even after days in the mail.

With two layers of pureed raisins and walnuts sandwiched between three thin layers of pastry, these squares aren't fancy or showy, but they sure are good. Serve them in the afternoon with tea (Madison says Earl Grey is especially nice) or a little glass of sherry. Or pack them up and ship them to a lucky friend.

makes 24 squares

FILLING

- 1 pound raisins, rinsed
- Grated zest and juice of 1 lemon
- 3–4 tablespoons sugar (optional)
- 1 cup boiling water
- 1 tablespoon all-purpose flour
- 1 cup finely chopped walnuts

DOUGH

- 8 tablespoons (1 stick) unsalted butter, at room temperature, plus more for the pan
- 1/2 cup plus 1 tablespoon sugar
- 2 large eggs, at room temperature
- 1 teaspoon pure vanilla extract
- 2 cups unbleached all-purpose flour
- 1 teaspoon baking powder
- 1/4 teaspoon salt
- 3 tablespoons sour cream
- 2 teaspoons ground cinnamon

MAKE THE FILLING:

Place the raisins, lemon zest, and sugar (if using) in a food processor. Start the machine, add the boiling water, and process to a coarse puree. Scrape into a small saucepan and add the lemon juice, flour, and walnuts. Cook over medium heat, stirring, until thick, about 5 minutes. Set aside to cool.

MAKE THE DOUGH:

Using an electric mixer (preferably a stand mixer fitted with the paddle), cream together the butter and 1/2 cup of the sugar until light and fluffy.

Crack 1 of the eggs into a small bowl, measure out 1 tablespoon of the egg white, and reserve for a glaze. Add what remains of the egg, the second whole egg, and the vanilla to the butter mixture and beat to combine.

Sift together the flour, baking powder, and salt in a small bowl. Set the mixer on low speed and gradually add the dry mixture to the butter mixture, alternating with the sour cream. The dough may become stiff and rather difficult to work. Remove it from the mixer and finish incorporating the dry mixture by hand until the dough is smooth. Place the dough in a resealable plastic bag and press into a thin rectangle. Refrigerate until firm.

Adjust the rack to the middle and preheat the oven to 350 degrees. Lightly butter a 9-x-13-inch baking pan.

Divide the cold dough into 3 equal pieces. Roll out the first piece into a 9-x-13-inch rectangle and place it in the prepared pan. Trim the dough, if necessary. Spread half of the cooled filling over the dough. Repeat the process for a second layer.

Roll out the third piece of dough and lay it neatly on top, brushing it with the reserved egg white. Combine the remaining 1 tablespoon sugar and the cinnamon and sprinkle over the top.

Bake for about 40 minutes, until the top is crisp and lightly browned. Let cool completely and cut into 24 squares. Store in a cookie tin, layered with wax paper.

notes from our test kitchen

- When rolling out the pastry, it may look as though you don't have enough to reach all the way to the edges of the pan. You will. The pastry layers are meant to be very thin and delicate.
- The top of the pastry will brown only lightly around the edges. Don't wait for it to become golden all over, or you'll risk overcooking the squares.

SOURCE: *Holiday Pumpkins*
by Georgeanne Brennan and Jennifer Barry

COOK: Georgeanne Brennan

pumpkin bars with lemon glaze

FILLED WITH DATES, walnuts, and warm spices and spread with a sweet-tart lemon glaze, these bars make a fine addition to any holiday cookie tray. They aren't thick and cakey like some bars, but elegantly thin and nicely chewy. The pumpkin puree makes them wonderfully moist and sweet without being cloying. These bars are good keepers, too, so we often wrap them in tins for friends and neighbors.

makes about 30 bars

BARS

- 1 cup canola or other light vegetable oil, plus more for the pan
- 1 large egg
- 1 cup sugar
- 1⅓ cups (8 ounces) pitted dates, finely chopped
- 1¾ cups all-purpose flour
- 1 teaspoon baking soda
- 1 teaspoon salt
- 1 teaspoon ground cinnamon
- 1 teaspoon ground cloves
- 1 cup homemade or canned pumpkin puree
- 1 cup chopped walnuts (4 ounces)

GLAZE

- 1 cup confectioners' sugar, sifted, plus more if needed
- 2 tablespoons fresh lemon juice

MAKE THE BARS:

Adjust the rack to the middle and preheat the oven to 350 degrees. Grease a 10-x-15-inch jellyroll pan. In a medium bowl, lightly beat the egg. Stir in the sugar, oil, and dates. In a large bowl, stir together the flour, baking soda, salt, and spices. Add one third of the egg mixture and the pumpkin puree alternately to the flour mixture, stirring well after each addition. Stir in the nuts.

Pour the batter into the prepared pan and spread it evenly with a spatula. Bake until well browned and a toothpick inserted in the center comes out clean, about 25 minutes. Transfer the pan to a wire rack and let cool for about 5 minutes.

MAKE THE GLAZE:

In a small bowl, mix the confectioners' sugar and lemon juice. If the glaze seems too thin, add a little more sugar.

Spread the glaze over the uncut bars. Let stand for 5 minutes, then cut into bars about 1½ x 3 inches.

note from our test kitchen

- If you don't have a 10-x-15-inch jellyroll pan, use a 9-x-13-inch baking dish. The bars will be thicker and take a little longer to bake. Cut them into smaller bars, about 1½ x 2 inches.

SOURCE: *Bon Appétit*

COOK: Elinor Klivans

lemon ripple cheesecake bars

FOR ELINOR KLIVANS, the author of several popular baking books, it all started with cheesecake. In her first pastry job, she was appointed "cheesecake specialist," and this recipe shows that she definitely knows a thing or two about it. Light, fluffy, and not quite as dense as most cheesecakes, these cheesecake bars are real winners. With fresh lemon juice and zest swirled into the filling and zest in the buttery crust, they have a bright lemony flavor that balances the sweetness. We also love how pretty they are with all those swirls of lemon curd.

makes 16 bars

CRUST

- 8 tablespoons (1 stick) unsalted butter, cut into 1/2-inch pieces and chilled, plus more for the pan
- 1 cup all-purpose flour
- 1/4 cup sugar
- 1 teaspoon finely grated lemon zest
- 1/8 teaspoon salt

FILLING

- 1 tablespoon plus 2 teaspoons cornstarch
- 1/2 cup cold water
- 2 large egg yolks
- 1 3/4 cups sugar
- 1/4 cup fresh lemon juice
- 1 teaspoon finely grated lemon zest
- 1 1/4 pounds cream cheese, at room temperature
- 2 tablespoons all-purpose flour
- 3 large eggs, at room temperature
- 1/4 cup sour cream
- 1 teaspoon pure vanilla extract

MAKE THE CRUST:

Adjust the rack to the middle and preheat the oven to 325 degrees. Butter a 9-inch square nonstick baking pan. In a food processor, pulse the flour, sugar, lemon zest, and salt. Add the butter and pulse until a soft, crumbly dough forms. Press the dough evenly over the bottom and a scant 1/2 inch up the sides of the pan. Bake for about 20 minutes, until golden and firm.

MEANWHILE, MAKE THE FILLING:

In a small bowl, dissolve the cornstarch in the water. In a medium saucepan, whisk the yolks with ¾ cup of the sugar and the lemon juice. Whisk in the cornstarch mixture and cook over medium heat, whisking gently, until the sugar dissolves and the mixture is hot, about 4 minutes. Boil over medium-high heat for 1 minute, whisking constantly, until the mixture is thick and glossy. Strain the mixture into a heatproof bowl. Stir in the lemon zest and let cool.

In a large bowl, using an electric mixer, beat the cream cheese with the remaining 1 cup sugar until smooth. Beat in the flour until blended. Add the eggs, one at a time, beating well between additions. Add the sour cream and vanilla and beat until the batter is smooth. Pour the cream cheese batter over the crust and smooth the surface with a spatula. Place the lemon mixture in dollops on the cheesecake batter and carefully swirl it into the batter using the tip of a knife or a skewer; take care not to cut into the crust.

Bake for about 40 minutes, until golden around the edges and just set. Run the tip of a knife around the edges to loosen the cheesecake from the sides of the pan. Let cool on a wire rack for 1 hour, then refrigerate until thoroughly chilled. Cut into 16 bars and serve.

notes from our test kitchen

- When it comes to cutting the cheesecake into bars, the colder the better. If the cheesecake begins to soften, it's a mess to cut.
- The cheesecake can be refrigerated in the pan for up to 3 days. Wait to cut it into bars until you're ready to serve them—or to pack them up to take on a picnic.

SOURCE: *An Embarrassment of Mangoes* by Ann Vanderhoof

COOK: Ann Vanderhoof

spicy island gingerbread

IN HER CHARMING ACCOUNT of a year spent cruising the Caribbean and sharing the lives of the locals she and her husband encountered, Ann Vanderhoof includes a number of recipes she picked up along the way (as well as a few beloved specialties from the Carolina Lowcountry). If you're used to the usual gingerbread, the kind based on pumpkin pie spices, this West Indian version will knock your socks off. There are four kinds of ginger here to kick it up—fresh, ground, crystallized, and even ginger beer. The cake is dense and moist, almost sticky in the English style, though not terribly sweet. The dark rum and sweet spices give it complexity. We had to hustle it out of the house shortly after we made it because we simply couldn't stop eating it.

makes about 20 squares, serves 10

- 8 tablespoons (1 stick) butter, plus more for the pan
- 3/4 cup unsulfured blackstrap molasses (see notes)
- 3/4 cup packed dark brown sugar
- 1/2 cup ginger beer
- 2 tablespoons grated fresh ginger
- 2 tablespoons chopped crystallized ginger
- 2 cups all-purpose flour
- 2 teaspoons baking powder
- 1 teaspoon baking soda
- 1 teaspoon ground ginger
- 1/2 teaspoon freshly grated nutmeg
- 1/2 teaspoon salt
- 3 large eggs, beaten
- 2 tablespoons dark rum

Adjust the rack to the middle and preheat the oven to 350 degrees. Butter a 9-inch square baking pan and cover the bottom with parchment paper. Combine the molasses, sugar, butter, ginger beer, fresh ginger, and crystallized ginger in a large saucepan. Stir over low heat until the butter melts, then set aside to cool.

Combine the flour, baking powder, baking soda, spices, and salt in a medium bowl. Stir the eggs and rum into the cooled molasses mixture, then stir in the flour mixture. Mix well.

Pour the batter into the prepared pan and bake for 30 to 40 minutes, until a toothpick inserted in the center comes out clean. Transfer to a wire rack. Cut into squares and serve warm or at room temperature.

notes from our test kitchen

- We find the flavor of blackstrap molasses a bit overwhelming, so we use regular golden molasses from the supermarket with excellent results.
- If you don't have parchment paper, cover the bottom of the pan with a square of wax paper.

SOURCE: *The Arrows Cookbook*
by Clark Frasier and Mark Gaier

COOKS: Clark Frasier and Mark Gaier

super-moist apple cake

THE ARROWS, located in the rather posh tourist town of Ogunquit, Maine, is one of those rare restaurants that manages to combine sophistication with honest, inspired food. That spirit springs from the owners' dedication to growing and harvesting: on the land surrounding the restaurant, they raise 90 percent of the herbs, vegetables, and fruits they serve—no mean feat in a rough, northern coastal climate.

This simple apple cake is traditional but not stodgy, unassuming but overwhelmingly delicious. What makes it so moist and tender is the heavy cream poured over the batter before it goes into the oven. It makes a great coffee cake, and we love a warm slice for dessert with a scoop of vanilla ice cream.

Make this in the fall using local apples. Frasier and Gaier suggest a mix of McIntosh and Cortland for flavor and taste, but any crisp, juicy apples will do.

makes one 10-inch cake; serves 10

- 12 tablespoons (1 1/2 sticks) unsalted butter, at room temperature, plus more for the pan
- 2 cups sugar
- 3 large eggs
- 1 cup plus 1 tablespoon cake flour
- 1 cup plus 1 tablespoon all-purpose flour
- 2 teaspoons baking powder
- Pinch kosher salt
- 3/4 cup whole milk
- 3/4 teaspoon pure vanilla extract
- 3 medium baking apples, peeled, cored, halved, and thinly sliced
- 3/4 cup heavy cream
- 1 1/2 teaspoons ground cinnamon

Adjust the rack to the middle and preheat the oven to 350 degrees. Butter a 10-inch-round, 2-inch-deep cake pan and line the bottom with parchment paper. With an electric mixer (preferably a stand mixer fitted with the paddle), beat 1 1/2 cups of the sugar and the butter for 3 to 5 minutes until light in color. Scrape the bowl as needed with a rubber spatula and continue to beat until very light in texture and color, several minutes more. Beat in the eggs, one at a time, scraping down the bowl between additions.

Sift together the flours, baking powder, and salt in a bowl. Gently mix the milk and the dry ingredients alternately into the sugar mixture, stopping to scrape the bowl as necessary. Add the vanilla and mix just until smooth; do not overbeat.

Pour the batter into the prepared pan and spread it evenly with a rubber spatula. Overlap the apple slices in concentric circles on top of the batter to cover it completely. Pour the cream evenly over the apples.

Stir together the remaining 1/2 cup sugar and the cinnamon and sprinkle the mixture over the top. Bake for about 45 minutes, until a toothpick inserted in the center comes out clean. Remove the pan from the oven, transfer to a wire rack, and let cool for about 15 minutes.

Invert the cake onto the rack, remove the parchment paper, and invert again, apple side up, onto a serving plate. Serve warm or at room temperature. Once cool, the cake can be stored, tightly covered, in the refrigerator for up to 3 days.

SOURCE: *Fine Cooking*

COOK: Gale Gand

chocolate pavlova with tangerine whipped cream

PAVLOVA, A CLOUDLIKE MERINGUE CAKE filled with whipped cream and fresh fruit, was one of the many lost-and-found recipes we came across this year. And as with any resurrected classic, pavlova comes in many shapes and flavors. Of all the versions we found, we were most taken by Gale Gand's. Her chocolate meringue doesn't rise as high as a plain meringue because of the cocoa powder, but it comes out of the oven with light, crackly sides and a soft, marshmallowy, almost brownie-like center. It's the perfect base for a pillow of tangerine-scented whipped cream and a mix of fresh fruit. The recipe calls for berries, mangoes, and kiwifruit, but feel free to use whatever looks good to you. You can also toy with changing the flavor of the whipped cream to match the fruit you find.

If you've never made pavlova and are intimidated by the meringue, don't be. It's surprisingly simple—as long as you have an electric mixer—and foolproof. You'll be amazed at how little effort this impressive dessert requires.

serves 8 to 10

- 4 large egg whites, at room temperature
- 1/8 teaspoon cream of tartar
- 1/8 teaspoon fine-grain salt
- 1 cup plus 2 tablespoons sugar
- 1 1/2 teaspoons cornstarch
- 1 tablespoon red wine vinegar
- 1/4 cup unsweetened Dutch-processed cocoa powder, sifted
- 1 cup heavy cream
- Finely grated zest of 1 tangerine (about 1 1/4 teaspoons)
- 1 1/2 cups fresh fruit, such as raspberries, sliced strawberries, or peeled and sliced mango, or a mixture
- 3 kiwifruit, peeled and sliced into half-moons

Adjust the rack to the middle and preheat the oven to 350 degrees. Cut a piece of parchment paper so that it fits flat on a baking sheet. With a pencil, draw a 9-inch circle in the center of the parchment (tracing a 9-inch cake pan works fine). Place the parchment pencil side down (you should still be able to see the circle) on the baking sheet.

With a hand-held electric mixer or a stand mixer (use the whisk attachment), whip the egg whites, cream of tartar, and salt in a large, dry bowl on medium speed until foamy, about 30 seconds. Gradually add 1 cup of the sugar and then the cornstarch and vinegar. Whip on medium-high speed until the whites hold stiff peaks and look glossy, 3 to 5 minutes.

Add the cocoa powder and mix on low speed until mostly combined, 20 to 30 seconds, scraping the bowl as needed. Finish mixing the cocoa into the meringue by hand with a rubber spatula until well combined and no streaks of white remain.

Pile the meringue inside the circle on the parchment. Using the spatula, spread the meringue to even it out slightly—it doesn't need to align perfectly with the circle, and it shouldn't be perfectly smooth or overworked. Natural swirls and ridges give it character.

Bake for 10 minutes, then reduce the heat to 300 degrees and bake until the meringue puffs and cracks around the edge, 45 to 50 minutes. Turn off the oven, prop the oven door open, and leave the meringue inside to cool to room temperature, at least 30 minutes. (The meringue won't collapse as much if it cools gradually.)

Just before serving, put the meringue on a serving plate. In a chilled, medium stainless-steel bowl, beat the cream with the remaining 2 tablespoons sugar until it holds soft peaks. Whip in the tangerine zest, making sure it's evenly distributed. Pile the whipped cream on the meringue, spreading it almost out to the edge, and top with the fruit. Slice into wedges with a serrated knife and serve.

note from our test kitchen

Once baked, the meringue can be kept for a day at room temperature if you live in a dry climate. If the humidity is high, it's best served soon after cooling.

five-spice angel food cake with maple glaze

CHINESE FIVE-SPICE POWDER SHOWED UP in all sorts of unexpected places this year, but this was without a doubt the most unusual—and perhaps the best. Five-spice powder is made of a few common baking spices—cinnamon, cloves, and even fennel. But it's the other things—star anise and Sichuan pepper—that give it its exotic and distinctive flavor.

In creating this cake, Roy Finamore, an innovative and talented cookbook author and editor, uses only enough of the spice powder to give the delicate cake a subtle, haunting perfume. And that's exactly why it works so well. In addition, the powder turns the cake a lovely shade of pale.

makes one 10-inch cake; serves 10 to 12

CAKE

- 1 cup cake flour
- 1 1/2 cups superfine sugar
- 1 teaspoon Chinese five-spice powder
- Freshly grated nutmeg
- 1 1/2 cups egg whites (11–12 large eggs), at room temperature
- 1 1/2 teaspoons cream of tarter
- 1/4 teaspoon salt
- 1/2 teaspoon pure vanilla extract

GLAZE

- 1 cup confectioners' sugar
- Pinch salt
- 1/3 cup pure maple syrup
- 1 teaspoon pure vanilla extract

MAKE THE CAKE:

Adjust the rack to the middle and preheat the oven to 350 degrees. In a medium bowl, sift the flour together with 1/2 cup of the sugar, the five-spice powder, and a few gratings of nutmeg 4 times to aerate.

Beat the egg whites in a large bowl with an electric mixer on medium-low speed until frothy. Add the cream of tartar and salt and beat on medium-high speed until soft peaks form. While beating, add the remaining 1 cup sugar gradually, in a slow, steady stream. Once all the sugar has been added, turn the mixer to the highest setting and beat until the whites are glossy and form stiff peaks. Whisk in the vanilla.

Sift half of the flour mixture over the whites and fold in gently. Sift the rest of the flour on top and fold in gently but thoroughly. Spoon the batter into an ungreased 10-inch tube pan and jiggle the pan just to settle the batter. Smooth the top. Bake for 30 to 35 minutes, until the top is lightly browned.

Invert the pan (onto a bottle if your pan doesn't have legs) and let cool completely. Run a knife around the edge of the pan and along the tube and pull the insert out, if the pan has one. Carefully release the cake from the bottom and slide it off. Set the cake bottom side up on a cake plate or pedestal stand.

MAKE THE GLAZE:

Combine the confectioners' sugar and salt in a medium bowl. Add the maple syrup and vanilla and beat with a fork until smooth. Spoon on top of the cake and spread just to the edge with a knife or small offset spatula. If the glaze hasn't started to drip down the sides on its own, nudge it to do so in a few places with the knife. Cut the cake into wedges using a serrated knife and a sawing motion (a standard knife will flatten the cake) and serve.

note from our test kitchen

As with all spices, five-spice powder fades over time. If your jar is more than six months old, it's time to get a fresh one.

SOURCE: *Bittersweet* by Alice Medrich

COOK: Alice Medrich

tiger cake

WE'LL ADMIT that it was the photograph that first caught our attention—a perfect chocolate marble pound cake with a moist crumb and golden crust. When we turned to the recipe and found it was made with extra-virgin olive oil and a pinch of white pepper, well, we knew we had to try it. The oil gives the cake its tenderness, and its flavor is perceptible only as a gentle fruity sweetness. As for the pepper, you won't know it's there, but Alice Medrich, the queen of chocolate, explains that it accentuates the cake's flavor. She also tells us that this cake is the favorite of a five-year-old boy, who named it for its stripes.

Make the cake in a tube pan, bundt pan, or two loaf pans. Let it cool completely before cutting. In fact, it's even better the next day.

serves 12

- Oil for the pan
- 3 cups all-purpose flour, plus more for the pan
- 2 1/2 cups sugar
- 1/2 cup natural cocoa powder (not Dutch-processed; see notes)
- 1/3 cup water
- 2 teaspoons baking powder
- 1/4 teaspoon salt
- 1 cup extra-virgin olive oil
- 1 teaspoon pure vanilla extract
- 1/2 teaspoon ground white pepper
- 5 cold large eggs
- 1 cup cold milk

Adjust the rack to the lower third and preheat the oven to 350 degrees. Oil and flour a tube or bundt pan or line two loaf pans with parchment paper. Whisk 1/2 cup of the sugar, the cocoa, and the water together in a small bowl until well blended. (Use a sturdy whisk, as the mixture tends to be rather thick.) Set aside.

In another bowl, mix the flour, baking powder, and salt thoroughly and sift together onto a piece of wax paper. Set aside.

In the bowl of a stand mixer (with the whisk attachment if you have it) or in a large bowl with a hand-held electric mixer, beat the remaining 2 cups sugar, oil, vanilla, and white pepper until well blended. Add the eggs, one at a time, beating well after each addition. Continue to beat until the mixture is thick and pale, 3 to 5 minutes. Stop the mixer and add one third of the flour mixture. Beat on low speed just until blended. Stop the mixer again and add half of the milk. Beat just until blended. Repeat with another third of the flour, the remaining milk, and then the remaining flour.

Pour 3 cups of the batter into another bowl (a large 1-quart measuring cup works as long as it's not too tall and narrow). Stir in the cocoa mixture. Pour one third of the plain batter into the prepared tube pan (or divide it between the loaf pans) and top with one third of the chocolate batter. Repeat with the remaining batters. Don't worry about marbling the batters—that happens magically during baking.

Bake until a cake tester comes out clean, about 1 hour and 10 minutes for either the tube pan or the loaf pans. Let the cake cool in the pan(s) on a wire rack for about 15 minutes. Slide a skewer around the tube pan or a thin knife around the loaf pans to release the cake(s). Invert the cake(s), peel off the parchment paper (if using), then invert again. Let cool completely, right side up, on the rack before serving.

notes from our test kitchen

- Medrich explains that natural cocoa powder is a must here. Dutch-processed cocoa will react badly with the oil and the leavening.
- Try toasting slices of this cake the second day for breakfast or afternoon tea.
- This cake keeps well, tightly wrapped in plastic, for a day or two.

SOURCE: *Bon Appétit*
COOK: Cindy Mushet

mango and lime chiffon cake

THIS YEAR WE SAW A RENAISSANCE OF LAYER CAKES—the fancy, towering, fluffy, quintessentially American confections that signify a special occasion. What enthralled us about this trend was the way innovative bakers like Cindy Mushet took the classic form and gave it a modern twist—as she does here by building a cake around the fresh, tropical flavors of lime, ginger, and mango.

This tender, golden chiffon cake is flavored with a hint of mango essence and lime zest. Then the layers are filled with a creamy lime-ginger curd and topped with a puff of mango-flavored whipped cream. And to complete this glorious creation, slices of fresh mango are fanned out on the whipped cream.

There are a few steps involved in making a chiffon layer cake. Fortunately, they can be spread out over time.

Makes one 9-inch layer cake; serves 10 to 12

LIME-GINGER CURD

- 1 cup sugar
- 3/4 fresh lime juice
- 4 large egg yolks
- 3 large eggs
- 1 tablespoon grated fresh ginger
- 6 tablespoons (3/4 stick) cold unsalted butter, cut into 1/2-inch cubes

CAKE

- 1 11.5-ounce can mango nectar (about 1 1/2 cups; see notes)
- 1 1/4 cups sifted cake flour (sifted, then measured)
- 12 tablespoons sugar
- 1 1/2 teaspoons baking powder
- 1/2 teaspoon salt
- 3 large egg yolks
- 1/4 cup canola oil
- 2 1/2 tablespoons grated lime zest
- 4 large egg whites

GLAZE AND TOPPING

- 1/4 cup sugar
- 1 tablespoon fresh lime juice
- 3/4 cup cold whipping cream
- 2 large firm ripe mangoes, peeled, pitted, and cut into 1/4-inch-thick slices (see notes)

MAKE THE LIME-GINGER CURD:

Whisk the sugar, lime juice, egg yolks, eggs, and ginger in a large metal bowl to blend. Set the bowl over a saucepan of simmering water (do not allow the bottom of the bowl to touch the water). Whisk constantly until the mixture thickens enough to coat a spoon and an instant-read thermometer reads 160 degrees, about 6 minutes. Remove the bowl from over the water. Quickly add the butter to the bowl and whisk until incorporated. Press a sheet of plastic wrap directly onto the surface of the curd and refrigerate overnight. (The curd can be made up to 3 days ahead. Keep covered and refrigerated.)

MAKE THE CAKE:

Simmer the mango nectar in a medium, heavy saucepan over medium heat until reduced to 3/4 cup, about 20 minutes. Let cool to room temperature.

Adjust the rack to the middle and preheat the oven to 325 degrees. Line the bottoms of two 9-inch-round, 1 1/2-inch-deep cake pans with parchment paper. (Do not grease the pans or the parchment.)

Sift the flour, 6 tablespoons of the sugar, the baking powder, and salt into a medium bowl. In a large bowl, whisk together the egg yolks, oil, lime zest, and 6 tablespoons of the cooled mango syrup (reserve the remaining syrup for the glaze). Add the dry ingredients to the wet; whisk to blend.

Using an electric mixer, beat the egg whites in another large bowl until soft peaks form. Add the remaining 6 tablespoons sugar, 1 tablespoon at a time, beating until soft and glossy. Fold one third of the egg whites into the yolk mixture until thoroughly combined. Then fold in the remaining whites in 2 additions.

Divide the batter between the prepared pans. Bake until golden and a cake tester inserted in the center comes out clean, about 22 minutes. Let cool completely in the pans on a wire rack. Run a small knife around the edge of each pan to loosen the cake. Carefully invert the cakes onto 9-inch cardboard rounds or tart pan bottoms; tap sharply on the work surface, if necessary, to release the cakes from the pans. Peel off the parchment.

MAKE THE GLAZE AND TOPPING AND ASSEMBLE:

Combine the sugar, lime juice, and reserved 6 tablespoons mango syrup in a small, heavy saucepan over medium-high heat. Boil until reduced to 1/4 cup, about 3 minutes. Chill the glaze until cold, about 15 minutes.

Place 1 cake flat side up on a cake plate. Spread 2 cups of the lime-ginger curd over the top of the cake (reserve the remaining curd for another use). Chill the cake until the curd firms up slightly, about 2 hours. Top with the second cake layer, flat side down this time, pressing gently to adhere.

Beat the whipping cream and 2 tablespoons of the chilled glaze in a bowl until firm peaks form. Spread the whipped cream over the top (not the sides) of the cake. Slightly overlap the mango slices in concentric circles on the cream. Rewarm the remaining glaze just to soften it enough to brush it over the mango slices. Refrigerate the cake for at least 2 hours. (The cake can be made up to 1 day ahead. Cover with a cake dome and keep refrigerated.) Cut into wedges and serve.

notes from our test kitchen

- If you can't find an 11.5-ounce can of mango nectar, buy whatever size you can find. You need about 1 1/2 cups to begin.
- Rolling the limes back and forth a few times under your palm makes them easier to juice—and you get a slightly better yield.
- To slice the mango, first peel the whole mango with a vegetable peeler. Then stand the fruit up on the stem end and slice off the 2 meaty "fillets." Place the fillets on the cutting board and slice lengthwise into 1/4-inch-thick slices.
- Be sure not to frost the sides of the cake with the whipped cream. The bare sides not only reveal the lovely lime-ginger filling, but they also afford just the right balance of airy whipped cream, tender cake, and creamy curd.

tip

David Karp, a self-proclaimed "fruit detective," explains that mangoes, like pears, are harvested firm and ripened off the tree. In fact, if picked ripe, they tend to rot near the pit. Mangoes are best ripened at room temperature and are ready when they yield to slight pressure at the narrow end.

The best way to dice a mango is to stand the fruit stem end down, holding it upright. Align the mango so that you are looking at one of its narrower faces—you'll see that every mango has two wider faces and two narrower, pointy ones. This shape reflects the shape of the large, flat pit inside. With a large knife, slice off the 2 "fillets"—the meaty halves on either side of the flat pit. You will leave some flesh above and below the pit, but there's no getting around this. Now crosshatch each fillet in the size dice you want by cutting down to, but not through, the peel with the tip of your knife. Turn the fillets inside out, and the dice will stand up like a porcupine's quills. Run the knife along the peel to release the dice. (From *Gourmet*)

SOURCE: *Fine Cooking Holiday Baking*
COOK: **Nicole Rees**

chocolate stout cake

WE CAN'T DECIDE whether it's the texture or the flavor of this cake that we love more. A cross between a dense pound cake and a light layer cake, it's tender, moist, hearty, and delicate all at once. The stout adds an almost winy character that offsets the sweetness, and the bits of semisweet chocolate make it pleasingly decadent. If, like us, you appreciate a little bitter with your sweet, this is your cake.

Thanks to the generous amount of butter and eggs, the cake will keep for up to a week, tightly wrapped in plastic. You can also freeze it for up to a month with no loss of quality. Nicole Rees, a professional baker in Seattle, gives her chocolate stout cakes away around the holidays. Don't we wish we were her neighbors!

makes 1 large bundt cake or 12 miniature bundt cakes

- 1 1/4 cups (2 1/2 sticks) unsalted butter, at room temperature, plus more for the pan
- 3/4 cup natural cocoa powder (not Dutch-processed), plus more for dusting
- 1 1/4 cups stout, preferably Guinness (don't include the foam when measuring)
- 1/3 cup dark molasses (not blackstrap)
- 1 2/3 cups all-purpose flour
- 1 1/2 teaspoons baking powder
- 1/2 teaspoon baking soda
- 1/2 teaspoon salt
- 1 1/2 cups packed light brown sugar
- 3 large eggs, at room temperature
- 6 ounces semisweet chocolate, very finely chopped
- Chocolate Glaze (optional; recipe follows)

Adjust the rack to the middle and preheat the oven to 350 degrees. Butter a 10- or 12-cup bundt pan (or twelve 1-cup mini bundt pans) and lightly dust with sifted cocoa powder. Tap out any excess cocoa. Bring the stout and molasses to a simmer in a small saucepan over high heat. Remove the pan from the heat and let cool while you prepare the cake batter.

Sift together the flour, cocoa powder, baking powder, baking soda, and salt. With a stand mixer fitted with the paddle attachment or a hand-held electric mixer, cream the butter in a large bowl on medium speed until smooth, about 1 minute. Add the brown sugar and beat on medium speed until light and fluffy, about 3 minutes. Stop to scrape the bowl as needed. Beat in the eggs, one at a time, stopping to scrape the bowl after each addition. With the mixer on low speed, alternately add the flour and stout mixtures, beginning and ending with the flour. Stop the mixer at least one last time to scrape the bowl and then beat at medium speed until the batter is smooth, about 20 seconds. Stir in the chopped chocolate.

Spoon the batter into the prepared pan(s), spreading it evenly with a rubber spatula. Run a knife through the batter to eliminate any air pockets. Bake until a wooden skewer inserted in the center comes out with only a few moist crumbs clinging to it, 45 to 50 minutes for the large cake or about 35 minutes for the mini cakes. Set the pan(s) on a wire rack to cool for 20 minutes. Invert the cake(s) onto the rack and remove the pan(s). Let cool until just barely warm. Drizzle with the glaze, if using, and let cool to room temperature. (If you're making the cake ahead or plan to freeze it, wrap it while still barely warm without the glaze. Don't glaze it until you're ready to serve it or give it to a friend.) Transfer to a cake plate, cut into wedges, and serve.

chocolate glaze

makes about 1 cup glaze

- 3/4 cup heavy cream
- 6 ounces semisweet chocolate, chopped

Bring the cream to a boil in a small saucepan over high heat. Remove the pan from the heat and add the chocolate. Let stand for 1 minute, then whisk until the chocolate is melted and smooth. Let cool for 5 minutes before drizzling over the barely warm or room-temperature cake.

SOURCE: *Forever Summer* by Nigella Lawson

COOK: Nigella Lawson

anglo-italian trifle

OUR FASCINATION WITH BRITISH FOOD CONTINUES, and this year it was the trifle that emerged as a star. We Americans have never quite known what to make of trifle, that boozy conglomeration of homemade custard, sponge cake, jam, fruit, and lavish amounts of cream. But it's time to take a closer look, as cooks everywhere are beginning to reinvent this classic dessert. This version owes a lot to tiramisu—no custard to make, no cooking at all, in fact. The blackberries are beautiful with the white mascarpone and superb with the limoncello. You can make it in about 15 minutes. Just be sure to assemble it in a big glass bowl for maximum dramatic effect, so everyone can see all the layers. This is the ultimate summertime party dessert, and it's even better made a day ahead.

serves 12 to 14

- 8–10 ladyfingers
- 3/4 cup plus 2 tablespoons black currant jam
- 7 ounces amaretti cookies (see notes)
- 1 cup plus 2 tablespoons limoncello or other lemon-flavored liqueur (see notes)
- Juice of 1/2 lemon
- 3 1/4 cups blackberries
- 2 large eggs, separated
- 1/3 cup sugar
- 1 3/4 cups mascarpone cheese
- Scant 1/4 cup slivered almonds

Split the ladyfingers and make little sandwiches using more than half of the jam. Press them into the base of a big glass bowl (preferably a pretty one). Reduce the amaretti to rubble in a food processor and scatter most of them evenly over the ladyfingers, reserving some for sprinkling on top at the end. Pour over all a generous 1/2 cup of the limoncello. Put the remaining 1/4 cup or so of jam in a wide saucepan with the lemon juice and melt over low heat. Tumble in the blackberries, stir gently, and heat for a minute or so, just until the juices start running. Tip these over the cookie-sprinkled, liqueur-soused sandwiches and leave this while you get on with the next bit.

Whisk the egg yolks with the sugar (with an electric mixer or by hand) in a large bowl until you have a thick, smooth yellow paste. Still whisking, drip in another 1/4 cup limoncello and continue whisking until you have a light, moussey mixture. Whisk in the mascarpone until everything is smoothly combined, then add the remaining limoncello. Finally, in another bowl, whisk the egg whites until firm but not dry and fold them into the mascarpone mixture. Now spread this gently over the blackberries in the bowl.

Cover the trifle with plastic wrap and refrigerate for at least 4 hours or up to 1 day to allow the flavors and textures to steep and meld. Take the trifle out of the refrigerator about 40 minutes before it's needed (depending on how cold your refrigerator runs) to achieve a coolish room temperature.

Not long before you want to eat, toast the slivered almonds by tossing them in a dry pan over medium heat until they begin to turn gold and are flashed bronze in parts. Tip them onto a plate. When they're cool, mix them with the reserved amaretti crumbs. Remove the plastic wrap from the bowl and scatter the nuts and crumbs over the pale, set surface. Dig in and serve, making sure to heap all three layers on each plate.

notes from our test kitchen

- The Italian elements in the trifle—mascarpone (halfway between cream cheese and butter) and amaretti (those paper-wrapped little almond cookies that come in tins)—are available in gourmet shops and many supermarkets. Amaretti cookies come in several sizes, depending on the manufacturer. Shop by weight—198 grams equals about 7 ounces if the package cites only metric amounts. Find limoncello at the liquor store.
- If you prefer a less boozy dessert, you can cut back the limoncello. Taste as you go along and use just enough liqueur to give it a good flavor. If you'd rather use rum, that's fine.
- This can also be a great winter trifle. Winter raspberries from California are quite good, and they work with these flavors perfectly.
- The shape of the bowl you choose may affect the way you assemble the trifle. If it's more tall than wide, you may need to make several layers. You can also adjust the quantities a bit to suit the bowl.

SOURCE: *Elle Decor*

COOK: **Daniel Boulud**

cinnamon sacristains

FROZEN PUFF PASTRY FROM THE SUPERMARKET is a gift to the home cook. But there's one problem: after you make something smashing, such as Savory Fig Tart (page 10), you usually have some leftover pastry, which unfortunately doesn't keep well. When that happens, make these wonderfully crunchy twists, which are perfect with ice cream, pudding, or a fruit compote.

All you need is a quarter box of puff pastry, and once you get the hang of making the sacristains, you can use even less. Although these are the work of a leading New York chef, they aren't at all tricky, and they always look charming. This reminds us of our grandmothers' frugal way of using up pie pastry scraps—cut them into strips and shake cinnamon sugar on top before baking them into instant treats.

makes 24 twists

- 4 ounces puff pastry dough
- 1 large egg, beaten with 1 teaspoon cold water
- Sugar
- Ground cinnamon

Cut the dough into a rectangle that measures about 6 x 7 inches. Place it on a parchment paper–lined or nonstick baking sheet. Brush with the beaten egg and sprinkle with sugar and cinnamon to taste. Fold the dough in half lengthwise and refrigerate for at least an hour.

Transfer the cold dough to a cutting board. With a very sharp paring knife or a pizza cutter, slice it into strips about 7 inches long and 1/4 inch wide (you should have about 24 strips).

One by one, place them on a flat surface and, using the palms of your hands to roll the ends of the dough in opposite directions, twist. Return them to the baking sheet and refrigerate for at least 1 hour.

Adjust the rack to the middle and preheat the oven to 400 degrees. Bake the twists for 8 to 10 minutes, until golden brown. Let cool on a wire rack.

notes from our test kitchen

- Look for all-butter puff pastry. Dufour is especially good.
- Make sure there's enough cinnamon in the twists. Mix the cinnamon into the sugar and taste until you find a balance you like.
- The twists are delicious right out of the oven, but they also keep well and will still be crunchy the next day, even if you forget to store them in a tin.

SOURCE: *It's All American Food* by David Rosengarten

COOK: David Rosengarten after *Southern Living*

bourbon, chocolate, and walnut pecan pie

DAVID ROSENGARTEN is the editor of the passionate foodie newsletter the *Rosengarten Report* and a veteran TV personality on the Food Network. It was on TV that he first tasted a pie like this one, made by an editor at *Southern Living,* and it knocked him out. It was not only the best *pecan* pie he'd ever eaten; it was one of the best pies of any kind. We have to agree that Rosengarten's version is stunning.

This pecan pie is not so much gooey as crunchy, with two kinds of nuts. There's also a lot of bittersweet chocolate, plus the bourbon, to give it a bit of an edge. Plenty of sugar—four kinds—along with the butter and eggs keep it authentic. This is the quintessential Thanksgiving dessert: a new twist on a classic that your guests will be talking about for days.

serves 6 to 8

- Dough for 1 pie crust, store-bought or homemade (see note)
- 1/2 cup coarsely chopped pecans
- 1/2 cup coarsely chopped walnuts
- 4 large eggs
- 1/2 cup light corn syrup
- 1/4 cup honey
- 1/3 cup sugar
- 1/3 cup packed light brown sugar
- 6 tablespoons (3/4 stick) unsalted butter, melted
- 3 tablespoons bourbon
- 1 tablespoon pure vanilla extract
- 1 tablespoon all-purpose flour
- Pinch ground nutmeg
- Pinch ground cinnamon
- 8 ounces good-quality bittersweet chocolate, broken into 1/2-inch-square chunks

Adjust the rack to the middle and preheat the oven to 350 degrees. Roll out the dough 1/8 inch thick, making the circle 1 inch larger than a 9-inch pie plate. Drape the crust over the rolling pin and carefully fit it into the pie plate. Trim the edge to 1/2 inch wider than the rim. Fold the excess under the rim, on the outside of the plate, and crimp, pinching the dough between your thumb and forefinger at 1-inch intervals.

Toast the pecans and walnuts in a small sauté pan over medium-high heat, stirring often with a wooden spoon, until they're evenly toasted and crisp, about 4 minutes.

In a medium bowl, whisk together the remaining ingredients, except the chocolate, and blend until the mixture is smooth. Stir in the nuts and chocolate. Pour and scrape the mixture into the pie crust.

Bake the pie until set and a cake tester inserted in the center comes out clean (unless you hit a chocolaty spot), 40 to 50 minutes. Serve slightly warm or at room temperature.

note from our test kitchen

Shirkers that we are, we used a frozen prepared pie crust from the supermarket, and the results were just fine. There's so much else going on here that no one will even notice the crust, but if you want to make it from scratch, it will be even better. Just use a favorite recipe or the one for Pumpkin, Sweet Potato, and Coconut Pie (page 266).

SOURCE: *Fine Cooking*

COOK: Regan Daley

pumpkin, sweet potato, and coconut pie

IMPROVING ON PUMPKIN PIE IS NO EASY FEAT, but leave it to the talented and inventive pastry chef Regan Daley to do just that. For starters, Daley combines pumpkin and sweet potato to add nuance to the filling. Then, to boost the flavor, instead of the usual pumpkin pie spices, she simmers the sweet potatoes with a cinnamon stick, cloves, star anise, and fresh ginger, a step that adds a remarkably warm backdrop. But what makes this pie stand head and shoulders above ordinary renditions is the addition of a little coconut milk to the custard. It contributes just the right amount of richness. In the end, the pie bears enough resemblance to the classic holiday version to make everyone happy, with one important difference—it's better.

There are a lot of steps here, but the various elements can be prepared in advance. If you're serving a throng, you can easily double the recipe. Just use 3 whole eggs in the filling.

makes one 9-inch pie; serves 8 to 10

- 1 1/4 pounds sweet potatoes, peeled and cut into 1-inch chunks
- 1 small cinnamon stick, broken into pieces
- 3 cloves
- 1 small star anise, crumbled into large pieces
- 1 1-inch piece fresh ginger, cut into 1/4-inch-thick slices
- 1 15-ounce can pure solid-pack pumpkin (not pumpkin pie filling)
- 1 large egg, lightly beaten
- 1 large egg yolk, lightly beaten
- 2 tablespoons unsalted butter, melted and cooled
- 1/2 cup sugar
- 1/2 cup packed light brown sugar
- 2 tablespoons all-purpose flour
- 3/4 teaspoon salt
- 1/2 cup canned unsweetened coconut milk (not coconut cream), well stirred
- 1 9-inch single pie crust (recipe follows), chilled
- 3/4 cup cold whipping cream, whipped to soft peaks with 1 1/2 tablespoons sugar for serving

In a medium saucepan, combine the sweet potatoes, cinnamon, cloves, star anise, and ginger with enough water to just cover. Bring to a boil over high heat. Reduce the heat and simmer, uncovered, until the sweet potatoes are very tender when pierced with a fork or skewer, about 10 minutes. Drain the potatoes, reserving the boiling liquid. Return the potatoes to the pot over low heat and toss to dry them a bit. Discard the cinnamon, cloves, and star anise. Force the warm potatoes through a ricer, food mill, or sieve. Boil the liquid, if necessary, until it is reduced to 1/4 cup. Let the sweet potato mash and the liquid cool separately. (The sweet potatoes and spiced liquid can be prepared up to 3 days ahead and refrigerated. See notes.)

Adjust the rack to the lower half and preheat the oven to 350 degrees. Whisk together the pumpkin and sweet potato puree in a large bowl. Whisk in the egg, egg yolk, melted butter, and reserved spiced liquid. In a separate bowl, stir together the sugars with a whisk until any large lumps of brown sugar are gone. Sift the flour and salt over the sugars; stir to blend. Add the sugar-flour mixture to the pumpkin and stir well until no pockets of sugar are visible. Blend in the coconut milk.

Scrape the filling into the chilled pie shell; smooth the top. Bake for 1 3/4 to 2 hours, turning the pie several times so that it bakes evenly. The filling should feel firm, not wobbly, and the point of a thin-bladed knife should come out clean when inserted into the center. The edge of the filling will be unevenly cracked. If the edge of the pastry darkens too much before the filling is cooked, cover with a pie shield or strips of foil. Transfer the pie to a wire rack and let cool completely before serving with mounds of the lightly sweetened whipped cream.

notes from our test kitchen

- If you make the sweet potato mash and spiced liquid in advance, bring them to room temperature before proceeding with the recipe. If you have frozen them, thaw them overnight in the refrigerator before bringing them to room temperature.
- If you use a metal pie plate rather than a glass one, the pie will take 10 to 15 minutes less time to bake.

tender pie crust

THIS RECIPE MAKES DOUBLE THE PIE DOUGH that you'll need for the pumpkin pie recipe, so freeze half to use another time.

makes two 9-inch pie crusts

- 3 cups all-purpose flour
- 1 teaspoon salt
- 1 cup solid vegetable shortening, chilled and cut into small pieces
- 1 large egg
- 2–3 tablespoons ice water, as needed
- 1 tablespoon white vinegar

Combine the flour and salt in a large mixing bowl or food processor. Add the shortening and cut it in with a pastry blender or two knives (or pulse in the processor) until the largest pieces of shortening are about the size of fat peas. Transfer to a large mixing bowl if using the processor.

In a small bowl, beat together the egg, 2 tablespoons of the ice water, and the vinegar. Add to the flour mixture. Work the liquid evenly through the dough with the tips of your fingers until it can be collected in a rough ball. If the dough is too dry to come together, gradually sprinkle a few drops of the remaining water over it and continue to work gently until it comes together.

Cut the dough in half and shape each half into a ball. Flatten each ball into a disk and wrap tightly in plastic. Chill for at least 4 hours or up to 3 days. Save 1 disk for another purpose.

About 2 hours before baking, remove the dough from the refrigerator to allow it to warm up just enough so it won't crack when you roll it. Unwrap the dough and roll it between two sheets of wax paper into a round about 12 inches in diameter. Peel off the top sheet of paper. Invert a 9-inch glass pie plate and center it on the dough. Slide one hand under the bottom sheet of wax paper, position your other hand flat on the pie plate, and quickly flip the plate and dough. Peel off the paper and gently press the dough down into the plate. With a paring knife, trim the dough to within 3/4 inch of the rim. Fold the dough under and crimp the edge. Use the trimmings to patch any cracks or bare spots. Wrap the shell loosely in plastic and chill for at least 2 hours or up to 1 day.

note from our test kitchen

Don't cheat on the chilling time before or after rolling the crust. A well-chilled crust won't shrink during baking. Plus, a well-chilled crust is less apt to burn during the long baking time this pie requires.

SOURCE: *Cooking by Hand* by Paul Bertolli

COOK: Paul Bertolli

tart of dried plums and walnut frangipane

DESCRIBING THIS AS A PRUNE TART (which it is) doesn't do it justice. For one thing, when Paul Bertolli makes it, he uses real Italian prune plums that he dries himself in a low convection oven for several hours. That's typical of Bertolli, a gifted and dedicated chef from Oakland, California, who makes his own salami, cures his own olives, mills his own polenta, and so forth. Fortunately for those of us less inclined to "cook from the bottom up" (as he calls it), this tart is stunning made with regular prunes.

The tart has three components: a rich tart crust, a walnut frangipane filling, and the prunes (aka dried plums), which are first plumped in lightly sweetened red wine syrup. As the tart bakes, the frangipane puffs up, cradling the prunes and becoming slightly chewy around the edges while remaining soft in the center.

The final glory of this dessert comes from reducing the leftover prune poaching liquid to a thick syrup. Serve the tart warm with a scoop of vanilla ice cream and a drizzle of the dark, winy syrup.

serves 8 to 10

TART DOUGH

- 3 1/3 cups all-purpose flour
- 1/3 cup sugar
- 1/3 teaspoon salt
- 1 1/2 cups (3 sticks) cold unsalted butter, cut into 1-inch cubes
- 1 large egg yolk

PRUNES

- 20 prunes, pitted
- 2 cups dry red wine
- 1/2 cup sugar

FRANGIPANE FILLING

- 1 1/4 cups walnuts, lightly toasted and ground (see notes)
- 1/2 cup sugar
- Pinch salt
- 6 tablespoons (3/4 stick) unsalted butter, melted
- 1 large egg
- 2 tablespoons heavy cream
- Vanilla ice cream for serving (optional)

MAKE THE DOUGH:

Place the flour, sugar, and salt in the bowl of a stand mixer fitted with a paddle. Mix in the butter on the lowest speed until the dough barely starts to come together in the middle of the bowl. Stop the mixer, add the egg yolk, and continue to mix until the dough is uniformly mixed. Divide the dough into 2 equal pieces. Wrap in plastic and refrigerate for at least 4 hours. Save 1 piece of dough for another use.

Roll out the dough into a 10-inch circle. Fit the circle into a 9-inch tart pan, pushing it all the way into the bottom so that the dough is not stretched. Trim off the excess dough. Refrigerate for at least 2 hours.

Adjust the rack to the middle and preheat the oven to 350 degrees. Bake the crust until it is well browned, about 30 minutes. Remove from the oven and set aside to cool. Leave the oven on.

MEANWHILE, PREPARE THE PRUNES:

Combine the prunes, red wine, and sugar in a small pot. Bring to a boil, reduce the heat to a simmer, and cook for about 5 minutes, until the prunes are tender but still hold their shape. Remove from the heat and let cool in the liquid.

MAKE THE FRANGIPANE FILLING:

Place the walnuts, sugar, and salt in a large bowl and stir with a rubber spatula to mix. In a small bowl, whisk together the butter, egg, and cream. Pour the wet ingredients into the dry and stir with the spatula just until the filling is combined and smooth.

ASSEMBLE AND BAKE THE TART:

Remove the prunes from the poaching liquid and place them on paper towels to drain. Reserve the poaching liquid. Pour the frangipane into the baked tart shell. Arrange the prunes on top, spacing them evenly. The tart shell should be quite full. (As it bakes, the filling will rise up around the fruit, partially covering it and keeping it from drying out too much.) Bake for about 30 minutes, until the edges of the frangipane feel set and the center is firm on top and soft underneath. Remove from the oven and let cool slightly.

Meanwhile, reduce the reserved poaching liquid over medium heat to a thick glaze, about 1/2 cup. Brush the top of the tart with the glaze, slice, and serve warm with vanilla ice cream (if using) and a drizzle of the glaze.

notes from our test kitchen

- We found the original tart dough to be a bit lean and difficult to handle, so we delved a little deeper into Bertolli's cookbook and found another dough with a bit more butter, which we've used here. Any buttery pie crust will work.
- To toast the walnuts, preheat the oven to 325 degrees. Spread the nuts on a baking sheet and toast, stirring once or twice, until toasty-smelling and a bit darker in color, about 10 minutes. Let cool completely before grinding.
- When making the frangipane, we like to grind the toasted walnuts in a food processor along with the sugar. The sugar prevents the nuts from turning to nut butter as you grind them.
- It's easier to combine the melted butter, egg, and heavy cream if they are all at room temperature.

SOURCE: *The Tante Marie's Cooking School Cookbook* by Mary Risley

COOK: Heidi Krahling

chocolate-pecan toffee

MARY RISLEY was in San Francisco at the dawn of the food revolution there and was inspired to start her own cooking school, Tante Marie's. A number of the former students at Tante Marie's have gone on to become chefs themselves, among them Heidi Krahling, who owns a restaurant called Insalata's in San Anselmo, California. When Risley eats there, all the waiters know that she wants a little plate of this sensational toffee after dinner—she doesn't even have to ask.

It's the perfect holiday treat—for after dinner, for a potluck, for gifts. Happily, the recipe makes a lot, and it's so easy that two batches are no big deal. As long as you have a candy thermometer, you're in business.

makes 2 pounds toffee

- 1½ cups sugar
- 6 tablespoons water
- 9 ounces light corn syrup
- 2 cups (4 sticks) butter, cut into 1-inch pieces
- 2½ cups chopped pecans, lightly toasted (see notes)
- 12 ounces semisweet or bittersweet chocolate
- 4 ounces milk chocolate

Heat the sugar and water in a large saucepan over low heat, swirling from time to time to dissolve the sugar. Add the corn syrup and butter and increase the heat to bring to a boil. Cook, stirring from time to time, until the mixture reaches the hard-crack stage (about 300 degrees on a candy thermometer), about 20 minutes. Quickly stir in 1 cup of the nuts and pour onto a Silpat-lined baking sheet (see notes). With a metal spatula, spread the candy as thinly as possible. Let cool to room temperature, then remove from the Silpat in one piece.

To finish the candy, melt the chocolates in a stainless-steel bowl set over a pan of gently simmering water. Spread the chocolate on the candy and sprinkle the remaining pecans on top. Let cool. When the chocolate has set, break the toffee into pieces. Store in an airtight container.

notes from our test kitchen

- Risley points out that you should always test a pecan before you buy some because they go rancid so quickly. And don't be tempted to substitute chocolate chips for the bulk chocolate. Chips contain too many stabilizers, so they don't work for candy.
- To toast the pecans, preheat the oven to 325 degrees. Spread the pecans on a baking sheet and toast, stirring once or twice, until fragrant and slightly darker, about 10 minutes.
- If you don't have a Silpat silicone baking mat, use heavy-duty foil to line the baking sheet and butter it well.

SOURCE: Gang e-mail

COOK: Patricia Brown after Margaret Knauer

peppermint popcorn

WHEN WE FIRST HEARD ABOUT THIS RECIPE, we were skeptical: peppermint and popcorn? But our source insisted that it was fabulous. The popcorn comes out irresistibly crunchy, a bit buttery, and sweet—just what you expect from candied corn—and the peppermint adds a pleasing flavor bonus. Be forewarned: this is one of those disappearing snacks. Anytime we put out a bowl, it goes in no time flat.

The original recipe appeared in the *Baltimore Sun* a few years ago in the "Recipe Finder" department. From there the recipe circulated among our friends and family before landing here. Packed in tins or pretty cellophane bags, it makes a welcome holiday gift and keeps well.

makes about 2 1/2 quarts popcorn

- 3 quarts unseasoned freshly popped popcorn (about 3/4 cup unpopped corn)
- 8 tablespoons (1 stick) butter
- 1 cup sugar
- 1/2 teaspoon salt
- 1/4 cup light corn syrup
- 1/2 teaspoon peppermint extract
- 1/8 teaspoon green food coloring (optional; see note)

Preheat the oven to 250 degrees. Drop the popcorn into a large, shallow roasting pan or onto a rimmed baking sheet.

Melt the butter in a medium saucepan over medium heat. Stir in the sugar, salt, and corn syrup. Cook, stirring constantly, until the mixture comes to a boil. Boil, without stirring, for 5 minutes. Remove from the heat and add the peppermint extract and food coloring (if using). Pour the mixture over the popcorn and stir well.

Bake for 1 hour, stirring 3 or 4 times. Let cool completely, then store in a tightly covered container.

note from our test kitchen

We don't cook with food coloring, so we don't bother adding it. Plus, we like to surprise people: when they taste it, the plain-looking caramel corn turns out to be delightfully minty.

tip

What if there were a way to get the convenience of microwave popcorn with none of the artificial flavorings and fats? Well, according to Jeanne McManus in the *Washington Post,* you can. Here's how: Put 1/4 to 1/2 cup popcorn in a brown paper bag. Close the top of the bag by folding it over twice. Stick it in the microwave for 3 minutes or so, until the sound of the popping stops. It's as easy as that. Be careful when you open the bag that the steam doesn't burn you—just as you would with store-bought bags.

drinks

SOURCE: *Celebrate!*
by Sheila Lukins with Peter Kaminsky

COOK: Sheila Lukins

fresh raspberry lemonade

IN SHEILA LUKINS'S NEW BOOK OF CELEBRATORY MENUS, she recommends this gorgeous deep pink lemonade for Mother's Day. We've also served it at a baby shower, and it always gets oohs and ahs, both for its loveliness and for its great taste.

There's not much work here for such kudos. Just squeeze some lemons, make a sugar syrup, and puree the raspberries.

makes 10 cups; serves 8

- 3 cups raspberries, gently rinsed
- 1 cup sugar
- 6 cups cold water
- Juice of 12 large lemons
- 8 large mint sprigs for garnish

Puree the raspberries in a blender or food processor. Strain into a medium bowl through a fine-mesh strainer to remove the seeds. Set aside.

Place the sugar and water in a saucepan over medium heat and cook, stirring occasionally, until the sugar has dissolved, about 5 minutes. Let cool to room temperature.

Combine the raspberry puree and sugar syrup in a large pitcher and stir in the lemon juice. Serve over ice in tall glasses, garnished with mint sprigs.

note from our test kitchen

You'll get a lot more raspberry flavor if you reverse the first two steps of the recipe: begin by making the sugar syrup and then puree and strain the raspberries. While the strainer is still filled with raspberry seeds, pour the syrup through the strainer as well. This will release any solids left behind and ensure that you get all the berry flavor.

SOURCE: *Saveur*
COOK: Oasis Date Gardens
STORY BY: Andrew Coe

date shakes

ROADSIDE STANDS all around date-growing country in California sell creamy, sweet date shakes in big to-go cups with thick straws. The rest of us have to be satisfied with making our own. Thankfully, it's as simple as can be to whip up a couple of these frosty treats, with their mellow caramel flavor. The combination of pureed dates and vanilla ice cream gives the shakes an incomparably smooth, rich texture and a lovely, pale coffee-with-cream color.

For the most intense flavor, Andrew Coe recommends using Medjool dates, a high-end date that originated in Morocco but is relatively easy to find in the United States. Medjools are recognizable by their large size and their soft, golden brown to molasses brown skin. For a less intense shake, go with the more delicate Deglet Noor dates. These smaller, caramel-colored dates account for about 75 percent of California's date crop and are often what we find in supermarkets.

If you don't have drinking straws in the cupboard, it might be worth buying a box. A shake always tastes best drawn up through a fat straw.

serves 2

1 cup dates, pitted and chopped (see above)
1 cup whole milk
2 cups good-quality vanilla ice cream (see note)

Combine the dates and milk in a blender and puree until smooth. Add the ice cream and puree again. Divide between two cups or glasses. Serve immediately.

note from our test kitchen

Don't skimp on the quality of the ice cream here. Lower-quality ice creams have too much air, and your shakes will be thin, not thick and creamy.

cranberry margaritas

BOBBY DOES IT AGAIN! Why did no one ever think of this before? Those of us who drink tequila in the summer usually say adios regretfully as the seasons change. But this not-too-sweet, not-too-tart "margarita" changes all that. Although it's shaken with ice briefly, it's not chilled, and it manages to be both refreshing and warming at the same time.

For holiday parties, you couldn't ask for a better crowd-pleaser. Fortunately, this drink goes together fast. However big a batch you make, we promise you won't have leftovers.

serves 10

- 2 cups tequila
- 1 1/3 cups cranberry juice
- 1 cup orange-flavored liqueur, such as Triple Sec or Cointreau
- 2/3 cup fresh lime juice

In a cocktail shaker filled with ice, shake all the ingredients and strain into margarita glasses or low cocktail flutes. Serve immediately.

notes from our test kitchen

- If you have neither margarita glasses nor low cocktail flutes, martini glasses are fine for this drink.
- We like silver tequila with mixed drinks. Jose Cuervo makes a reasonably priced one.

SOURCE: *Westchester Magazine*
COOK: Jonathan Dorf
STORY BY: John Bruno Turiano

turkeytini

IT'S NOT A COSMOPOLITAN, IT'S NOT A MANHATTAN, but it has a similar kind of addictive appeal. The turkeytini is the perfect Thanksgiving cocktail, with cranberry juice, warming bourbon, and a delightful jolt of fresh lime. Lime is both the perfect accent and highly appropriate: this gorgeous cocktail first saw the light of day at the Lime Restaurant in Larchmont, New York.

Jonathan Dorf likes to garnish the drinks with sun-dried cranberries and a slice of lime.

serves 1

2 ounces Wild Turkey bourbon
2 1/2 ounces cranberry juice
1 ounce simple lime syrup (see notes)
Sun-dried cranberries and lime slices for garnish (optional)

In a cocktail shaker filled with ice, combine all the ingredients. Mix well and strain into a chilled martini glass. Garnish with cranberries and/or lime slices, if desired, and serve.

notes from our test kitchen

- A bon vivant friend with professional bartending training showed us how to shake a cocktail properly. Fill the shaker full of ice (don't worry that you'll be diluting the drink; that's part of the point) and shake vigorously for longer than you think you should.
- To make the simple lime syrup, combine 2 tablespoons fresh lime juice with an equal measure of superfine sugar. Stir to dissolve the sugar.

SOURCE: *Cosmopolitan* by Toby Cecchini

COOK: Toby Cecchini

dry negroni

THE MUCH-NEGLECTED NEGRONI made a huge comeback in this year of retro cocktails, and of all the versions we saw, this one turned out to be our favorite. Toby Cecchini, a New York bartender, plainly loves his negronis ("one of the most perfect drinks in existence") and prepares them not in the classic ratio of equal parts gin, Campari, and sweet vermouth but something more like 3-1-1, with a predominance of gin. This strategy results in a drier cocktail—the usual sweetness tends to be cloying on the refill.

Cecchini is generous with interesting opinions: the negroni and the Manhattan are the only cocktails that shouldn't be shaken. Instead, they should be stirred in the shaker, just until the shaker frosts on the outside. A coil of citrus peel goes into the glass of gorgeous ruby liquid, and a slice of orange, preferably blood orange, perches on the rim.

master formula for any number of cocktails

- 3 parts Campari
- 3 parts sweet vermouth, such as Carpano Antica Formula or Martini & Rossi
- 8 parts gin
- Orange slices, preferably from blood oranges, for garnish
- Strips of lemon and/or orange zest/lemon zest

In a shaker filled liberally with ice, combine the liquors. Stir until the exterior of the shaker beads with frost.

To serve, strain the liquid into a chilled cocktail glass and garnish with an orange slice. Squeeze a lemon and/or an orange twist above the drink, then rub the rim of the glass with the peel and either dip it in the drink and then discard (to leave just a slick of citrus oil) or leave it in, as Cecchini does when he's making negronis for himself.

note from our test kitchen

The Seattle chef Tom Douglas is another passionate negroni admirer. Douglas makes his the classic way but fills the shaker only half full of ice, shakes the drink, and makes only 2 drinks at a time. He chills the martini glasses in the freezer for a few minutes, then rubs each rim with a lemon twist, dropping the twist into the glass before pouring the drinks.

SOURCE: *Washington Post*
COOK: **Ellen Ficklen**

caribbean coolers

WHEN THE DOG DAYS HIT, few combinations are as refreshing as watermelon, ginger, and lime. This slushy drink is just the ticket for that kind of day, and if you can think an hour or so ahead to freeze the watermelon, making it is a breeze.

There are a lot of gingery ginger ales around, everything from Blenheim (see page 182) to Jamaican ginger beer. Choose one of those for the best flavor. Or grate a little fresh ginger into the drinks and use regular old ginger ale for a similar effect.

serves 2

- 3 cups chopped seeded watermelon, rind removed
- 2–4 tablespoons fresh lime juice, to taste
- 2 tablespoons sugar, plus more to taste
- 1/2 cup Jamaican-style ginger ale

Place the watermelon in a single layer on a rimmed baking sheet. Cover and freeze until solid, at least 1 hour. Remove from the freezer and set aside at room temperature to soften slightly, about 5 minutes.

In a small bowl, combine 2 tablespoons of the lime juice and sugar and stir until the sugar dissolves. In a blender, combine the lime-sugar mixture and the ginger ale and, with the motor running, add the watermelon, a few cubes at a time, until the mixture turns to slush. Taste and adjust the amount of lime juice and/or sugar accordingly. Serve immediately.

notes from our test kitchen

- No one says you can't add some rum or vodka to this cooler.
- Frozen watermelon is so good that you might want to freeze some extra just to munch on. Give it a 5-minute rest outside the freezer before you bite into it.

SOURCE: *New York Times*

COOK: Suzanne Hamlin

kentucky derby mint juleps

EVERY FEW YEARS, the press seems to get julep fever, and this year was one of them. We saw many, many recipes for the "authentic" Kentucky Derby mint julep, full of eyebrow raisers such as Tennessee whiskey, lots of lemon juice, and whacking big ice cubes.

The food writer Suzanne Hamlin, who was Raised Right in Louisville, Kentucky, has been on a decades-long crusade to set the record straight. None of these aberrations is the real thing (they're just bourbon highballs), and the real thing is so incredibly good that it must be preserved. We'll drink to that, and not just on Derby Day—this is a terrific excuse for any spring or summer party.

The only element likely to give you pause is the julep cups, which must, says Hamlin, be slightly flared metal, preferably silver. The cups give the julep its glorious frosted coating, and the slightly metallic taste, says Hamlin, is the perfect balance to the warm, smoky, sweet bourbon and the spicy spearmint. Price isn't an issue; you can find fairly heavy silver foil cups with gold wash inside for less than twenty cents each at party stores.

This mint julep really *is* the one first served to Derby guests in 1875 by Colonel Meriwether Lewis Clark, Jr., the founder of Churchill Downs. Let the word go forth.

makes up to 20 mint juleps

- Metal julep cups, about 9 ounces each, preferably silver
- 1 cup spring or bottled water
- 1 cup sugar
- 1/2 cup small spearmint leaves, stems removed
- Fresh sprigs for garnish
- Finely crushed or shaved ice, enough to fill the cups completely
- Good-quality (90-proof) Kentucky bourbon, such as Maker's Mark or Woodford Reserve

The day before serving or even earlier, put the julep cups in the freezer. Put the water and sugar in a small saucepan, bring to a boil without stirring, and boil for about 2 minutes, until the sugar is completely dissolved. Let cool slightly.

Put the mint leaves in a glass jar or cup and pour the slightly cooled syrup over them. Let cool, then cover and refrigerate for 12 hours or longer. When ready to use, strain out the mint leaves.

About 30 minutes before serving, pack the julep cups tightly up to the rim with crushed ice and return them to the freezer.

For each julep, pour 3 ounces of bourbon over the ice, followed by 2 teaspoons of mint syrup. Do not stir or agitate. Use a cloth to hold each cup by the rim so you don't disturb the frost. Use a short straw or a chopstick to make a hole in the ice on the side of the cup and insert a mint sprig. Serve immediately, preferably on a silver tray.

note from our test kitchen

- If you don't have an ice crusher, one of those new powerful blenders will do the trick (but an old blender won't).

SOURCE: *Santé*

COOK: Kim Owens

the vip
(vodka-infused-pineapple cocktail)

THIS AMAZING LITTLE DRINK COMES FROM KIM OWENS, a bartender at Del Frisco's in Las Vegas. Owens says it's the perfect Vegas cocktail because it's so light and refreshing. In our book, that makes it a perfect just-about-anywhere cocktail.

A marvelous little bit of alchemy happens to the vodka as it sits with fresh pineapple for 10 days. In the end, the vodka retains enough pineapple flavor and sweetness that it tastes more like a mixed drink than a straight-up cocktail. Which leads to our only word of caution: these slide down easily.

makes about 1 liter (enough for 8 to 12 cocktails)

1 ripe golden pineapple, cut into 1-inch-thick slices

1 liter premium vodka

Orange twists for garnish

Combine the pineapple and vodka in an airtight jar or other nonreactive container and let sit for 8 to 10 days.

Carefully strain off the vodka. Scoop the pineapple into a triple layer of cheesecloth set over a bowl and squeeze it to extract as much juice as possible. Discard the pineapple.

Pour 5 to 6 ounces of the pineapple-infused vodka into a shaker half filled with ice. Shake vigorously and strain into a chilled 10-ounce martini glass. Garnish with an orange twist and serve.

notes from our test kitchen

- If you prefer to leave the vodka in the refrigerator to infuse, that works equally well.
- Be sure to squeeze the pineapple chunks well. They will have absorbed a lot of vodka.
- Big drinks are big business in bars, but we're happier with a smaller (3- to 4-ounce) cocktail. It doesn't warm up before you're finished sipping it.

tip

In his latest book, *Hawaii Cooks,* Roy Yamaguchi has his own version of pineapple vodka. The technique is very much the same, with the exception that he garnishes the cocktail with fresh mint. We're partial to a mint garnish in warm weather, reserving the orange for winter.

credits

Cheese Ball with Cumin, Mint, and Pistachios. Copyright © 2003 by The New York Times Co. Reprinted with permission.

Spicy Eggplant Dip. Copyright © 2003 by Nawal Nasrallah. Originally published as Spicy Puréed Eggplant (Misaqua'at Betinjan) in *Delights from the Garden of Eden*. Reprinted by permission of Nawal Nasrallah.

Baba Ghanoush tip (originally published as Microwave Baba Ghanoush). San Francisco Chronicle Index. Newspaper Index [staff-produced material only] by Tara Duggan. Copyright © 2003 by *San Francisco Chronicle*. Reproduced with permission of *San Francisco Chronicle* in the format Other Book via Copyright Clearance Center.

Giant Goat Cheese Gougère. Copyright © 2003 by Anne Willan. Originally published as Goats' Cheese Gougère in *Good Food No Fuss*. Reprinted by permission of Stewart, Tabori, & Chang.

Parmesan Crackers. Copyright © 2003 by The New York Times Co. Reprinted with permission.

Mustard-Cheese Crackers. Copyright © 2003 Condé Nast Publications Inc. All rights reserved. Originally published as Mustard and Cheese Crackers in *Gourmet*. Reprinted by permission.

Savory Fig Tart. Copyright © 2003 by Whole Foods Market. Originally published in the *Winter 2003 Whole Foods Holiday Entertaining Guide*. Reprinted by permission of Whole Foods Market.

Anchoiade with Figs and Walnuts tip. Copyright © 2003 by Tasha DeSerio. Originally published in *Fine Cooking*. Reprinted by permission of Tasha DeSerio.

Roasted Pepper Boats with Pancetta and Pecorino. Copyright © 2003 by Micol Negrin. Originally published on the Rustico Cooking Web site. Reprinted by permission of Micol Negrin.

Cumin-Baked Parsnips with Salmon Roe. Excerpted from *Kitchen of Light*. Copyright © 2003 by Andreas Viestad. Used by permission of Artisan, a division of Workman Publishing Co., Inc., New York. All rights reserved.

Roasted Asparagus with Panko Bread Crumbs by Arlene Jacobs. Copyright © 2003 by Sheryl Julian and Julie Riven. Originally published in *The Way We Cook*. Reprinted by permission of Houghton Mifflin Company.

Caribbean-Style Shrimp Cocktail with Jalapeño-Lime Dipping Sauce. Copyright © 2003 by the Editors of *Cook's Illustrated*. Originally published in *The Quick Recipe*. Reprinted by permission of *Cook's Illustrated*.

Charred Pesto Shrimp. From *The Summer House Cookbook* by Debra Ponzek and Geralyn Delaney Graham, copyright © 2003 by Debra Ponzek and Geralyn Delaney Graham. Used by permission of Clarkson Potter/Publishers, a division of Random House, Inc.

Pickled Salmon by Patricia Unterman after Joyce Goldstein. Copyright © 1992 by Joyce Goldstein. Originally published in *Back to Square One*. Reprinted by permission of Joyce Goldstein.

Roman Meatballs in "Fake" Sauce. Copyright © 2003 by Jo Bettoja. Originally published as Polpette con Sugo Finto in *In a Roman Kitchen*. Reprinted by permission of Wiley Publishers.

Polenta tip. Copyright © 2003 by Jo Bettoja. Originally published as Polenta per le Spuntature in *In a Roman Kitchen*. Reprinted by permission of Wiley Publishers.

Chorizo and Apples in Hard Cider. Reprinted with permission from *César* by Olivier Said and James Mellgren with Maggie Pond. Copyright © 2003 by Olivier Said and James Mellgren, Ten Speed Press, Berkeley, CA.

Melt-in-the-Mouth Lamb Kebabs (originally published as Ground Lamb "Galavat" Kebabs). From *From Curries to Kebabs* by Madhur Jaffrey, copyright © 2003 by Madhur Jaffrey. Used by permission of Clarkson Potter/Publishers, a division of Random House, Inc.

Fresh Cilantro Chutney (originally published as Green Sauce or Cilantro Chutney). From *From Curries to Kebabs* by Madhur Jaffrey, copyright © 2003 by Madhur Jaffrey. Used by permission of Clarkson Potter/Publishers, a division of Random House, Inc.

Chilled Potato-Chive Soup. Copyright © 2003 by Marcus Samuelsson. Originally published in *Aquavit*. Reprinted by permission of Houghton Mifflin Company.

Minted Pea Soup with Crispy Pancetta, Bread, and Sour Cream. From *Jamie's Kitchen* by Jamie Oliver. Copyright © 2003 by Jamie Oliver. Reprinted by permission of Hyperion.

Tomato Soup with Spanish Smoked Paprika. Reprinted with the permission of Scribner, an imprint of Simon & Schuster Adult Publishing Group, from *The Good Fat Cookbook* by Fran McCullough. Copyright © 2003 by Fran McCullough.

Roasted Butternut Squash Soup with Bacon (originally published as Butternut Squash Soup with Minced Bacon). Reprinted with the permission of Scribner, an imprint of Simon & Schuster Adult Publishing Group, from *Tom Valenti's Soups, Stews, and One-Pot Meals* by Tom Valenti and Andrew Friedman. Copyright © 2003 by Tom Valenti and Andrew Friedman.

Butternut Squash Puree tip. Reprinted with the permission of Scribner, an imprint of Simon & Schuster Adult Publishing Group, from *Tom Valenti's Soups, Stews, and One-Pot Meals* by Tom Valenti and Andrew Friedman. Copyright © 2003 by Tom Valenti and Andrew Friedman.

French Country Cabbage Soup. Copyright © 2003 by Marlena Spieler. Originally published as Country Cabbage Soup in the *San Francisco Chronicle*. Reprinted by permission of Marlena Spieler.

Creamy Roasted Poblano Soup (originally published as Roasted Poblano Soup). From *Gulf Coast Kitchens* by Constance Snow, copyright © 2003 by Constance Snow. Used by permission of Clarkson Potter/Publishers, a division of Random House, Inc.

Queso Blanco tip. From *Gulf Coast Kitchens* by Constance Snow, copyright © 2003 by Constance Snow. Used by permission of Clarkson Potter/Publishers, a division of Random House, Inc.

Spanish Almond Soup. Copyright © 2003 Condé Nast Publications. All rights reserved. Originally published in *Gourmet*. Reprinted by permission.

Roasted Cauliflower Soup by Donna Meadow. Copyright © 2003 by Gruner + Jahr USA Publishing. Originally published in *Family Circle*. Reprinted by permission of Gruner + Jahr USA Publishing.

North African Tomato Bulgur Soup (Shorba). From *Moosewood Restaurant Celebrates*, copyright © 2003 by Moosewood, Inc. Used by permission of Clarkson Potter/Publishers, a division of Random House, Inc.

Oyster Stew with Ginger and Leeks (originally published as Salt Creek Oyster Stew). From *Cooking from the Heart: 100 Great American Chefs Share Recipes They Cherish*. Foreword by Richard Russo, edited by Michael J. Rosen, copyright © 2003 by Michael J. Rosen and Share Our Strength. Used by permission of Broadway Books, a division of Random House, Inc.

Pacific Rim Chicken Noodle Soup (originally published as Chicken and Noodle Soup—Pacific Rim). Reprinted with permission from *A Taste of the Tropics* by Jay Solomon. Copyright © 2003 by Jay Solomon, Ten Speed Press, Berkeley, CA.

Heirloom Tomatoes with Orange Zest. From *Flavor* by Rocco DiSpirito. Copyright © 2003 Rocco DiSpirito. Reprinted by permission of Hyperion.

Baby Greens with Broiled Lemons. From *Lemon Zest* by Lori Longbotham, copyright © 2002 by Lori Longbotham. Used by permission of Broadway Books, a division of Random House, Inc.

Baby Romaine with Green Goddess Dressing. Copyright © 2003 by Fanny Singer. Originally published in *Food & Wine*. Reprinted by permission of Fanny Singer.

Tomato and Fresh Green Bean Salad with Crisp Prosciutto. Copyright © 2003 by Joanne Weir. Originally published in *Fine Cooking*. Reprinted by permission of Joanne Weir.

Crunchy Cucumber, Celery, and Red Bell Pepper Salad with Cumin and Fresh Mint. From *Once Upon a Tart* by Frank Mentesana and Jerome Audureau with Carolynn Carreño, copyright © 2003 by Frank Mentesana and Jerome Audureau. Used by permission of Alfred A. Knopf, a division of Random House, Inc.

Sweet Pepper Salad with Manchego and Almonds. Copyright © 2003 by Laura Chenel. Originally published in *Food & Wine*. Reprinted by permission of Laura Chenel.

Ricotta and Pine Nut Salad. Copyright © 2003 by The New York Times Co. Reprinted with permission.

Moroccan Herb Salad by Paula Wolfert. Copyright © 2003 by Andrew Dorenburg and Karen Page. Originally published as Shalda de Baqqoula in *The New American Chef*. Reprinted by permission of Wiley Publishers.

Roasted Pear, Blue Cheese, and Bibb Salad with Cranberry Vinaigrette. Copyright © 2003 by Didi Emmons. Originally published in *Entertain-*

ing for a Veggie Planet. Reprinted by permission of Houghton Mifflin Company.

Potato and Haricot Vert Salad by James O'Shea after Kevin Thornton. Copyright © 2003 by James O'Shea. Originally published in the *Washington Post*. Reprinted by permission of James O'Shea.

Spinach and Tabbouleh Salad with Feta and Olives by Frank Melodia. Copyright © 2003 by Hearst Communications, Inc. Originally published as Yummy Spinach-Tabbouleh Salad in *Redbook*. Reprinted by permission of *Redbook*.

Mac and Cheese Salad with Buttermilk Dressing from *Tom's Big Dinners* by Tom Douglas. Copyright © 2003 by Tom Douglas and Jackie Cross. Reprinted by permission of HarperCollins Publishers Inc., William Morrow.

Sardinian Rice Salad with Tuna, Olives, and Capers. Copyright © 2003 by Paula Disbrowe. Originally published as Sardinian Rice Salad in *Food & Wine*. Reprinted by permission of Paula Disbrowe.

Chicken Salad à la Danny Kaye. Copyright © 2003 by Jacques Pépin. Originally published in *The Apprentice: My Life in the Kitchen*. Reprinted by permission of Houghton Mifflin Company.

Killer Granola. Reprinted with permission from *Cheese Board: Collective Works—Bread, Pastry, Cheese, Pizza* by The Cheese Board Collective. Copyright © 2003 by The Cheese Board Collective, Ten Speed Press, Berkeley, CA.

Killer Granola Cookies. Reprinted with permission from *Cheese Board: Collective Works—Bread, Pastry, Cheese, Pizza* by The Cheese Board Collective. Copyright © 2003 by The Cheese Board Collective, Ten Speed Press, Berkeley, CA.

Baked Eggs in Maple Toast Cups. Copyright © 2003 by Dakin Farm. Originally published on the Dakin Farm Web site. Reprinted by permission of Dakin Farm.

George Jones Sausage Balls. Copyright © 2004 by Julia Reed. Reprinted with permission of The Wylie Agency, Inc.

Crunchy Breaded Bacon (originally published as Breaded Breakfast Bacon). From *The Big Book of Breakfast*. Copyright © 2003 by Maryana Vollstedt. Used with permission of Chronicle Books LLC, San Francisco. Visit ChronicleBooks.com.

Grits in the Slow-Cooker. Copyright © 2003 by John Thorne and Matt Lewis Thorne. Originally published as True Grits, My Way, in the *Simple Cooking* newsletter. Reprinted by permission of John Thorne and Matt Lewis Thorne.

Tomato, Goat Cheese, and Focaccia Pudding. Copyright © 2003 by Kerry Leigh Heffernan. Originally published in the *San Francisco Chronicle*. Reprinted by permission of Kerry Leigh Heffernan.

Cottage Street Bakery Dirt Bombs. From *The Cape Cod Table*. Copyright © 2003 by Lora Brody. Used with permission of Chronicle Books LLC, San Francisco. Visit ChronicleBooks.com.

Iced Cinnamon Bun Scones. Copyright © 2003 by Marcy Goldman. Originally published in the BetterBaking.com eZine. Reprinted by permission of Marcy Goldman.

Cinna-Myron Caramel Sweet Rolls by Myron Sikora. Copyright © 2003 by *Saveur*. Originally published as Cinna-Myron Caramel Rolls in *Saveur*, June/July 2003. Reprinted by permission of *Saveur*.

Cardamom Swirl Coffee Cake from *Brown Sugar* by Joyce White. Copyright © 2003 by Joyce White. Reprinted by permission of HarperCollins Publishers Inc.

Cremini Mushrooms with Chive Pasta. From *High Heat: Grilling and Roasting Year-Round with Master Chef Waldy Malouf* by Waldy Malouf and Melissa Clark, copyright © 2003 by Waldy Malouf Hospitality Concepts, Inc., and Melissa Clark. Used by permission of Broadway Books, a division of Random House, Inc.

Three-Ingredient Fettuccine Alfredo by Alfredo of Rome in New York City and Orlando. Copyright © 2003 by Russell Bellanca. Originally published in *Everyday Food, from the Kitchens of Martha Stewart Living*. Reprinted by permission of Russell Bellanca.

Tex-Mex Macaroni and Cheese with Green Chiles. Copyright © 2003 by Robert Del Grande. Originally published as Tex-Mex Macaroni and Cheese in *Fine Cooking*. Reprinted by permission of Robert Del Grande.

Sear-Roasted Salmon Fillets with Lemon-Ginger Butter. Copyright © 2003 by Isabelle Alexandre. Originally published in *Fine Cooking's Quick and Delicious Recipes*. Reprinted by permission of Isabelle Alexandre.

Salmon with Yogurt and Cardamom (originally published as Slow-Roasted Salmon with Yogurt and Cardamom). From *Big City Cooking*. Copyright © 2003 by Matthew Kenney. Used with permission of Chronicle Books LLC, San Francisco. Visit ChronicleBooks.com.

Soy-Glazed Salmon Burgers with Ginger-Lime Aïoli. From "Fear of Grilling" from *Cookoff: Recipe Fever in America* by Amy Sutherland, copyright © 2003 by Amy Sutherland. Used by permission of Viking Penguin, a division of Penguin Group (USA) Inc.

Baked Snapper with Potatoes, Oregano, and White Wine. Copyright © 2003 by La Cantinella. Originally published in *Bon Appétit*. Reprinted by permission of La Cantinella.

Sautéed Swordfish with Fresh Tomato Chutney by

Mary Sue Milliken and Susan Feniger (originally published as Sautéed Swordfish with Pickled Tomatoes and Couscous). Reprinted with the permission of Simon & Schuster Adult Publishing Group from *The Tante Marie's Cooking School Cookbook* by Mary Risley. Copyright © 2003 by Mary Risley.

Shrimp Baked with Tomato Sauce and Feta Cheese. Copyright © 2003 by The New York Times. Originally published as Shrimp Baked with Feta Cheese in *The New York Times Seafood Cookbook* edited by Florence Fabricant. Reprinted by permission of St. Martin's Press, LLC.

Chicken Saltimbocca with Escarole and Beans. Copyright © 2003 by Wegmans Food Markets, Inc. Originally published in *Wegmans Menu Magazine*. Reprinted by permission of Wegmans Food Markets, Inc.

Fried Chicken Littles. Copyright © 2003 by Leonard Schwartz and Michael Rosen. Originally published in *Food & Wine*. Reprinted by permission of Leonard Schwartz and Michael Rosen.

Stewed Chicken with Chipotles and Prunes. From *Ready When You Are* by Martha Rose Shulman, copyright © 2003 by Martha Rose Shulman. Used by permission of Clarkson Potter/Publishers, a division of Random House, Inc.

Country Captain. Copyright © 2000 by John Martin Taylor. Originally published in *Hoppin' John's Lowcountry Cooking*. Reprinted by permission of Houghton Mifflin Company.

Drunken Steak by Seth and Angela Raynor. Copyright © 2003 by *Boston* magazine. Originally published in *Boston* magazine. Reprinted by permission of *Boston* magazine.

Port-and-Soy-Glazed Beef Tenderloin. Reprinted with permission from *Caprial and John's Kitchen* by Caprial and John Pence. Copyright © 2003 by Caprial and John Pence, Ten Speed Press, Berkeley, CA.

Beef Stew with Tequila (originally published as Spicy Tequila Chuck). Reprinted with the permission of Simon & Schuster Adult Publishing Group from *The Weekend Chef* by Barbara Witt. Copyright © 2003 by Barbara Witt.

Braised Beef Short Ribs Chinese Style. Copyright © 2003 by Leslie Revsin. Originally published as Braised Beef Short Ribs with Chinese Flavor in *Come for Dinner*. Reprinted by permission of Wiley Publishers.

Braised Beef Short Ribs with Leeks tip. Copyright © 2003 by Leslie Revsin. Originally published as Asian-Style Beef Short Ribs with Julienned Leeks in *Fine Cooking*. Reprinted by permission of Leslie Revsin.

Ticino-Style Pot Roast by Margrit Biever Mondavi. Reprinted with permission from *Annie and Margrit* by Annie Roberts, Margrit Biever Mondavi, and Victoria Wise. Copyright © 2003 by Annie Roberts, Margrit Biever Mondavi, and Victoria Wise, Ten Speed Press, Berkeley, CA.

Millionaire's Brisket with Coffee and Beer Mop Sauce (originally published as Millionaire Brisket with Coffee and Beer Mop Sauce). Excerpted from *BBQ USA*. Copyright © 2003 by Steven Raichlen. Used by permission of Workman Publishing Co., Inc., New York. All rights reserved.

Smithfield Inn's Roasted Peanut Pork Chops. Copyright © 2003 by David Walker. Originally published in *The Best of Virginia Farms*. Reprinted by permission of David Walker.

Three-Way Pork Burgers (originally published as Pork Burgers). Copyright © 2003 by The New York Times Co. Reprinted with permission.

Jerk Pork Tenderloin. Copyright © 2003 by Arlene Weston. Originally published in *Bon Appétit*. Reprinted by permission of Arlene Weston.

Chili Verde. From *Firehouse Food*. Copyright © 2003 by George Dolese and Steve Siegelman. Used with permission of Chronicle Books LLC, San Francisco. Visit ChronicleBooks.com.

Sausage and Mushroom Risotto with Raisins by Jimmy Bradley. Copyright © 2003 by Sam Sifton. Originally published in the *New York Times Magazine*. Reprinted by permission of Sam Sifton.

Creole Ham and Shrimp Jambalaya. Copyright © 2003 by James Villas. Originally published in *Crazy for Casseroles*. Reprinted by permission of Harvard Common Press.

Carnitas by Marilyn Tausend and Ricardo Muñoz Zurita. Copyright © 2003 by Marilyn Tausend. Originally published as Crispy Pork with Avocado Salsa and Tomato Salsa in *Bon Appétit*. Reprinted by permission of Marilyn Tausend.

Tacos with Chorizo and Potato Filling. From *From My Mexican Kitchen: Techniques and Ingredients* by Diana Kennedy, copyright © 2003 by Diana Kennedy. Used by permission of Clarkson Potter/Publishers, a division of Random House, Inc.

Grilled Butterflied Leg of Lamb with Fresh Mint-Pepper Jelly. From *Foster's Market Cookbook* by Sara Foster, copyright © 2002 by Sara Foster. Used by permission of Random House, Inc.

Asparagus Baked in Parchment with Caper Mayonnaise. Copyright © 2003 by Paula Wolfert. Originally published in *The Slow Mediterranean Kitchen*. Reprinted by permission of Wiley Publishers.

Oven-Roasted Asparagus with Fried Capers. Copyright © 2003 by Rozanne Gold. Originally published in *Cooking 1–2–3*. Reprinted by permission of Stewart, Tabori, & Chang.

Green Beans with Crisp Shallots, Chile, and Mint.

Copyright © 2003 Condé Nast Publications. All rights reserved. Originally published in *Gourmet.* Reprinted by permission.

Dry-Fried Green Beans tip (originally published as Dry-Fried Green Beans 2). From *Land of Plenty* by Fuchsia Dunlop. Copyright © 2001 by Fuchsia Dunlop. Used by permission of W. W. Norton & Company, Inc.

Roasted Maple-Glazed Baby Carrots with Dried Grapes. Copyright © 2003 by The New York Times Co. Reprinted with permission.

Pan-Roasted Cauliflower with Capers by Egi Maccioni with Peter Kaminsky. Copyright © 2003 by Egi Maccioni. Originally published in *The Maccioni Family Cookbook.* Reprinted by permission of Stewart, Tabori, & Chang.

Corn Cooked in Milk with Chiles and Coconut. Copyright © 2003 by *Saveur.* Originally published as Makai Nu Shaak in *Saveur,* August/September 2003. Reprinted by permission of *Saveur.*

Vanilla "Creamed" Corn. Copyright © 2003 by Michel Nischan. Originally published in *O, the Oprah Magazine.* Reprinted by permission of Michel Nischan.

Greens and Oranges. Copyright © 2003 by Eric Gower. Originally published in *The Breakaway Japanese Kitchen.* Reprinted by permission of Kodansha International Ltd.

Armenian Chickpeas and Spinach by Moustache Restaurant. Copyright © 2003 by Jonathan Reynolds. Originally published as Chickpea-and-Spinach Salad in the *New York Times Magazine.* Reprinted by permission of Jonathan Reynolds and the Moustache Restaurant.

Braised Fennel. From *Bistro Cooking at Home* by Gordon Hamersley with Joanne McAllister Smart, copyright © 2003 by Gordon Hamersley. Used by permission of Broadway Books, a division of Random House, Inc.

Parsnip Crisps by Renee Schettler. Copyright © 2003, *The Washington Post,* reprinted with permission.

Roasted Sugar Snap Peas with Fleur de Sel. Copyright © 2003 by Betty Rosbottom. Originally published in *Bon Appétit.* Reprinted by permission of Betty Rosbottom.

Glazed Pearl Onions with Mustard and Brown Sugar. Copyright © 2003 by Sarah Leah Chase. Originally published as Pearl Onions Glazed with Mustard and Brown Sugar in the *Cincinnati Post Online Edition.* Reprinted by permission of Sarah Leah Chase.

Mashed Potatoes with Sage and White Cheddar Cheese. Copyright © 2003 Condé Nast Publications. All rights reserved. Originally published in *Bon Appétit.* Reprinted by permission.

Roasted Potatoes with Anchovies and Lemon. Copyright © 2003 Condé Nast Publications. All rights reserved. Originally published in *Gourmet.* Reprinted by permission.

Whipped Chipotle Sweet Potatoes. Copyright © 2003 Condé Nast Publications. All rights reserved. Originally published in *Gourmet.* Reprinted by permission.

Ginger Ale–Spiked Sweet Potatoes. Copyright © 2003 by John T. Edge. Originally published as Blenheim-Spiked Sweet Potatoes in *The New Great American Writers Cookbook,* edited by Dean Faulkner Wells. Reprinted by permission of University Press of Mississippi.

Spinach and Artichoke Casserole. Copyright © 2004 by Julia Reed. Reprinted by permission of The Wylie Agency, Inc.

Roasted Tomatoes and Onions (originally published as Riad's Roasted Tomatoes and Onions). Excerpted from *Celebrate!* Copyright © 2003 by Sheila Lukins. Used by permission of Workman Publishing Co., Inc., New York. All rights reserved.

Butternut Squash Rounds with Sage. Reprinted with the permission of Scribner, an imprint of Simon & Schuster Adult Publishing Group, from *Everyday Greens* by Annie Sommerville. Copyright © 2003 by Annie Sommerville.

Island Rice with Cumin and Coconut. From *At Blanchard's Table* by Melinda Blanchard and Robert Blanchard, copyright © 2003 by Melinda Blanchard and Robert Blanchard. Used by permission of Clarkson Potter/Publishers, a division of Random House, Inc.

Wild Rice for Lots of People. Copyright © 2003 by Louise Erdrich. Originally published in *The New Great American Writers Cookbook,* edited by Dean Faulkner Wells. Reprinted by permission of University Press of Mississippi.

Green Chile–Cheese Grits. Copyright © 2003 by Grady Spears. Originally published in *The Texas Cowboy Kitchen: Recipes from the Chisholm Club.* Reprinted by permission of Texas Monthly Custom Publishing.

Crisp Arugula-Polenta Cakes by Charlie Trotter. Copyright © 2003 by Jeremiah Tower. Originally published in *America's Best Chefs Cook with Jeremiah Tower.* Reprinted by permission of Wiley Publishers.

Baked Beans in Cider by Annie Proulx and Lew Nichols. Copyright © 2003 by Storey Publishing LLC. Originally published in *Cider.* Reprinted by permission of Storey Publishing.

Easy Biscuits by the Indianapolis Christian School. Copyright © 2003 by Lari Robling. Originally published in *Endangered Recipes.* Reprinted by permission of Stewart, Tabori, & Chang.

Popovers with Sage Butter. Copyright © 2003 by Elizabeth and Susan Allen. Originally published in *Bon Appétit*. Reprinted by permission of Elizabeth and Susan Allen.

Stuffin' Muffins. Copyright © 2003 by Jay Murray. Originally published as Grill 23 & Bar Stuffin' Muffins in the *Boston Herald*. Reprinted by permission of Jay Murray.

Cranberry Cornbread (originally published as Cranberry Corn Bread). Copyright © 2003 by The New York Times Co. Reprinted with permission.

Cheese Shortbread. Reprinted with permission of Simon & Schuster Adult Publishing Group from *Bernard Clayton's New Complete Book of Breads: The 30th Anniversary Edition* by Bernard Clayton. Copyright © 1973, 1987, 1995, 2003 by Bernard Clayton, Jr.

Tom Cat Rosemary Matzoh (originally published as Mediterranean Matzoh). From *The Bread Bible* by Rose Levy Beranbaum. Copyright © 2003 by Rose Levy Beranbaum. Used by permission of W. W. Norton & Company, Inc.

Popcorn Focaccia from *The Cornbread Book* by Jeremy Jackson. Copyright © 2003 by Jeremy Jackson. Reprinted by permission of HarperCollins Publishers Inc., William Morrow.

Fresh Apricot-Berry Crumble. Copyright © 2003 by Greg Patent. Originally published as Apricot-Berry Crumble in *Baking in America*. Reprinted by permission of Houghton Mifflin Company.

Apple and Dried Fig Cobbler. Copyright © 2003 Condé Nast Publications. All rights reserved. Originally published as Hudson Valley Apple and Dried Fig Cobbler in *Bon Appétit*. Reprinted by permission.

Pear and Hazelnut Gratin. Copyright © 2003 by Leslie Revsin. Originally published in *Fine Cooking*. Reprinted by permission of Leslie Revsin.

Citrus Compote by Carolyn Miller. Copyright © 2003 by Weldon Owen Inc. and Williams-Sonoma Inc. Originally published in *Williams-Sonoma Christmas*. Reprinted by permission of Weldon Owen Inc.

Grapefruit and Star Anise Granita (originally published as Star Anise & Grapefruit Granita). Excerpted from *Granita Magic*. Copyright © 2003 by Nadia Roden. Used by permission of Artisan, a division of Workman Publishing Co., Inc., New York. All rights reserved.

Food Dance Café's Double-Chocolate Pudding. Copyright © 2003 by Ari Weinzweig. Originally published in *Zingerman's Guide to Good Eating*. Reprinted by permission of Houghton Mifflin Company.

Mocha Fudge Pudding tip. Copyright © 2003 by Jan Newberry. Originally published in *Food & Wine*. Reprinted by permission of Jan Newberry.

Chunky Peanut Butter and Oatmeal Chocolate Chipsters. Copyright © 2003 by Dorie Greenspan. Originally published in *HMCo Cooks*. Reprinted by permission of Dorie Greenspan.

Martha's Mother's Cookies. Excerpted from *Home Baking*. Copyright © 2003 by Jeffrey Alford and Naomi Duguid. Used by permission of Artisan, a division of Workman Publishing Co., Inc., New York. All rights reserved.

Coffee-Walnut Pinwheels by Coretta Williams. Copyright © 2003 by *Dallas Morning News*. Originally published in *Dallas Morning News*. Reprinted by permission of *Dallas Morning News*.

Linzer Cookies. Reprinted from *One Smart Cookie: All Your Favorite Cookies, Squares, Brownies and Biscotti...with Less Fat!* by Julie Van Rosendaal. Copyright © 2000, 2004 by One Smart Cookie, Inc. For U.S. rights: Permission granted by Rodale, Inc., Emmaus, PA 18098. Available wherever books are sold or directly from the publisher by calling (800) 848-4735 or visit our website at www.rodalestore.com. For Canadian rights: Copyright © 2003 by Julie Van Rosendaal. Reprinted by permission of Carlisle & Co.

Chocolate Pecan Pie Bars by Rick Bayless. Copyright © 2003 by Frontera Grill. Originally published in *El Mundo,* the Frontera Grill newsletter. Reprinted by permission of Frontera Grill.

Apricot and Oat Squares by Monica Sharpe, Glenorchy Café. Copyright © 2003 by *Saveur*. Originally published as Apricot and Oat Slices in *Saveur,* January/February 2003. Reprinted by permission of *Saveur*.

Deborah Madison's Grandmother's Raisin Squares (originally published as Raisin Squares). From *Cooking from the Heart: 100 Great American Chefs Share Recipes They Cherish*. Foreword by Richard Russo, edited by Michael J. Rosen, copyright © 2003 by Michael J. Rosen and Share Our Strength. Used by permission of Broadway Books, a division of Random House, Inc.

Pumpkin Bars with Lemon Glaze. Reprinted with permission from *Holiday Pumpkins* by Georgeanne Brennan. Copyright © 2003 by Georgeanne Brennan, Ten Speed Press, Berkeley, CA.

Lemon Ripple Cheesecake Bars. Copyright © 2003 by Elinor Klivans. Originally published in *Food & Wine*. Reprinted by permission of Elinor Klivans.

Spicy Island Gingerbread. From *An Embarrassment of Mangoes: A Caribbean Interlude* by Ann Vanderhoof, copyright © 2003 by Ann Vanderhoof. For U.S. rights: Used by permission of Broadway Books, a division of Random House, Inc. For Canadian rights: Published by Doubleday Canada. Reprinted by permission of the author.

Super-Moist Apple Cake. Reprinted with the permission of Scribner, an imprint of Simon & Schuster Adult Publishing Group, from *The Arrows Cookbook* by Clark Frasier and Mark Gaier with Max

Alexander. Copyright © 2003 by Clark Frasier and Mark Gaier.

Chocolate Pavlova with Tangerine Whipped Cream. Copyright © 2003 by Gale Gand. Originally published in *Fine Cooking*. Reprinted by permission of Gale Gand.

Five-Spice Angel Food Cake with Maple Glaze. Copyright © 2003 by Roy Finamore. Originally published as Five-Spice Angel Food Cake at www.tastycentral.com. Reprinted by permission of Roy Finamore.

Tiger Cake. Excerpted from *Bittersweet*. Copyright © 2003 by Alice Medrich. Photographs copyright © by Deborah Jones. Used by permission of Artisan, a division of Workman Publishing Co., Inc., New York. All rights reserved.

Mango and Lime Chiffon Cake. Copyright © 2003 by Cindy Mushet. Originally published in *Bon Appétit*. Reprinted by permission of Cindy Mushet.

Chocolate Stout Cake. Copyright © 2003 by Nicole Rees. Originally published in *Fine Cooking Holiday Baking*. Reprinted by permission of Nicole Rees.

Anglo-Italian Trifle. From *Forever Summer* by Nigella Lawson. For U.S. rights: Copyright © 2003 Nigella Lawson. Reprinted by permission of Hyperion. For Canadian rights: Copyright © 2002 Nigella Lawson. Reprinted by permission of Alfred A. Knopf Canada.

Cinnamon Sacristains. Copyright © 2003 by Daniel Boulud. Originally published in *Daniel's Dish: Entertaining at Home with a Four-Star Chef* (Filipacchi, 2003). Reprinted by permission of Daniel Boulud.

Bourbon, Chocolate, and Walnut Pecan Pie. From *It's All American Food* by David Rosengarten. Copyright © 2003 by David Rosengarten. By permission of Little, Brown and Company, Inc.

Pumpkin, Sweet Potato, and Coconut Pie. For U.S. rights: Excerpted from *In the Sweet Kitchen*. Copyright © 2003 by Regan Daley. Used by permission of Artisan, a division of Workman Publishing Co., Inc., New York. All rights reserved. For Canadian rights: Extracted from *In the Sweet Kitchen* by Regan Daley. Copyright © 2000 by Regan Daley. Reprinted by permission of Random House Canada.

Tart of Dried Plums and Walnut Frangipane. From *Cooking by Hand* by Paul Bertolli, text copyright © 2003 by Paul Bertolli. Used by permission of Clarkson Potter/Publishers, a division of Random House, Inc.

Tart Dough (originally published as Tart Dough from Tomato Jam Tartlets). From *Cooking by Hand* by Paul Bertolli, text copyright © 2003 by Paul Bertolli. Used by permission of Clarkson Potter/Publishers, a division of Random House, Inc.

Chocolate-Pecan Toffee by Heidi Krahling. Reprinted with the permission of Simon & Schuster Adult Publishing Group from *The Tante Marie's Cooking School Cookbook* by Mary Risley. Copyright © 2003 by Mary Risley.

Fresh Raspberry Lemonade. Excerpted from *Celebrate!* Copyright © 2003 by Sheila Lukins. Used by permission of Workman Publishing Co., Inc., New York. All rights reserved.

Date Shakes by Oasis Date Gardens. Copyright © 2003 by *Saveur*. Originally published in *Saveur*, November 2003. Reprinted by permission of *Saveur*.

Cranberry Margarita by Bobby Flay. Copyright © 2003 by Boy Meets Grill, Inc. Originally published in *InStyle Magazine*. Reprinted by permission of Boy Meets Grill, Inc.

Turkeytini. Copyright © 2003 by Jonathan Dorf. Originally published in *Westchester Magazine*. Reprinted by permission of Jonathan Dorf.

Dry Negroni (originally published as The Negroni). From *Cosmopolitan: A Bartender's Life* by Toby Cecchini, copyright © 2003 by Toby Cecchini. Used by permission of Broadway Books, a division of Random House, Inc.

Caribbean Cooler. Copyright © 2003 by Ellen Ficklen. Originally published in the *Washington Post*. Reprinted by permission of Ellen Ficklen.

Kentucky Derby Mint Juleps. Copyright © 2003 by The New York Times Co. Reprinted with permission.

The VIP (Vodka-Infused-Pineapple Cocktail). Copyright © 2003 by Kim Owens. Originally published in *Santé* magazine.

index

C

L

M

R

S